Nigel Rees is a writer and broadcaster. On radio and television he has presented and appeared in a large number of programmes ranging from current affairs to comedy. BBC Radio's *Quote . . . Unquote*, which he first devised in 1976, has given rise to a series of books on aspects of the popular use of language — and especially the humour that derives from it. The books include three *Quote . . . Unquote* collections, the enormously successful *Graffiti* series, and *Sayings of the Century*.

THE NIGEL REES BOOK OF

Slogans & Catchphrases

THE NIGEL REES BOOK OF

London
UNWIN PAPERBACKS
Boston   Sydney

UNWIN® PAPERBACKS
40 Museum Street, London WC1A 1LU, UK

Unwin Paperbacks
Park Lane, Hemel Hempstead, Herts HP2 4TE, UK

George Allen & Unwin Australia Pty Ltd
8 Napier Street, North Sydney, NSW 2060, Australia

British Library Cataloguing in Publication Data

Rees, Nigel
   The Nigel Rees book of slogans and catchphrases.
1. Slogans
I. Title
659.13'22   PN6311
ISBN 0-04-827108-X

Set in 10 on 11 point Palatino by A. J. Latham Ltd
and printed in Great Britain by
Cox and Wyman Ltd, Reading

CONTENTS

PREFACE

Everyday speech is frequently rendered more pithy and colourful by our use of phrases taken from entertainment and advertising. After a while, we may find that we are using the phrases, having forgotten whatever it was they once alluded to. One of the purposes of this book is to provide a note of the sources of catchphrases and slogans which have − for however short a time − passed into the language.

The other purpose is to record, where possible, something of the circumstances in which notable catchphrases and slogans originated and how the phrases have been taken up and used.

The first part of the book is devoted to nearly a thousand catchphrases and stock phrases that have come into the language from entertainment. The second part records nearly a thousand slogans taken from advertising and politics. It is possible, of course, for a slogan to become a catchphrase − even for a catchphrase to take on the force of a slogan − so, at times, the way I have presented the phrases is somewhat arbitrary. Definitions of the words 'catchphrase' and 'slogan' − at least as I have interpreted them − are contained in the introductions to the two parts of the book.

The catchphrases section is based on my earlier *Very Interesting . . . but Stupid!* (Unwin Paperbacks, 1980) − but this has been completely revised and reorganised. The number of entries has almost doubled. The slogans section is a revised and expanded version of my *Slogans* (George Allen & Unwin, 1982). I am grateful to the many people who have provided corrections to − and suggestions for expanding − these two works. A list of acknowledgements can be found at the end of the book.

London, 1984

11

Catchphrases

Catchphrases

An Introduction

In the broadest sense of the word, a catchphrase is simply a phrase that catches on. In the show business sense — which is what we are concerned with here — it is a phrase that helps identify a particular performer or show and which the audience takes up and uses until it becomes, for a time, a part of the language. At best, a catchphrase lives on, evoking an era and its pleasures, and brightening the language. So, you will find here a catalogue of catchphrases drawn mostly from British and American show business — some you will know, some you will have forgotten, and some you never knew existed (which means they did not catch on in a big way). The bulk comes from radio and TV, there is a sprinkling from music-hall, variety and the cinema, and a handful from advertising. Literary catchphrases have been included only where they have been popularized through the media.

At worst, a catchphrase is a mechanical device. The temptation is for an aspiring comedian to kit himself out with one and din it into his audience. From then on he can be sure of a round of applause whenever he utters it (an affectionate, if sheeplike, show of recognition between performer and public). If he is careful, however, and the phrase does have some appeal to the public, he can record a song incorporating it; use it as the title of a film or TV series; and, if he lasts long enough, he can use it as the title of his autobiography.

How catchphrases evolve and why they exert a peculiar hold over people is, to my mind, an interesting and not always explicable phenomenon. It was not until the rise of the mass media that the catchphrase became a staple part of show business. True, in the heyday of music-hall certain performers were noted for their little phrases. Going back even further, it appears that Shakespeare was familiar with something akin to the phenomenon. In the first quarto version of *Hamlet* we can read:

> You have some again, that keepes one suit of jests, as a man is known by one suit of apparel, and gentlemen quote his jests down in their tables before they come to the play, as thus: Cannot you stay till I eat my porridge? and, You owe a quarter's wages; and, Your beer is sour.

Not until the 1930s, however, and the arrival of a particular type of radio comedy show, were conditions ripe for catchphrases to become commonplace. Shows like *Band Waggon* and *ITMA*, on British radio, had two key ingredients: regularity and feedback. Catchphrases could be used every week (whereas a music-hall performer doing his rounds might be seen in one place at most a couple of times a year). The studio audiences helped them catch on by their enthusiastic response. This then spread to listeners at home. Because this kind of repetition and feedback has been lacking, comparatively few phrases have come out of the cinema.

The heyday of the catchphrase undoubtedly occurred when radio was at its peak in Britain and America — from the mid-30s to the mid-50s. When TV became the main form of entertainment, a certain reaction against the catchphrase seems to have set in. Individual performers launched their own, a good number came out of situation comedies, but TV largely managed without catchphrases in the radio manner. In addition, a new breed of comedian often eschewed them altogether, out of a feeling that they belonged to an alien showbiz world (though *Monty Python* gave rise to one or two). The big exception to this trend was *Rowan and Martin's Laugh-In* produced in the United States during the late 60s and early 70s. Although the use of catchphrases may have waned somewhat there are still plenty of *stock* phrases to be heard on radio and TV: the greetings, the sign-offs, the verbal formats beloved of disc jockeys, quiz show hosts and the like. These are not catchphrases in the strict sense — they can hardly be said to have entered popular speech — but they are well-known in association with particular performers and shows. So I have included a good number of them, as

also some 'verbal tics' — the sort of mannerisms impressionists seize upon. In addition, I draw attention to one or two
'visual' catchphrases and — purely for interest's sake — a
number of sayings that have resolutely *failed* to catch on.

True catchphrases — ones that have entered the language
— are by and large those which can be employed with some
regularity in day-today situations, to cover social embarrassment — for example, when performing a service, accepting
the offer of a drink, or going through a doorway with another
person. The shared knowledge implied by the use of catchphrases somehow lessens the embarrassment and obscures
the difficulty.

This quality of sharing an 'in' thing lies at the heart of the
use of catchphrases in ordinary conversation. They become
verbal lubricants: an exchange of recognition tokens. People
also like a little mindless repetition. Silliness is an important
ingredient of a good catchphrase. So, too, is the possibility of
a double meaning.

Many of the best catchphrases came about by accident.
They suddenly emerged, were seized on by the audience,
and took off. But quite a few have been deliberately and successfully concocted. Bob Monkhouse avers that a gilt-edged
catchphrase should be 'perfectly in character, arise naturally,
be short, funny in any setting, and *useful*' and yet he admits
that **Bernie, the bolt** was carefully engineered like an industrial product.

One should say that a lot of these phrases were in use long
before they became associated with a particular performer.
Where an entertainer's name is mentioned it is because he
popularized the words and made them, for a while, his own.

My attempts at finding out the extent to which catchphrases exist in foreign languages have gone largely unre-
warded. Foreigners I have approached assured me that
catchphrases did exist in their languages but could not think
of any examples. However, an observer of languages in
Belgium and the Netherlands finally came to my rescue. In
Dutch, he quoted: 'Als het aan de kat lag, dan kocht ze X' — a
line from a TV commercial, meaning 'If the cat could decide,
she (it) would buy X.' This came to be used by people who
felt that a decision concerning them was actually taken by
others. A Dutch singer-comedian Paul Van Vliet once

launched the phrase "'t Zijn leuke dingen voor de mensen', meaning 'These are funny things for the people', which was then applied ironically to things which were 'not quite nice.'

In Belgium, there are many local dialects, so a phrase has to be in the standard language to catch on. One such, not from entertainment, came from politics. In 1978, coalition Prime Minister Tindemans was so fed up that he declared in the Chamber of Representatives (and on television): 'Ik heb er genoeg van, ik ga naar de koning!' − 'I've had enough of it, I'm going to the king!' The words caught on. When Belgians had had enough of a discussion in their families or at work, they would use the Tindemans phrase but, by 1983, it had fallen into disuse.

These examples seem to suggest that the process of phrases catching on is not confined to the British and American fields which I have largely concentrated on exploring.

A work like this is, in a manner of speaking, a series of footnotes to show business history − a history which is largely unwritten. My own memories of the pleasures of entertainment only go back to about 1951, when I was seven. So I have had to rely on a number of sources to help me in the more archaeological parts of my quest and especially with regard to American catchphrases. I would mention in particular a number of useful conversations I have had with entertainers about their catchphrases − which, by and large, they discuss like proud parents.

So **that's the way it is, folks.** I shall **say no more.** And **orft we jolly well go then!**

HELLO, GOOD EVENING, AND WELCOME

If there are indeed, according to Paul Simon's song, 'Fifty Ways To Leave Your Lover' — there are even more to get into and out of a radio or TV show. Various examples are scattered throughout the book in the chapters devoted to specific programmes and comedians. Here, to start with, are just forty salutations, from more than one country of origin:

Ah, there's good news tonight (even if there wasn't) — Gabriel Heatter (b.1890), American radio newscaster of the 1930s and 40s.

And that's the top of the news as it looks from here Fulton Lewis Jr (1903-66) — American radio newscaster of the 1930s and 40s.

And that's the way it is Walter Cronkite (b.1916) retired from anchoring the CBS TV Evening News after 19 years. His sign-off on that occasion was 'And that's the way it is, Friday March 6, 1981. Goodnight . . .'

Attention all shipping On BBC radio, the weather forecast for ships was introduced with these words for many years when rough conditions were imminent. Then: 'The following Gale Warning was issued by the Meteorological Office at 06.00 hours G.M.T. today . . .' (or similar).

Be a good bunny Sign-off by Wendy Barrie, on her US TV chat show c1949/50.

Be good to yourself Sign-off from Don McNeill, homely American radio star, on the air from 1934-68.

Don't forget to switch off your set I suppose any TV

announcer could have said it on British television where round-the-clock programming has rarely been attempted. But somehow I always associate it with David Hamilton (b.1939), an announcer with a number of ITV companies, including Tyne Tees, ABC and Thames, before concentrating as a DJ on radio. It was such a contrast to his romantic sign-off **And a special goodnight to you** which became so distinctive he even made a record with the title 'A Special Good Night to You' (c1967). This sign-off was also used by Barry Aldiss (B.A.), a DJ on Radio Luxembourg, at about the same time.

Glad we could get together Sign-off by John Cameron Swayze (b. c1913), American radio and TV newscaster of the 1940s and 50s. His customary opening was: **And a good evening to you**.

God love you The Most Reverend Fulton J. Sheen was Auxiliary (Roman Catholic) Bishop of New York and presented highly-popular religious TV shows called *Life is Worth Living* and *The Bishop Sheen Programme* in the period 1952-68. This was his famous sign-off.

Goodbye, everyone, goodbye Jennifer Gay was a nicely-spoken teenager and would-be ballet-dancer who introduced BBC Children's Television for a year or two in the early 1950s.

Good . . day Upbeat conclusion to broadcasts by US radio and TV newscaster and commentator Paul Harvey (especially in the 1950s.)

Good evening, everyone The customary salutation of A.J. Alan the radio storyteller of the 1920s and 30s. He was a civil servant (real name: Leslie Lambert) who eschewed personal publicity and always broadcast wearing a dinner-jacket. He never went into a BBC studio without having a candle by him in case the lights fused.

Good evening, Mr and Mrs North America and all the ships at sea — let's go to press Walter Winchell (1892-1972) was an ex-vaudevillian who became a top American radio newscaster. This was how he introduced his zippy fifteen-minute broadcast on Sunday nights, starting in 1932. By 1948 it was the top-rated radio show in the US with an average audience of 20 million people. A television version ran 1952-55, when Winchell surprised viewers by wearing his hat throughout. A variation of his greeting was 'Mr and Mrs North *and South* America.' Winchell also ran a syndicated newspaper gossip column and narrated the TV series, *The Untouchables*. Many of his stories were pure fabrication.

Goodnight . . . and good luck Edward R. Murrow (1908-65), the leading US broadcaster, used this farewell at the end of such programmes as *See It Now* (1951-55) and *Person to Person* (1953-61).

Goodnight, Chet / Goodnight, David Famous exchange between Chet Huntley and David Brinkley on NBC TV News and *The Huntley-Brinkley Report* from approximately 1956 to Huntley's retirement in 1970.

Good night, everybody . . . goodnight This was the distinctive pay-off at the end of the day's radio from Stuart Hibberd (even in the days when BBC announcers were anonymous.) Hibberd (1893-1983) would count four after saying 'Goodnight, everybody' in order that listeners could say 'goodnight' back to him if they felt like it.

Goodnight, gentlemen, and good sailing Another example of informality from a BBC announcer in the starchier days of radio presentation — the customary end to a shipping forecast read by Frank Phillips (1901-80).

Goodnight . . . God bless Benny Hill, as himself, at the end of his TV comedy shows in the UK from 1969 on. Latterly, Hill has become equally well-known in the US, where this farewell was once associated with comedian Red Skelton.

Goodnight, good luck, and may your God go with you Customary farewell from Dave Allen, the Irish-born comedian, on UK TV during the 1970s and onwards.

Hello, everyone — old ones, new ones, loved ones, neglected ones The pianist Semprini's opening patter on his BBC radio shows in the 1960s and 70s (referring to the music he was going to play).

Hello, good evening, and welcome is a greeting well-known on both sides of the Atlantic. It derives from the period when David Frost (b.1939) was commuting back and forth to host TV chat shows in London and New York. It may contrive to say three things where only one is needed but it became an essential part of the Frost-impersonator's kit.

He was certainly saying it by 1970 and he was still saying it in 1983 (with a brief alteration to 'Hello, *good morning* and welcome' at the shaky debut of TV-AM, the breakfast TV station, in February of that year.)

Having been on the receiving end of his presentational style — 'Super . . . wonderful . . . it's been a *joy* having you here!' — I can only say that what may seem peculiar to the viewer is very disarming to the interviewee.

Frost's variation on the traditional lead-in to a commercial-break — 'We'll be right back after this break/ after this word' — has been **We'll be back in a trice.**

Hello, hello, and a very good, good morning to you all Edmundo Ros, the Venezuelan-born band leader who came to Britain in 1937, introduced Latin-American music programmes on BBC radio until the mid-1970s. He would say things like 'You're listening to a programme of Latin-American music played by my ballroom orchestra — which we most sincerely hope you are enjoying.' Whatever the type of dance-music he was about to lead the orchestra into he always seemed to say: **Ah, three — four!**

Hello, me old mates Presenter/disc jockey Brian Matthew on early BBC radio pop programmes in the 1960s, like *Easy Beat* and *Saturday Club*. In 1983 he was still referring to himself as 'Your old mate, Brian Matthew.'

Here is the news — and this is Alvar Liddell reading it Until the war, and for about twenty years after it, newsreaders on the BBC were anonymous, but for a period during the war they did identify themselves. This was to lessen the possibility of impersonation by English-speaking news-readers on German propaganda stations or if Britain was invaded. Hence, when Alvar Liddell (1908-81), a regular broadcaster from 1932-69, died, it was suggested that he had made this format famous. Indeed, he may have done, having had one of the most famous of the old-style BBC voices and having read the news at some key points in the course of the war.

How *do* you do, ladies and gentlemen, how *do* you do? Carroll Levis, a Canadian-born showman, introduced a talent contest on British radio for a number of years. From a typical edition broadcast in 1946: after a fanfare, the announcer said, 'The Carroll Levis Show! We're back again with our feast of fun for everybody, bringing you the family show which is equally welcome to outlaws and in-laws. The founder of the feast, Carroll Levis!' Levis then intoned his welcome. Along the way he called people 'Brother' and referred to 'My brother Cyril's favourite comedy couple . . .' At the end of the show he said: 'Same day, same time, same spot on the dial . . . so long, good luck and happy listening!'

How do you do? (without the emphasis put in by Levis) was also used by Arthur Askey (who had a radio series with the title in 1949), by Terry-Thomas, Jimmy James, and — for many years, in another sphere — by Roy Plomley, compère of radio's *Desert Island Discs:* 'How do you do, ladies and gentlemen. Our castaway this week is . . .'

Jeez, Wayne From McPhail and Gadsby's New Zealand TV show, set in the bar of a hotel. Current in 1980.

Love you madly Duke Ellington (1899-1974), the composer, pianist and band-leader, used to say 'We'd like you to know that the boys in the band all Love You Madly' — also the title of one of his songs.

Nice one, Stew From a children's programme on New Zealand TV in the mid-70s. Stew Dennison wore a schoolboy's cap and would say it to himself. Kids around him would then echo it.

So long . . . until tomorrow Lowell Thomas (1892-1981), a top American radio newscaster from 1930 to the mid-1970s.

(Before this he had helped promote the legend of T.E. Lawrence on lecture tours.)

This *is* Henry Hall speaking and tonight is my guest night
What was the reason for the peculiar emphasis on 'is'? In 1934, the BBC Dance Orchestra had been playing while Henry Hall (b.1899) was away in America and yet it was still announced as 'directed by Henry Hall'. A journalist wrote: 'Why do the BBC allow this to happen? How can Henry Hall possibly be conducting the orchestra when we know for a fact that at this very moment he is on the high seas?' Hence, on his return, he said: 'Hello, everyone, this *is* Henry Hall speaking!'

His sign-off was **Here's to the next time** − the title of his signature tune and autobiography.

This . . . is . . . London was a greeting familiar to American listeners to wartime reports given by Ed Murrow from London. It was a natural borrowing from BBC announcers who had been saying **This is London calling** from the earliest days of station 2LO in the 1920s. One of them, Stuart Hibberd, entitled a book of his broadcasting diaries *This is London*.

A very good night to you all Alan Keith presenting *Your Hundred Best Tunes* on BBC Radio from the early 1960s onwards.

We'll take a break there . . . in part 2 . . . Customary way of ending part 1 of ITN's *News at Ten* and for promoting news to be featured in the following section. Any time after the programme was launched in 1967, but chiefly in the late 1970s.

Well, if you have been, thank you for listening John Ebdon concluding one of his BBC Radio 4 talks (70s onwards).

'The time now − **when you hear the gong** − is six o'clock!' Radio Luxembourg in the 1950s and 60s.

THE SHOW MUST GO ON

The tradition that *the show must go on* grew out of circus. Whatever mishap occurred, the band was told to go on playing and the cry went up *send in the clowns* – for the simple reason that panic had to be avoided, the audience's attention had to be diverted, and the livelihood of everybody in the circus depended on not having to give the audience its money back. Later, Noel Coward wrote a song which posed the question '*Why* Must the Show Go On?'

From the many acts that appeared in music-hall and variety before TV completely took over as the main medium of popular entertainment, the following phrases linger:

Here we are again   Perhaps the oldest catchphrase it is possible to attach to a particular performer. Joseph Grimaldi (1779-1837) used it as Joey the Clown in pantomime and it has subsequently been used by almost all clowns on entering the circus ring or theatre stage . . . for example by Harry Paine in the 1870s and 80s. He would turn a somersault on entering and declare it.

Gentlemen, be seated   The great age of the black Minstrels in the UK was from 1840 until 1900. Mr Interlocutor, the white compère, would say this to the minstrels, as in the US.

I don't wish to know that – kindly leave the stage   The traditional response to a corny joke. Impossible to say when or with whom it started, but in the 1950s the phrase was given a new lease of life by the Goons on radio and by other British entertainers who still owed much to the routines and spirit of music-hall. Of equally obscure origin is the comedian's lead-in to a joke: **a funny thing happened (to me) on the way to the theatre (tonight) . . .**

Get your hair cut 'Johnnie Get Your Hair Cut' was the title of a late Victorian song sung by the comedian, George Beauchamp (1863-1901).

Daddy-o From the Gaiety Palace of Varieties in Leicester in the 1880s. The proprietor, Sam Torr, would dance around the stage with a dummy horse, singing about being 'on the back of Daddy-o'. He addressed remarks to it, rather like a ventriloquist's dummy, and 'Daddy-o' became a well-known catchphrase of the day.

By jingo From G.W. Hunt's music-hall song 'We Don't Want to Fight', 1878.

Where did you get that hat? A catchphrase of the 1890s, this originated in a comic song by J.J. Sullivan.

Hop along, sister Mary, hop along This saying originated in a song called 'Sister Mary Walked Like That', written by Gus Levaine and sung by John Nash (1830-1901), who called himself Jolly Nash. It was uproariously encored whenever Nash sang it in late Victorian times because he illustrated the words by imitating, with exaggeration, the mincing steps of a young girl. It was published as sheet music and had a vogue as a comic song into Edwardian times.

How's your poor (old) feet? Origin obscure — perhaps from nineteenth century music-hall?

Oh, no, there isn't In pantomime, an actor traditionally speaks to the audience with his back to something which he denies exists. The following kind of exchange then takes place: 'There isn't a bear behind me, is there, children?' Audience: 'Oh, yes, there is!' Actor: 'Oh, no, there isn't!' and so on. (The phrase was also used as bill matter by The Two Pirates variety act.) There is the story of a curtain-speech made by the manager of a provincial theatre half-way through a panto: 'I'm very sorry, ladies and gentlemen, but we cannot continue the performance as our leading lady has just died.' Children in the audience: 'Oh, no, she hasn't!'

Always merry and bright Comedian Alfred Lester (1872-1925) — who was always lugubrious — was associated with this phrase, although it crops up in all sorts of other places.

Peter Doody, a lugubrious jockey in the Lionel Monckton/ Arthur Wimperis musical comedy *The Arcadians* (1909) had it as a motto in a song. Somerset Maugham in a letter to a friend (1915) wrote: 'I am back on a fortnight's leave, very merry and bright, but frantically busy — I wish it were all over.' An edition of *The Magnet* from 1920 carries an ad. for 'Merry and Bright' — a comic paper. And Larry Grayson suggests that it was the billing of Billy Danvers.

Meredith, we're in　A shout of triumph which originated in a music hall sketch called 'The Bailiff' (or 'Moses and Son'), performed by Fred Kitchen (1872-1950), the leading comedian with Fred Karno's company. The sketch was first seen in 1907. The phrase was used each time a bailiff and his assistant looked like gaining entrance to a house. Fred Kitchen even had it put on his gravestone.

'Sno use　Harry Weldon (1881-1930) — the 's' pronounced with a loud whistle. From the title of a song.

If it's h-h-hokay with you, it's h-h-hokay with me　The stuttering catchphrase of Tubby Turner (1882-193?), the Lancashire-born music-hall artist.

How's your father?　The music-hall star, Harry Tate (1872-1940).

A little of what you fancy does you good　Innuendo-laden phrase from a song by Fred W. Leigh and George Arthurs, popularized with a wink by Marie Lloyd (1870-1922).

Not tonight, Josephine　Napoleon did not actually, as far as we know, utter the words which have become linked with him. The suggestion that he had better things to do than satisfy his wife's famous appetite, or was not inclined or able to, must have grown up in the nineteenth century. There was a saying attributed to Josephine: 'Bon-a-parte est Bon-à-rien' ('Bonaparte is good for nothing'). On the other hand, he did manage to father a son by his second wife and had a mistress during his last exile on St Helena.

The expression 'Not tonight, Josephine' probably arose through music-hall in Victorian times. Quite when this happened, it is impossible to say. However, a good example of the phrase in use occurs in a knockabout sketch filmed for the Pathé Library c1932 in which Lupino Lane plays Napoleon and Beatrice Lillie, Josephine. After signing a document of divorce (which Napoleon crumples up), Josephine says: 'When you are refreshed, come as usual to my apartment.' Napoleon says (as the tag to the sketch): 'Not tonight, Josephine', and she throws a custard pie in his face.

John Willie, come on George Formby Senior (1877-1921) included in his act monologues from a typical Lancashire character called 'John Willie'. The phrase 'John Willie, come on' swept the country, so I'm told. Audiences waited for the line and knew just when it was coming — so they could join in:

> We went to Madame Two Sword's waxwork show and it
> were grand,
> And there we saw all t'waxworks, kings and queens all
> shakin' hands,
> There was Mary Queen of Scots and Queen Elizabeth you
> see —
> They rather took my fancy when the wife said to me:
> 'John Willie, come on! It's closin' time, you see.'
> The lights went out and all was dark and quiet as could be.
> On turnin' round to my surprise I found the wife had gone,
> And I'm sure I heard Queen Elizabeth say, 'John Willie,
> come on!'

Formby also used a tragically true remark about himself: **Coughin' well tonight**. He had a convulsive cough, the result of a tubercular condition, which eventually killed him.

Desist One of a number of mock-disapproving phrases employed by Sir George Robey, 'The Prime Minister of Mirth' (1869-1954). 'If there is any more hilarity you must leave. Pray temper your hilarity with a modicum of reserve. Desist! I am surprised at you, Agnes!' (pronounced 'Ag-er-ness'). Also: Desist, refrain and cease', 'Go *out!*' and 'Get *out!*' or simply '*Out!*' Robey also used the expression: **I meanter say** (this was quite a common expression, however — I have come across it in a Frank Richards Billy Bunter story in a 1915 edition of *The Magnet*.)

Bang goes saxpence   The origins of this line lie in a *Punch* cartoon of 1868. A Scotsman who has just been on a visit to London says: 'Mun, a had na' been the-rre abune two hours when — bang — went saxpence!' It was repopularized by Sir Harry Lauder, the professional stage Scotsman.

Boom, boom   Verbal underlining to the punchline of a gag. Ernie Wise suggests that it is like the drum-thud or trumpet-sting used, particularly by American entertainers, to point a joke. Music-hall star Billy Bennett (1887-1942) may have been the first to use this device to emphasize his comic couplets. Morecambe and Wise, Basil Brush, and many others have since taken it up.

I say, I say, I say   Hard to know whether Murray and Mooney, the variety duo, invented this interruption, but they perfected the routine in their act during the 1930s. Mooney would interrupt with, 'I say, I say, I say!' To whatever he had to impart, Murray would reply with the traditional 'I don't wish to know that — kindly leave the stage!' Harry Murray died in 1967, Harry Mooney in 1972.

Mrs Ginocchi, SOS   Said by Arthur Lucan, who used to appear as Old Mother Riley, to his wife Kitty McShane, who played the daughter (in the 1930s/40s). Also: **Where've you been, who've you been with, what've you been doing, and why?**

Oh, I should love to polish you off   Todd Slaughter (1885-1956) as Sweeney Todd, the Demon Barber of Fleet Street.

By gum, she's a hot 'un   Frank Randle, the variety star of the 1930s and 40s, used this phrase in a sketch in which he appeared as an aged hiker, obsessed with ale and girls' legs. Randle (1901-57), whose fame was largely restricted to the North of England, would also say **Any more fer sailing?** and **By gum ah've supped sum ale toneet.** Offering a tin of fag-ends, he would ask: **Would y'care for a Woodbine?**

On behalf of the working classes!   Bill matter and phrase used in routines by the music-hall comedian Billy Russell (1893-1971).

Good morning, boys   Opening line from Will Hay (1888-

1949) as the Headmaster of St Michael's. His pupils would reply wearily: 'Good morning, sir!'

Don't you know there's a war on?   Response to complaints used by (Will) Hatton and (Ethel) Manners as a cockney chappie and Lancashire lass in their variety act of the 1930s/40s.

Let's get on with it   Nat Mills and Bobbie were a variety act that flourished in the 1930s and 40s portraying 'a gumpish type of lad and his equally gumpish girl friend.' Nat recalled in 1979: 'It was during the very early part of the war. We were booked by the BBC to go to South Wales for a *Workers' Playtime*. Long tables had been set up in front of the stage for the workers to have lunch on before the broadcast. On this occasion a works foreman went round all the tables shouting, "Come on, let's get on with it," to get them to finish their lunch on time. I was informed he used this phrase so many times, the workers would mimic him among themselves. So I said to Bobbie, "You start the broadcast by talking to yourself and I'll interject and say, 'Let's get on with it'." Lo and behold it got such a yell of laughter we kept it in all our broadcasts. Even Churchill used our slogan to the troops during the early part of the war.'

Play the game, cads   The Western Brothers (who were in fact cousins) would begin their act with 'Hello, cads!' and end it with, 'Cheerio, cads, and happy landings!'

Somebody pinched me puddin'   Variety act Collinson and Breen. The explanation was that 'Somebody said "All put your puddins out for treacle", and I put mine out and somebody pinched it!'

God, what a beauty   Leon Cortez (1898-1970) was billed as The 'Coster' Comedian. Also **As you may know . . . or as you may not know.**

Aren't plums cheap?   The catchphrase of comedy acrobat/contortionist Bob Nelson − 'The Naval Comic'. He would entangle himself in a number of balancing bentwood chairs and make the remark to hold the audience's interest while he had another go at disentangling himself.

Show us your rabbit   Curious but inspired phrase used by (Raymond) Bennett and (Harry) Moreny in their variety act.

Take a kick in the pants   George Doonan, comedian (d.1973) who also asked: **'Smatter wit chew?**

We bring you melodies from out of the sky/ My brother and I   From the signature tune of Bob and Alf Pearson.

Very tasty, very sweet   Kenway and Young (Nan Kenway and Douglas Young) used to say this, smacking their lips. E.g. Kenway: 'My nephew's getting on well in the Navy. He's a ship's carpenter. They say he's a very efficient chips.' Young: 'Fish and chips? I like them with a dollop of the old vinegar and a sprinkle of old salt. Goes down a treat I reckon. Very tasty, very sweet!'

What a performance   Comedian Sid Field (1904-50).

I've got a letter from a bloke in Bootle   was one of a number of expressions used by Jimmy James, the variety comedian (1892-1965). Others were: **Excuse me, is this the place? Are you the bloke?**; **Somebody come** (said by James in his 'drunk' bedroom sketch — though he himself was a teetotaller); **Give me a note, please . . . Er-fa-a-fa-a fah . . . fah . . . fah** — trying to get the note at the start of a song, when drunk; **How do you do?** — said with a slight nod.

The splendidly named Hutton Conyers would say to James: **Hey, are you putting it round that I'm barmy?**

Over the garden wall   was the billing given to Norman Evans, the North country comedian (1901-62) who specialised in take-offs of garrulous women. Among his phrases were: **It's daft** and **I'll separate you from your breath**.

George, don't do that   Not from variety or music-hall, but a phrase from intimate revue. Joyce Grenfell (1910-79) would do entire solo evenings of monologues and songs. This line came from her Nursery School sketch in which she played a slightly harrassed but unflappable teacher. Part of its charm lay in our never knowing precisely what it was that George was being asked not to do.

Wotcher, mates   Danny La Rue (b.1928) carried some of the vivacity of music-hall and variety into the television age.

First in clubs and then in quite lavish spectaculars and pantomimes his drag act depended on our knowing that, underneath, all was not lost.

Aw, don't embarrass me Ventriloquist Terry Hall (b.1926) first created Lenny the Lion from a bundle of fox-fur and papier-mache (with a golfball for a nose) in 1954. He gave his new partner a gentle lisping voice, added a few mannerisms and a catchphrase which began thus:

> He's ferocious! *(drum roll)*
> He's courageous! *(drum roll)*
> He's the king of the jungle!

– Aw, don't embarrass me! *(with a modest paw over the eyes)*

Unusually, given the success of the catchphrase, Terry Hall told me (in 1979) that he drops it from time to time – arguing that it's no bad policy to rest certain material and then resuscitate it.

Roger de Courcey (b.1944) came along with a bear called Nookie, giving the slang word for sexual activity further currency. T-shirts appeared with pictures of the bear and the slogan **I like Nookie.** Ray Alan (b.1930) appears with the monocled Lord Charles who exclaims **Silly Ass!**

Pre-dating these exponents of the art, there was the odd case of Harry Hemsley who – like Peter Brough and Archie Andrews – found fame as that contradiction in terms, a radio ventriloquist (though Edgar Bergen with Charlie McCarthy had great success on American radio). Hemsley conducted dialogues with his family (of three, I think): two girls, Winnie and Elsie, and baby Horace who spoke gibberish that only Winnie could translate. Hence, **What did Horace say?**

While we're on the subject, let me just record that **Gottle o' geer, gottle o' geer** has become a standard showbiz way of mocking the inadequacies of so many vent acts (it represents 'Bottle of beer' as said with teeth tightly-clenched.)

MAKE 'EM LAUGH
MAKE 'EM LAUGH

Individual British and American comedians and their catch-phrases:

Hylda BAKER (b.1908)

Diminutive comedienne Baker used to say about Cynthia, her mute giraffe-like butt: **She knows, y'know**. Her **Be soon** was used as the title of a TV series in the 1950s.

Jack BENNY (1894-1974)

He would give a pregnant pause and exasperatedly say **Well!** and that was his trademark, so why not call it a catchphrase? Hence, also: **Now cut that out! Yipe! Hmmm!**

Harold BERENS (b.19——)

This Glasgow-born comedian, often believed to be a Cockney, became known through the late 1940s radio show *Ignorance is Bliss*. He acquired one of his catchphrases from a woman who used to sell him carnation buttonholes. To everything he said she would reply: **Now, there's a coincidence.** Likewise, when Berens was living near the Bayswater Road in London he would buy his daily newspaper from a vendor who always asked him what the latest joke was. When told, his customary reaction — taken up by Berens — was **'Ee, wot a geezer.**

Max BYGRAVES (b.1922)

Launched on a sea of catchphrases in *Educating Archie* (q.v.), Max later became chiefly known for a phrase wished upon him by an impersonator. It is possible that he may have said of his own accord **I wanna tell you a story** (with the appropriate hand-shaking gestures) but it was Mike Yarwood who drew attention to it. Now Bygraves uses it himself in self-parody and even chose it as the title of his autobiography. Still, as he says, he once went into a competition for Max Bygraves impressionists — and came fifth!

Of having successful catchphrases in general, Bygraves told me (1980): 'It's like having a hit record!'

Tommy CANNON (b.1938) and Bobby BALL (b.1944)

The precise origin of **Rock on, Tommy** goes unremembered by Bobby Ball but he thinks it came from places like Wigan and Oldham when he was spurring on Tommy Cannon. Depending on who is telling the story, it may also have occurred when Cannon was singing and be related to the David Essex song 'Rock on'. Bobby recalled (1980): 'About three years ago Tommy was singing a rock and roll number. I was fooling about and just happened to say it. To my astonishment it got a big laugh, such a tremendous response that we decided to try it again.' Tommy added: 'After a couple of years we thought of dropping it because it might be losing its impact. But we decided to keep it in for our TV show. We could never drop it now.'

Frank CARSON (b.1926)

'You've heard them all before, but . . . **it's the way I tell 'em'** The Ulster comedian's line became famous from the mid-70s. Also **It's a cracker** (pronounced 'crocker').

Charlie CHESTER (b.1914)

The phrase 'a right Charlie' probably grew out of rhyming slang 'Charlie Hunt', used to describe a fool or simpleton. I think it must have arisen during the Second World War – it may have been a simultaneous British and American coinage, too. **Proper Charlie** was commandeered, however, by Charlie Chester who was prominent as a radio comedian in Britain immediately after the war. The phrase was later used by him as the title of a radio show although he first became known through *Stand Easy*.

From *that* show came the name of **Whippit Kwick**, a catburglar in a radio strip cartoon. Leslie Bridgmont, the producer recalled how the name swept the country. Wherever he went on bus, tube or train he would hear someone say, 'Who's that over there?' to which would come the reply, 'Whippit Kwick!' Chester remembered (1979): 'Bruce Woodcock, the boxer, used to run around the streets chanting the jungle chants from the same strip cartoon, **Down in the jungle, living in a tent, better than a pre-fab – no rent**, that sort of thing. Once at Wembley, just before he threw a right to put the other fellow out for the count, some wag in the audience yelled out, "Whippit Kwick!" He did – and it went in.'

Also from *Stand Easy* came **Don't force it, Phoebe** and one other phrase: 'This was really a joke on my missus. My wife broke her arm and was sitting in the audience. I told Len Marten to keep coming up to me with the line **I say, what a smasher**. Then, at the end of the programme, the resolving gag was: "Len, what do you mean by all this 'I say, what a smasher business'?" He said, "The blonde in the third row!" And there's this broken arm sticking out like a beacon. Strangely enough, I went down to Butlin's not long after and somebody dropped a pile of crockery. Of course the noise resounded all over the place and everybody shouted "I say, what a smasher!"'

Chester also used **I can hear you** which arose when he noticed somebody talking about him in a rehearsal room.

Another of his radio shows was called *Come to Charlee-ee!* – a title which grew out of a catchphrase: 'I would talk to somebody from the stage and say, "Are you all right, Ada? Speak to Charlee-ee. Charlie spoke to *you!*" ... You'd be surprised how many people still ask, "Say that phrase for me – say, **Come to Charlee-ee!**" It's just one of those things they like to hear.'

In his more recent role as a presenter on Radio 2, Chester developed an elaborate sign-off (from about 1970): **There we are, dear friends, both home, overseas and over the borders.**

Tommy COOPER (1922-84)

Tommy Cooper's **Just like that** was not a premeditated catch-phrase. He only noticed it when impressionists and others singled it out from his conjuring act. Said in the appropriate gruff tones and accompanied by small paddling gestures, it was a gift to mimics. Inevitably the phrase was used by Cooper as the title of his autobiography. There is also a song incorporating it.

Paul DANIELS (b.1938)

The Yorkshire magician and comedian says he found the catchphrase **Not a lot** early on in his career. He was being heckled by somebody who didn't like his act. 'A pity,' he retorted, 'because I like your suit. Not a lot, but I like it.' Which became: 'You'll like this. Not a lot, but you'll like it.' 'I feel it has done a lot to establish my identity with the public,' Daniels adds.

Jim DAVIDSON (b.1954)

Davidson got off to an early start in show business. His **Nick, nick** phrase provided an aural counterpart for the revolving light on the top of police vehicles. 'As kids we all shouted it whenever Old Bill appeared on the horizon,' he says.

In 1980, having been fined for using threatening behaviour at a football match and for obstructing the police, Davidson said he was giving the phrase a rest. He took up a new one: **Too risky!**

Reg DIXON (1915-84)

'I didn't feel well, I didn't. I felt poorly — **proper poorly.**' Also noted, on early 1950s radio shows like *Variety Bandbox*, for his 'Confidentially' theme song.

Ken DODD (b.1927)

'I was once a salesman and I've always been fascinated by sales techniques,' Ken Dodd told me in 1979, 'and catchphrases are like trade marks — they are attention-getting details which in my case make people exclaim, "Ah yes, Ken Dodd." The disadvantage of catchphrases is that they get worn — like tyres. So I wanted a catchphrase that was better than a catchphrase . . . I narrowed it down to the fact that it had to be a greeting like "Hello, folks" or something like Fanny Brice's **Are you all right? Fanny's all right**. I thought of the word "tickled" and all the permutations and combinations one could get from that. So I devised **How tickled I am** as a phrase that could be varied by the addition of a joke — "Have you ever been tickled, Mrs?" and so on. But it was out of the need for a catchphrase that the tickling stick actually came.' (**Hello, Mrs** is also a hangover from his days as a travelling hardware salesman.)

'Like most performers I'm always trying out material on friends and relatives. One night after recording my radio show in London, we rushed to catch the train back to Knotty Ash from Euston. I was trying on various daft voices and saying, "Where's me case? Where's me shirt?" and the people who were with me laughed — so it went into the next show.' The pronunciation is approximately **Whairs me shairt?** Also **I'm a shairt short**.

Other Doddisms include:

By Jove, I needed that after a quick burst on the banjo, to relieve tension. (Also used on *The Goon Show*.)

Diddy 'Diddy Uncle Jack' was how the family used to describe Ken's great-uncle. Ken now uses the word to describe anything 'quaint, small and lovable'. 'My family,' he says, 'always impressed on me the importance of being original in my act and I suppose these words I use, like "diddy", "full of plumptiousness" and "tattifalarious", are an attempt at having something which is mine and nobody else's.'

Discumknockerating Means that something bowls you over.

Nikky, nokky, noo Nonsense phrase. 'Humour is anarchic, I suppose. So, like a child, from time to time you revolt against the discipline of words and just jabber!'

Tatty-bye!   Ken inherited this form of farewell from his dad.

What a beautiful day for_____   Another example of a catch-phrase which allows for variety by the addition of a new punchline.

On 31 December 1981 the *Liverpool Echo* reported Ken's reaction to being awarded the OBE: 'I am delighted. It's a great honour and wonderful news. I am full of plumptious-ness. The jam butty workers are discumknockerated and the Diddymen are diddy-delighted.'

Jack DOUGLAS (b.1927)

For his character of Alf Ippititimus, Jack Douglas created what for me is one of the most compelling visual and verbal catchphrases of all. The bodily twitch that accompanies his **Wu-hey!** defies description. The combination was born when Jack was appearing in a double act with Joe Baker at a holiday camp many years ago. Joe managed to get himself locked out of the theatre and Jack found himself alone on stage. 'My mind went completely blank and in sheer des-peration I began twitching and falling about.' I recall seeing Jack in pantomime at Oxford in the mid-60s — one just waited for him to come on and do his twitch.

Charlie DRAKE (b.1925)

His husky, baby-voiced greeting was **Hello, my darlings!** from the early 1950s

Jimmy 'Schnozzle' DURANTE (1893-1980)

The big-nosed American comedian had a gaggle of phrases he employed regularly:

I'm mortified
Everybody wants to get into the act

He used to sign off his radio and TV shows in the 1940s and

50s with the phrase **Goodnight, Mrs Calabash . . . wherever you are** — Calabash was a pet name for his first wife, Maud, who had died in 1943, and is an American idiom for 'empty head' (calabash=gourd). However, Durante always resisted explaining the phrase. His biographer, Gene Fowler writing in 1952, could only note: 'When he says that line his manner changes to one of great seriousness, and his voice takes on a tender, emotional depth . . . when asked to explain the Calabash farewells, Jim replied: "That's my secret. I want it to rest where it is".'

Of Gary Moore, the MC on US radio's *The Camel Caravan* (1943-7) — and 22 years his junior — Durante would say **Dat's my boy dat said dat!**

Them's the conditions that prevail! or **Dese are de conditions dat prevail!** or **It's da conditions dat prevail!**

I've got a million of 'em! (also used by Max Miller).

Stop da music! Stop da music!

Dick EMERY (1917-83)

After an apprenticeship in radio comedy shows such as *Ray's a Laugh*, Emery established himself as a versatile comedian on TV in a wide variety of disguises including characters with these catchphrases:

Are you married? The amorous Hetty.

Hello, honky-tonks! Clarence, the camp gentlemen.

Oooh, you are awful — but I like you! Emery in drag as Mandy, the man-hungry spinster. The last word was followed by a quick bash with her handbag. Also the title of a song and a feature film. Emery recalled (1980): 'We were filming at Ealing. I was in drag as Mandy and when the prompt man came out with something outrageous I snapped back: "Ooh, you are awful." Everyone thought it was hilarious.'

Arthur ENGLISH (b.1919)

A necessary exhortation to audiences from Arthur English in his late 1940s spiv character was **Sharpen up there, the quick**

stuff's coming! He would spiel at some three hundred words a minute. However, Arthur commented in 1979: 'It didn't really get off the ground. One of my scriptwriters put it in — but strangely enough it was the catchphrases we didn't plan that caught on.'

For example: 'During my first show at the Windmill I finished up my act halfway through a joke, looking at the front row and saying "You'll be here next house — I'll tell you the end then!" But when I was asked to do a further six week season at the "Mill", I thought, "I can't do the same ending" and as I can't sing all that well I was stuck for a finish. So I started rambling on with the senseless chatter I became known for and my wife, Joy, said, "That's funny — finish with that." So I did and when I got to the end of my act I suddenly realised I had no finish to the chatter! I don't know what made me say it, but I said, "I don't know what the devil I'm talking about. **Play the music and open the cage!**" and ran off.'

Another such arose like this : 'On my entrance during my first broadcast I had my big tie rolled up and proceeded to unfurl it. There was a great laugh and, to cover it, I said, **Mum, mum, they are laughing at me.** I repeated this in a couple of broadcasts, then Brian Sears (the producer) said, "I shouldn't do that line about your mother any more." So I said, "It's my mother's birthday today — can I do it just once?" The following week I started getting letters saying, "As soon as we hear 'Mum, mum' we know we are in for a good laugh" — so naturally it became my catchphrase.'

Bud FLANAGAN (1896-1968)

His way of rounding off a joke or explanation in his routines with Chesney Allen was to exclaim: **Oi!** If Flanagan muffed a line or committed a malapropism he would at last correct himself with Chesney's help, shout 'Oi', and the orchestra would shout it back. Used as the title of a biographical show on the London stage in 1982. Also used by Lupino Lane.

Cyril FLETCHER (b.1913)

Fletcher recalled (1978) that he was persuaded to broadcast 'Dreaming of Thee', a poem by Edgar Wallace, in 1938. He did it in an extraordinary voice — a cockney caricature — and the constant refrain at the end of each verse — **I'm dreaming oh my darling love of thee** — got 'yells of delight'. It 'made' him, he says, and later when he returned to London for a repeat performance he was on a bus and the conductor was saying 'Dreaming of thee' to every passenger with a passable imitation of Fletcher's funny voice as he gave them their tickets.

Fletcher's customary cry before embarking upon one of his Odd Odes has been **Pin back your lugholes!** Other Fletcher-isms have included **Thanking you!** (pronounced 'thenking yew') and **Ours is a nice 'ouse ours is!**

George FORMBY (1904-61))

Formby was not exactly a comedian but he exuded personal-ity and, singing slightly naughty songs to a ukelele accompaniment, he became one of the great stars of the variety stage between the wars and also in a highly-successful series of cinema films. It was in these films that two phrases featured: **Ooh, mother!** — scuttling away from trouble — and **It's turned out nice again!** Formby disclaimed any credit for originating the latter phrase with which he always opened his act. 'It's simply a familiar Lancashire expression,' he once said. 'People use it naturally up there. I used it as part of a gag and have been doing so every since' — particularly in films after emerging from some disaster or other. It was used as the title of a film in 1941 (as well as being the punchline of it) and as a song title.

Bruce FORSYTH (b.1928)

Once during Forsyth's time as compère of the ATV show *Sunday Night at the London Palladium* (from 1958) he was supervising 'Beat the Clock', a game involving members of the audience. A young couple was in a muddle, throwing plates at a see-saw table. Bruce recalled (1980): 'We had a particularly stroppy contestant. In the end I just turned round and told him, "Hold on a minute . . . **I'm in charge!**" It just happened, but the audience loved it and it caught on.' Lapel badges began appearing with the slogan, foremen had it painted on their hard hats. The phrase suited Brucie's mock-bossy manner to a tee.

In his later incarnation as host of the hugely-popular *Generation Game* on BBC TV during the mid-70s, Forsyth again had the nation parroting his phrases:

Anthea, give us a twirl! To hostess Anthea Redfern, who later became his wife for a while (inviting her to show off her dress here, perhaps one should add.)

Didn't he do well? This compliment to contestants was off the cuff, according to Brucie — made when one finalist recalled almost all the items that had passed before him on the conveyor belt. However, it is said to have originated c1973 with what a studio attendant used to shout down from the lighting grid during rehearsals.

Good game . . . good game! Encouragement to contestants.

Nice to see you, to see you . . . / Nice! Exchange of greetings with studio audience — something that Bruce admits was worked out in advance and not spontaneous.

Ken GOODWIN (b.19– –)

A catchphrase cleverly based on the observation that if you tell people not to laugh they will only do so the more (cf. George Robey's 'Desist!') was Ken Goodwin's attempt to quieten laughter at his own jokes: '**Settle down now, settle down!** . . . I don't want you to make a noise, I've got a headache.' Ken recalled (1979): 'I first said "Settle down" in a working men's club after the so-called compère/chairman had announced me to the audience. They didn't hear him and they didn't know I was on stage till I let them know. They were so noisy that, to get attention, I said, "Come on, you lot, settle down now." One or two began to smile and say to themselves, "What's this unknown commodity?" They were all waiting for bingo! It really took off after I did the Royal Variety Show, a summer season at the Palladium and *The Comedians* on TV.'

'Monsewer' Eddie GRAY (1898-1978)

This Crazy Gang member who spoke in a delightful mishmash of Anglicised French and English would comment, if he got a laugh: **They're working well tonight!** Other Crazy Gang phrases included: **Aye, aye, taxi!** and **Shut up, Cecil!** — both usually from Jimmy Nervo — and **Suck it and see**, usually from Charlie Naughton, though it is of older, music-hall origin.

Larry GRAYSON (b.1930)

Once upon a time, Grayson appeared as 'Billy Breen' and used to say **Thank you, mother, for the rabbit!** In his later persona he had a rapid rise to fame in the early 1970s. The first time he used the phrase **Shut that door!** was on stage at the Theatre Royal, Brighton in 1970 'when I felt a terrible draught up my trouser legs. I turned to the wings and said it.' I really meant it — but the only response was giggles from the wings and a roar of laughter from the audience. So I kept it in my act. I can't go anywhere now without taxidrivers or shopkeepers telling me to "Shut that door".'

His mock-camp routine included such effusions as **What a gay day! The place is alive!** and **I just don't care any more!** As host of BBC TV's *Generation Game* from 1978, he would comment knowingly on contestants, saying: **He seems like a nice boy, doesn't he?** — 'It's the expression mothers always use when they describe their daughter's boyfriend and I never dreamt it would catch on like it did.'

Dickie HASSETT (————.————)

I didn't know why he said it until quite recently, but it's wonderful: **Large lumps!** I'm told he even did a radio show with this phrase as the title c1940, but this was before my time. Ned Sherrin advances the case by saying that the full phrase was 'large lumps, they're lovely'. Then a correspondent tells me that it occurred in a sketch about London street cries, also including: 'Don't fergit yer mohair laces . . . **Sarsparillar** . . . Mmatches, two-fer-a-h'penny!' It was the cry of the iced-coconut man.

Lenny HENRY (b.1958)

Dudley-born Henry, Britain's youngest black comedian, was noticed first on ITV's *New Faces* show as a 16-year-old comic. His send up of a woolly-hatted Rastafarian — Algernon Winston Spencer Churchill Gladstone Disraeli Pitt the Younger Razzmatazz — has given the West Indian catchphrase **Ooookaaaay** to a whole generation of schoolchildren. On TV's *O.T.T.* (1982) he introduced another black character with the catchphrase **Katanga!** (which, as one paper commented, 'half the population already seems to have taken up in an attempt to drive the other half mad.') As presenter of a record programme on Radio 1 he also came up (1982) with

Delbert Wilkins, the garrulous DJ from a Brixton pirate radio station who says **Well, basic, Well, crucial, man!** and **Diamond!**

Frankie HOWERD (b.1922)

Howerd, rightly, refers to his catchphrases more as 'verbal punctuation marks'. 'While other shows used catchphrases almost as characters, I was a character who used catchphrases,' he says. **Ladies and gentle-*men!*** is an opening phrase to which he gives special emphasis. Howerd explains that when he was starting in radio just after the war he thought a good gimmick would be for him to give unusual emphasis to certain words. Hence **I was a-*mazed!*** He also claims to have given the phrase **And the best of luck** to the language: 'It came about when I introduced into radio *Variety Bandbox* those appallingly badly sung mock operas, starring the show's bandleader Billy Ternent (tenor), Madame Vera-Roper (soprano), and Frankie Howerd (bass — "the lowest of the low"). Vera, while singing, would pause for breath before a high C and as she mustered herself for this

musical Everest I would mutter, "And the best of luck!" Later it became: "And the best of British luck!" The phrase is so common now that I frequently surprise people when I tell them it was my catchphrase on *Variety Bandbox*.'

Eric Partridge suggests, however, that the 'British' version was originally a Second World War army phrase ironically meaning the exact opposite of what it appeared to say and compares it with a line from the First World War: 'Over the top with the best of luck/ Parley-voo.'

Similarly, Partridge dates **Not on your Nellie!** from the late 1930s and says that it is abbreviated rhyming slang for 'puff' (breath), as in 'Not on your Nellie Duff!' meaning 'not on your life'. Howerd undoubtedly popularized both these expressions after the Second World War, however.

Other Howerdisms include: **No, don't laugh! Titter ye not! Chilly! 'Ere, mush! Listen! Let's get myself comfy! Please yourselves!** (used as the title of a radio series) and **Poor soul – she's past it!** (said of his supposedly deaf accompanist – alternatively, **Poor old thing – she'll have to go!**) not to be confused with **Er, thing you know**, when speaking of the person responsible for or in charge of the show.

Shut your face perhaps demonstrates what Howerd is all about – taking phrases that are already in circulation and somehow giving them a special twist (this one was also given a going over on a hit single as **Shadda up your face** by the Australian-Italian entertainer Joe Dolci in 1980.)

Barry HUMPHRIES (b.1934)

With entertainers like Humphries, the word comedian seems inappropriate – especially when his most famous creation Dame Edna Everage, the Housewife Superstar from Australia, is so convincing a personality that the word comedienne might seem more fitting. Although frequently seen on television, this is an act that is nevertheless in the great stand-up comic tradition of music-hall and variety. It is built on confidence – even managing to fill the Royal Albert Hall – and eminently flexible – playing with and not just to an audience like any great comic had to do before the days of studio audiences and laughter tracks. Perhaps there is no outstanding catchphrase, though Australianisms like **possums!** have become closely linked with the character. The ritual waving of gladdies has become a visual catchphrase.

Jimmy JEWEL (b.1912)

Jimmy Jewel, of the double-act Jewel and Warriss, would refer to his cousin Ben as 'Harry Boy' (for reasons lost in the mists of time) and say **'Carry on, 'Arry Boy!** Tell 'em, boy. Has Harry Boy been up to something naughty?' When some dreadful tale had been unfolded, Jewel would cap it with **What a carry on!** In his autobiography (1982) Jewel remarked that Tommy Trinder 'stole' the line 'and later we almost came to blows over it.'

LIBERACE (b.1919)

The twinkly pianist was as famous for his phrases in the 1950s as he was for his candelabra. He seemed to say **Ladies and Gentlemen** between every sentence, frequently mentioned his **Mom**, and thanked us **on behalf of my brother George.**

Syd LITTLE (b.1942) and Eddie LARGE (b.1942)

Little and Large have had two words they slipped into routines since their TV appearances began in the mid-70s — **sorree!** and the otherwise Sloane Rangerish **brill** (short for brilliant) as in 'It's a brill idea!' Eddie Large's nickname for Syd Little has been **Soopersonic!** However, Eddie Large explained (1980) that the words were born before the duo got together: 'Syd was entertaining in the pubs in Glasgow. I was a bit of a tearaway and used to go round the pubs just to heckle him. I called him "Soopersonic" because his nose is the same shape as Concorde. We teamed up and we've been together ever since.'

Max MILLER (1895-1963)

'The Cheeky Chappie' did not exactly have a catchphrase but he had stock phrases with which he became associated:

'**Here's a funny thing!** Now this is a funny thing. I went home the other night . . . *there's* a funny thing!'
When I'm dead and gone, the game's finished!
'Miller's the name, lidy. **There'll never be another!'**
You're the kind of people who give me a bad name! (when an audience readily perceived a double-entendre without it being emphasized.)

Albert MODLEY (1901-79)

The north country comedian achieved nationwide fame through radio's *Variety Bandbox* in the late 1940s. A former railway porter he employed several northern expressions, including: 'Heee!' 'Flippin' 'eck!' and his own **'Ee, in't it grand to be daft!** Towards the end of his life I also heard him refer to an inexplicable catchphrase he had used on *Variety Bandbox:* **Ninety-two!**

Jack PEARL (–––––.–––––)

Known on US radio as Baron Munchausen, Hungarian-born Pearl would tell tall stories to Charlie, a straight man. If Charlie expressed doubt, the Baron would inquire **Vas you dere, Sharlie?** This was in the early 1930s. He later dropped the character.

Joe PENNER (1904-41)

Penner, a Hungarian-American, rocketed to fame on US radio in 1934 with rapid-fire one-liners and a number of catchphrases including **Wanna buy a duck?** and **You naaasty man!** He carried a real duck, called Goo Goo, in a basket. Almost as rapidly his fame declined, but the duck phrase is still remembered.

Ken PLATT (b.1922)

I won't take me coat off – I'm not stopping! Ken Platt, the nasal-voiced slightly lugubrious northern comedian, was handed this catchphrase on a plate by Ronnie Taylor, producer of radio's *Variety Fanfare* in January 1951. Says Ken: 'I told him rather grudgingly that I thought it was "as good as anything" . . and I've been stuck with it ever since. People are disappointed if I don't say it. I tease them and pretend not to know what they're talking about if they ask me to "say it"!'

Platt also adapted the northern expression 'Soft as a brush': 'I started saying **daft as a brush** when I was doing shows in the Army in the early 1940s. People used to write and tell me I'd got it wrong!' Also in *Variety Fanfare* he would comment: **Hasn't it been a funny day, today?**

Gillie POTTER (1887-1975)

Potter's radio talks, delivered with an assumed pedagogic and superior air, recounted the doings of the Marshmallow family of Hogsnorton Towers — a delight from the 1940s and early 50s. He would begin by saying **Good evening, England! This is Gillie Potter speaking to you in English.** He would conclude with **Goodbye, England, and good luck!**

This reminds me of a favourite broadcasting story. When Radio 1 began in 1967, the BBC had yet to cultivate newsreaders who could fit in with the prevailing tone of the station. As I recall it, on the very first day, someone not a million miles from Alvar Liddell was given the job of reading a news summary in the middle of a noisy rock show introduced by a DJ with the mandatory mid-Atlantic accent. The newsreader began: 'And now here is the news — *in English*.'

Sandy POWELL (1900-82)

'It was in about 1932-3,' Sandy Powell told me in 1979, 'when I was doing an hour's show on the radio, live, from Broadcasting House in London. I was doing a sketch called "Sandy at the North Pole". I was supposed to be broadcasting home and wanting to speak to my mother. When I got to the line, "Can you hear me, mother?" I dropped my script on the studio floor. While I was picking up the sheets all I could do was repeat the phrase over and over. Well, that was on a Saturday night. The following week I was appearing at the Hippodrome, Coventry, and the manager came to me at the band rehearsal with a request: "You'll say that, tonight, won't you?" I said, "What?" He said, "**'Can you hear me, mother?'** Everybody's saying it. Say it and see." So I did and the whole audience joined in and I've been stuck with it ever since. Even abroad — New Zealand, South Africa, Rhodesia, they've all heard it. I'm not saying it was the first radio catchphrase — they were all trying them out — but it was the first to catch on.'

Al READ (b.19––)

The north country comedian was big on radio in the 1950s and then disappeared almost completely. His speciality was monologues — or, rather, dialogues — with him playing all the parts. He used a number of standard Lancashire expressions and made them for a while his own — like **Give over! You'll be lucky . . . I say, you'll be lucky! Dad . . . dad! Ooh, an 'e was strong!** and **My reply is on a piece of paper!**

Above all, Read was known for two catchphrases: **Cheeky monkey!** and **Right monkey!** For example: 'She said, "Did he say anything about the check suit?" and I thought, "Right monkey!"'

Gerry Collins of Manchester's Music Hall Association added (1979): 'My mother used to say this to me *years* before Al Read's pro-time. When I refused to go an errand because I was busy playing, she'd say, "Right, monkey, wait till your father comes home" — which shows how talented Al Read was to store up these Lancashire gems and, in after years, be able to reproduce them.'

From a theatre poster once seen in Blackpool: 'HENRY HALL PRESENTS AL READ IN "RIGHT MONKEY".'

Another Readism I have been told is when he played a drunk staggering homeward and shouting through his neighbours' letter boxes: **We've soopped soom stoof tonight** — but he may have obtained this from Frank Randle, the music-hall star.

Mike REID (b.19––)

The cockney comedian pronounced the word 'terrific' in the distinctive way: **Terr-if-ic!** Perhaps he would also say the word **Wallop!** — or, at least, a correspondent encourages me to believe this. However, from a letter to the London *Evening News* (17 February 1978): 'May I ask Mike Reid to drop his latest catchphrase **Migraine** whenever he gets a burst of applause? I would have written earlier but I have been in a blacked out room for eight days suffering from a migraine attack. In 30 years, migraine has caused enough havoc in my life without a comedian trying to make it a laughing-matter, which it isn't. Mrs H.K., Putney.'

TERRY-THOMAS (b.1911)

The gap-toothed toff with the cigarette-holder would say **Oh, good show!** in his late 40s, early 50s monologues. Also: **How do you do?** (or, on TV in the early 50s, as the title of a show, **How Do You View?**) I also seem to remember him saying **You're an absolute shower!** in the film *Private's Progress* (1956).

Tommy TRINDER (b.1909)

Trinder rode on a wave of publicity in the early 1940s. He even took space on advertising hoardings to declare, 'If it's laughter you're after, Trinder's the name. **You lucky people!**' The phrase (which arose in concert party) was used as the title of a film in 1954 and gave rise to one of his fastest ad-libs. Trinder was appearing at a London club. He would give his photographs out and walk round the tables in a hurried manner, saying, 'Trinder's the name, you lucky people!' One night, he walked towards Orson Welles who had recently been divorced from Rita Hayworth. Welles said, somewhat aggressively, 'Why don't you change it, then?' Quick as a flash, Trinder replied: 'Are you proposing?'

Norman VAUGHAN (b.1927)

Rather as the upper classes tend to rely on two adjectives — 'fascinating' and 'boring', so, too, did Vaughan in the 1960s. Accompanied by an upward gesture of the thumb his **Swinging!** was the equivalent of the upper-class 'fascinating' and (with a downward gesture of the thumb) his **Dodgy!**, the equivalent of the upper-class 'boring'. Norman told me in

1979: 'The words "Swinging" and "Dodgy" came originally from my association with jazz musicians and just seemed to creep into my everyday conversation. Then when I got the big break at the Palladium (introducing ITV's *Sunday Night at the London Palladium* in 1962) they were the first catch-phrases that the papers and then the public seized upon.'

According to *The Making of the Prime Minister 1964* by Anthony Howard and Richard West, the Labour Party considered using the word 'Swinging' with an upraised thumb as the basis of its advertising campaign prior to the 1964 General Election. However, doubts were expressed as to whether everyone would get the allusion and only the thumb was used. Although not, of course, the first person to use the word, Norman's use of 'Swinging' helped to characterise an era — the Swinging Sixties.

During his Palladium stint, he also used the stock phrase **It's all been happening this week!** and introduced the verbal format of **A touch of the** _____ ('A touch of the Nelson Riddles', etc.) Later he had a TV series called *A Touch of the Norman Vaughans*.

And just one more: 'On the *The Golden Shot* from 1971, for eighteen months, I developed the catchphrase **These are the jokes, folks!** Often the studio audience — perhaps overawed by the occasion — would sit in silence as we cracked a few funnies. Either that or the jokes weren't very good! The first time I used the line every joke after it got a laugh. It was later used by two other "name" comics.'

Max WALL (b.1908)

'Hello everyone — **Wall's the name** — Max Wall. You've heard of the Great Wall of China. He was my grandfather. He was a brick . . .' — that is how he would start his act. He would exclaim **Success!** on getting applause for a particularly funny gag, or say **That's it!** Almost a catchphrase: **It don't arf make you larf!**

Jimmy WHEELER (1910-73)

Wheeler was a cockney comedian with a fruity voice redolent of beer, jellied eels and winkles. He would appear in a bookmaker's suit, complete with spiv moustache and hat, and play the violin. At the end of his fiddle piece he would break off his act and intone the words: **Aye, aye, that's yer lot!**

Dave WILLIS (d.1973)

In a Sherlock Holmes sketch, Scots comedian Willis would slope on stage with a huge magnifying glass. Peering through it, he would go up to an imaginary flower and without bending his knees would balance and hover over it, examining it through the glass, getting closer and closer until he fell over. **I've failed!** he would wail in a wee voice. In a song about an air-raid he would sing:

Then all run helter-skelter
But don't run after me,
You'll no get in my shelter
For it's far too wee!

Hence, he would declare of others: **You're far too wee**. From the same source came 'An aeroplane, an aeroplane, away, way up 'a kay.' Hence: **Way up a' ky** (English: 'Way up in the sky.')

Robb WILTON (1881-1957)

His famous opening routine — '**The day war broke out**, my missus said to me, "It's up to you . . . you've got to stop it." I said, "Stop what?" She said, "The war"' — was created for radio. When circumstances changed, it was amended to 'the day *peace* broke out.'

As Mr Muddlecombe he would say to Lauri Lupino Lane (as Adolphus): **You shouldn't have done that!**

His usual comment on anything: '**Ee, what a to-do!**

Mike YARWOOD (b.1941)

Such a self-effacing individual, never at rest unless disguised as someone else, could hardly be expected to have his own catchphrases — except **And this is me** when finally revealing himself. However, as has been noted under Max Bygraves, Yarwood brought about the 'I wanna tell you a story' catchphrase.

In another sphere, he seized on **Silly Billy** for Denis Healey, the Labour politician.

See also ERIC AND ERNIE and BIG-HEARTED ARTHUR, THAT'S ME, etc.

YOU HEARD IT
ON THE RADIO

In the 1920s, John Henry became the first wireless comedian in Britain, playing a henpecked Yorkshireman with a domineering wife called Blossom. Out of their lips came one of the earliest radio catchphrase exchanges: **John Henry, come here! / Coming, Blossom!**

Circa 1944 there was a real curiosity — a radio magician called Sirdani. He would say **Don't be fright!**

The following are the *programmes* which gave rise to catch-phrases on British radio. The BBC had a fifty year start over commercial radio — which did not begin until 1973 but has not produced a single notable catchphrase. Perhaps this is because it is locally-based broadcasting; perhaps because it is not principally devoted to individual programmes but to strip broadcasting. Hence, the programmes listed here are all BBC ones:

ARCHERS, THE   The agricultural soap-opera — **An every-day story of country-folk** — has been running nationally since 1951. The nearest it has come to a catchphrase has been Walter Gabriel's **Oooo arr, me ol' beauty, me ol' pal!** How-ever, as Norman Painting (who has written many of the episodes and played Phil Archer since the beginning) told me (1983), a number of cliché/catchphrases have crept in, namely, **Why are you telling me all this?** and **I see what you mean.**

BILLY COTTON BAND SHOW, THE   This programme ran on radio and TV for over twenty years. For one seven-year period it was broadcast on radio without a break for fifty-two weeks of the year. First would come a fanfare, then Billy Cotton's cry **Wakey-wakey!** (without any 'rise and shine'), and this was followed by a brisk, noisy rendering of 'Somebody Stole My Gal'. The programme was first broadcast on 6 February 1949 at 10.30 a.m. Because of this unsocial hour, rehearsals had to begin at 8.45 – not the best time to enthuse a band which had just spent six days on the road. 'Oi, come on,' said Cotton on one occasion, 'Wakey-wakey!' It worked and eventually led to such a cheerful atmosphere that the producer said the show might as well start with it. 'I thought of all those people lying in their beds,' said Cotton (1899-1969), 'and I remembered the sergeant who used to kick my bottom when I was a kid – and out came the catchword.' So it remained – even when the programme moved to its better-remembered spot at Sunday lunchtime.

BRAINS TRUST, THE This was a discussion programme first broadcast in 1941, taking its title from President Roosevelt's nickname for his circle of advisers (in American, more usually, '*brain* trust') Kenneth Clark, one of the regular participants, later described it as 'a form of popular entertainment second only to Tommy Handley'. Other regulars became national figures, most notably C.E.M. Joad (1891-1953) – often called 'Professor' though he was not entitled to be. Joad was, according to Clark, 'a quick-witted, bumptious disciple of Bertrand Russell, who treated the *Brains Trust* as a competitive sport and a chance of showing off'.

His technique was to jump in first and leave the other speakers with little else to say. Alternatively, he would try and undermine arguments by using the phrase with which he became famous: **It all depends what you mean by . . .** When the chairman once read out a question from a listener, Mr W.E. Jack of Keynsham – 'Are thoughts things or about things?' – Joad inevitably began his answer with 'It all depends what you mean by a "thing".' Joad's broadcasting fame ended rather abruptly when he was found travelling by rail using a ticket that was not valid. The BBC banished him.

Of the other regular participants: Julian Huxley's characteristic interjections began with **Surely . . .** and Commander A.B. Campbell with **When I was in Patagonia . . .!** In fact this latter phrase first arose on an earlier version of the programme when it was still entitled *Any Questions*. Donald McCullough, the chairman, said: 'Mr Edwards of Balham wants to know if the members of the Brains Trust agree with the practice of sending missionaries to foreign lands.' Joad and Huxley gave their answers and then Campbell began 'When I was in Patagonia . . .'

In a book which used the phrase as its title, Campbell recalled: 'I got no further, for Joad burst into a roar of laughter and the other members of the session joined in. For some time the feature was held up while the hilarity spent itself. For the life of me I could not see the joke . . . I got hundreds of letters and it cost me a small fortune in stamps . . . Even today (1951), years after, I can raise a laugh if I am on a public platform and make an allusion to it.'

BURKISS WAY, THE   This was a zany Radio 4 comedy show that ran on Radio 4 intermittently from 1976-80. I was one of the cast, so I should know. However, I have left it to others to suggest to me that it should be included here. One correspondent has volunteered that **There now follows a short intermission** was one of our stock phrases that verged on the catchphrase.

My own favourite line was a submerged catchphrase – by which I mean that it was obvious only to the cast and writers. But **Isn't he a panic?** was almost always included in the dialogues between Fred Harris and Eric Pode of Croydon (Chris Emmett). The mention of the name **Eric Pode of Croydon!** by the man himself was always engineered to cause ecstatic cheering and applause.

I just remember that it was also impossible to say 'Third' on the programme – always it was 'Thrid'). David Renwick and Andrew Marsall, who wrote the scripts, just liked leaving the typing errors in, I expect.

CHILDREN'S HOUR   Derek McCulloch and Mary Elizabeth Jenkin were Mac and Elizabeth among the original

'Uncles' and 'Aunts' on BBC radio. In the early days, birthday greetings were read out over the air (until they were dropped in 1932 because they took up nearly half the 'hour') and the simultaneous cry of **Hello . . . twins!** (or occasionally 'Hello triplets') became a catchphrase.

Uncle Mac developed the special farewell **Goodbye, children . . . everywhere!** during the Second World War when many of the programme's listeners were evacuees (Vera Lynn recorded a song based on it.)

CLITHEROE KID, THE   Jimmy Clitheroe (1916-73) was a person of restricted growth with a high-pitched voice who played a naughty boy until he died. The radio programme which ran from 1957-72 popularized an old Lancashire saying **Don't some mothers have 'em?** In the form 'Some mothers do 'ave 'em', the phrase was used in the first edition of TV's *Coronation Street* in 1960 and later used as the title of Michael Crawford's TV series.

CLUB NIGHT   This comedy series from the BBC's North Region in the 1950s was hosted by the pebble-lensed 'manager', Dave Morris. He would be pestered repeatedly by a northern eccentric with **'As 'e bin' in, whack?** ('E never 'ad, of course.) (Morris also originated the saying **Meet the wife — don't laugh!** What the real Mrs Morris thought of this is something we may perhaps never know.)

EDUCATING ARCHIE   Bizarre though the idea of a radio ventriloquist is, this show, starring Peter Brough and his wooden dummy Archie Andrews, was first broadcast on 6 June 1950 and ran for many years.

The 'catchphrase of the year' in 1951, according to Peter Brough, was spoken by Tony Hancock as one of the dummy's long line of tutors. **Flippin' kids!** he would say. Indeed, 'The Lad 'imself' was billed as 'Tony (Flippin' Kids) Hancock' before moving on to his own shows, which more or less eschewed the use of catchphrases.

During his period as Archie's tutor in the early 1950s, Max Bygraves made a big splash with **I've arrived — and to prove it, I'm here!** (which formed part of his bill matter when he appeared at the Palladium in 1952) and **A good idea, son!** (also incorporated in a familiar song). Bygraves told me (1980): 'None of them were planned. They just came up in the reading. When Archie read a line, it was so stilted, I would ape him. This happened a couple of times and people sensed I was reading the line rather than saying it. They're still saying it today, a lot of people.'

He also used the term **Dollar lolly!** when the free-spending American serviceman was particularly noticeable in post-austerity Britain.

A moment from a programme in 1956:

Ken Platt: I suppose you don't know this fellow coming in with the big head?
Archie Andrews: Big head? Yes, of course I know him. Hello, Mr Bygraves.

Max Bygraves ran into a little trouble with educationalists who thought he ought to pronounce the 'h' in **Big 'ead!** but he persisted with a song ('Why Does Everybody Call Me Big 'Ead') and with an act which lasts to this day, cleverly based on a form of mock conceit.

Quite the saddest catchphrase in this book is **Oh, get in there, Moreton!** Robert Moreton (b.1922) had a brief taste of fame as one of Archie's tutors and was noted for his *Bumper Fun Book* out of which he would quote jokes. Did he also say **Crisp — very crisp?** Alas, after only a year he was dropped from the show, was unable to get other work, and committed suicide.

For a while, Beryl Reid played Monica — Archie's posh, toothsome schoolgirl friend, who would introduce herself by saying **My name's Monica.** In her hands, the traditional double-entendre 'As the Bishop said to the actress . . .' became **As the art mistress said to the gardener!** (I have always used it in preference to the original!) Monica also would say **I'm absolutely fed up** and **Priscilla, she's my best friend — and I hate her!** Beryl told me in 1979: 'Even though I've done so many other things, straight acting parts and so on, people always remember these little phrases and want me to say them still.' Above all, Beryl's Monica seems to have given rise to the expression **Jolly hockey sticks!** — first used as an exclamation and then adjectivally to describe a type of woman — public school, games-playing, and enthusiastic. Beryl Reid claims to have coined it. 'I can't write comedy material . . . but I know what sort of thing my characters should say!' In this case she seems to have lighted upon a masterly phrase which has entered the language.

Having established Monica, Beryl wanted to find another character from a different social class. This turned out to be Marlene (pronounced 'Marleen') from Birmingham, complete with Brum accent and girl friend Deirdre. She helped establish the American import **It sends me** as the archetypical 1950s phrase for the effect of music on the hearts and minds of the young and had a wonderful way of saying **Good evening, each** and **It's terrific** (pronounced 'turreefeek').

Following his success as the gormless private in TV's *The Army Game*, Bernard Bresslaw was a natural choice as another of Archie's educators. Usually preceeded by heavy footsteps he would arrive and give his 'thicko' greeting: **Hello, it's me — Twinkletoes!** He would also say **Smashin'!** and **I'm not stupid, you know!** Bernard commented (1979): 'This phrase came up spontaneously because it was entirely in character.'

Towards the end of the run, Dick Emery made his mark as more than one character in the show. As Mr Monty he would say **We've got a right one, 'ere!** — a familiar phrase also employed at one time or another by Tony Hancock, Frankie Howerd and Bruce Forsyth. As Grimble, Emery would say: **I hate yew!** and 'Oh **I was livid** . . . livid I was . . . I wasn't half livid . . . I was!'

FAMILY FAVOURITES A potent memory of Sunday mornings in the 1950s: the smell of roast and gravy wafting out of the kitchen and from the radio: **It's twelve o'clock in London, one o'clock in Cologne — at home and away it's time for Two-Way Family Favourites** (or words to that effect) followed by the sweeping strings of the signature tune — the André Kostelanetz version of 'With A Song In My Heart' . . .

The programme began on 7 October 1945 as a link between home and the British occupying troops in Germany. Cliff Michelmore, who used to introduce the programme from Hamburg and later met and married the London presenter, Jean Metcalfe, recalls the origin of the phrase **Bumper bundle**: 'It was invented by Jean. Her road to Damascus was at the crossroads on Banstead Heath one Sunday morning when driving in to do the programme. It was used to describe a large number of requests all for the same record, especially "Top Ten" hits, *circa* 1952-53.'

GARRISON THEATRE This programme was first broadcast on 6 January 1940 and was based on producer Harry S. Pepper's memories of such theatres in the First World War. In it, Jack Warner as Private Warner spawned some notable phrases: **Little gel!** (which he would say to Joan Winters when exchanging saucy chat); **Veree good, sir!** (as Private Warner); and **Blue pencil** (which he helped establish as a synonym for censorship.) Recitations from blue-pencilled letters from his 'brother' at the Front led to expletives being deleted ('not blue pencil likely!') and to Warner's actual

mother boasting that 'My John with his blue pencil gag has stopped the whole nation from swearing.' **Di-da-di-da** was substituted for 'etcetera' when reading from the letters.

In his autobiography, Warner recalls a constable giving evidence at a London police court about stopping 'Mr Warner, a lorry driver.' The magistrate inquired, 'Did he ask what the blue pencil you wanted?' 'No, sir,' replied the constable, 'this was a different Mr Warner . . .'

Most famous of Warner's phrases however was **Mind my bike!** In his autobiography *Jack of All Trades* he wrote: 'When I dropped the phrase for two weeks, I had 3,000 letters from listeners asking why . . . the only other complaint came from a father who wrote, "I am very keen on your *Garrison Theatre* show, but I have spent several hundreds of pounds on my son's education and all he can do is shout 'Mind my bike!' in a very raucous Cockney voice. I'm trying to break him of the habit, so will you please stop saying it?"'

Warner also recalled that when his producer, Charles Shadwell, was once fined at Bristol for causing an obstruction with his car, his solicitor pleaded: 'Mr Shadwell became engrossed in conversation with Mr Jack Warner . . . they were discussing that gentleman's bicycle, about which you have no doubt heard.'

GRANDE GINGOLD   Quite impossible to represent these catchphrases in print — but Hermione Gingold (b.1897) had a most extraordinarily baroque way of saying almost anything. At the end of this show, *circa* 1955, she was asked (by David Jacobs) 'How shall I describe the programme?' Said she: **It's indescribabbbbble!** Gingold also had a wonderful way of asking people if they would like a cup of tea: **Tea, Gregory?**

HANCOCK'S HALF-HOUR   Co-scriptwriter Ray Galton said of this show's start in 1954: 'Alan Simpson and I wanted a show without breaks, guest singers and catchphrases — something that hadn't been done before. After the first week with Kenneth Williams in the show, bang went our idea of no funny voices and no catchphrases!' Although Williams's delightful cameos occupied a very tiny part of the show, they were enough to bring him to everyone's attention. His insidious **Gewd evenin'!** and **Stop messin' abaht!** began with

Hancock. Later the second of the two was used as the title of a radio series in which he himself starred.

Hancock also developed distinctive phraseology — and in the subsequent TV series (from 1956): **A man of my calibre** (pronounced 'cal-aye-ber'), **Have you gone raving mad? Are you looking for a punch up the bracket?** and **Stone me!**

Supporting actor, Australian Bill Kerr, also had a line: **I've only got four minutes** when unconfidently starting his solo act on programmes like *Variety Bandbox*. Also **I don't want to worry you, but . . .** followed by an account of the dreadful things that might happen, including the collapse of the theatre balcony.

HAPPIDROME   During the Second World War this programme featured Harry Korris as Mr Lovejoy, a theatre manager, Cecil Fredericks as Ramsbottom, and Robby Vincent as Enoch, the call-boy. Hence the phrase from the opening song: **Ramsbottom, Enoch and me.** Also from the show came **Take 'im away, Ramsbottom!** and **Let me tell you!** Enoch would say the latter before revealing some startling fact to Mr Lovejoy.

HAVE A GO   'Ladies and gentlemen of Bingley, **'ow do, 'ow are yer?**' — that was how Wilfred Pickles introduced the first edition of this folksy, travelling show in 1946. Within a year the show had an audience of 20 million and ran for twenty-one years. It was to the 40s and 50s what TV's *Generation Game* was to the 1970s — a simple quiz which enabled the hosts (Pickles and Bruce Forsyth), both accompanied by their respective wives, Mabel Pickles and Anthea Redfern, to indulge in folksy chatting-up of contestants. Pickles (1904-78) spent most of the programme chatting to the quiz contestants and fishing for laughs with questions like **Have you ever had any embarrassing moments?** One reply he received was from a woman who had been out with a very shy young man. Getting desperate for conversation with him she had said: 'If there's one thing I can't stand, it's people who sit on you and use you as a convenience.' And — chatting up spinsters of any age from nineteen to ninety, Pickles would ask: **Are yer courtin'?** But, after all, this is what the programme set out to provide: **a spot of homely fun, presenting the people to the people.**

Whereas winners in the later TV programme took away covetable consumer goods of the 1970s, *Have a Go* offered only the simplest of prizes like pots of jam and the odd shilling or two. **Give 'im/'er the money, Barney!** was the cry when a winner was established. The Barney in question was Barney Colehan, a BBC producer, who later went on to produce TV's *The Good Old Days* and *It's a Knockout*. Later Mabel Pickles supervised the prizes — hence the alternative **Give 'im/'er the money, Mabel!** and the references to **Mabel at the table** and **What's on the table, Mabel?**

'And so we come to the end of this week's *Have a Go*, which came to you from Blackburn, with Violet Carson at the piano. This is your old pal, Wilfred Pickles, wishing you good luck and **good neet!**' (Chorus of 'Come round any old time and make yourself at home'. End of programme.) Pickles had first put this northern expression in the nation's ears, however, during his brief and controversial stint as a radio newsreader. Brendan Bracken at the wartime Ministry of Information had concluded that a voice such as that of Pickles would be less easy for the Germans to copy, so he was brought in and on one occasion ended the news (which till then had been read in God-like Oxbridge tones) with 'Good-night everybody — and to all northerners wherever you may be, good neet!'

HI GANG!   The former Hollywood star Ben Lyon and his wife Bebe Daniels hosted two popular radio series in Britain. *Life with the Lyons* was a regular programme in the 1950s, while from 26 May 1940 they brought a whiff of American radio to Britain in *Hi Gang!* At the start, Ben would call out **Hi gang!** and the audience would reply 'Hi, Ben!' At the close of the show: 'So long, gang!' — 'So long, Ben!' An incidental line of Ben's, addressed to members of the studio audience, was: **Not you, momma, siddown!** (once reported as having appeared as a piece of graffiti on the underside of a train lavatory seat.)

HITCH HIKER'S GUIDE TO THE GALAXY, THE   This sci-fi comedy by Douglas Adams, first broadcast in 1978, had two catchphrases: Marvin the robot's **I'm so depressed** and the injunction **Don't panic** (which appeared on the cover of the fictitious *Guide*.)

HOUSEWIVES' CHOICE   For some reason George Elrick, the former Scots bandleader, chose to introduce himself when doing DJ stints on this programme as **Mrs Elrick's wee son George.**

I'M SORRY I'LL READ THAT AGAIN   The newsreader's traditional apology for a stumble — **I'm sorry, I'll read that again** — was registered as a cliché when the phrase was taken as the title of a long-running comedy show, largely staffed by ex-Cambridge Footlights performers (from 1964 to the 70s).

The show also gave further currency to the phrase **Hello sailor!** — a difficult one to fathom, that. It may always have been around with varying degrees of homosexual and hetero-sexual emphasis (cf. the old naval saying: 'Ashore it's wine, women and song; aboard, it's rum, bum and concertina.') Nevertheless, as a camp catchphrase it had quite a vogue in the early 1970s, promoted in various branches of the media.

The first appearance of the phrase that I have come across is in Spike Milligan's script for 'Tales of Men's Shirts' in *The Goon Show* (31 December 1959). 'Hello, sailor!' is spoken for no very good reason by Minnie Bannister. In 1978, however,

Spike told me that he thought he started the revival in one of his *Q* TV shows. To fill up space, he just sat and said it a number of times. Dudley Moore used it. Perhaps all were influenced by there being a number of newsworthy sailors about in the early 1970s, including Prince Philip, Prince Charles, and the Prime Minister, Edward Heath.

IN TOWN TONIGHT   From 1933 to 1960, this was the nearest BBC radio came to a chat show. It was introduced by what sounds like a very quaint montage of 'Knightsbridge March' by Eric Coates, traffic noises, the voice of a violet-seller in Piccadilly Circus, and then a stentorian voice — which I always believed (wrongly) to be that of Lord Reith — shouting **Stopppp!** Then an announcer would intone: **Once again we stop the mighty roar of London's traffic and from the great crowds we bring you some of the interesting people who have come by land, sea and air to be "In Town Tonight"**. At the end of the programme, to get the traffic moving again, the stentorian voice would bellow: **Carry on, London!** Various people were 'The Voice' but I am told that Freddie Grisewood was the first to do it.

IT'S ALL YOURS   Willie Joss would say **Arriverderci!** in this Scottish radio show, c1952/3. Stanley Baxter as Bella Vague would say, as an exit line, 'Don't forget, I'm in the book — so **if you want me, thingmy, ring me!**' (she called everyone 'Thingmy'.) Or perhaps it was Jimmy Logan who would say **If you want anything, ring me!** Beyond that, I know nothing of this programme.

LISTEN WITH MOTHER   **Are you sitting comfortably? Then we'll begin** — this was the customary way of beginning a story on BBC radio's programme for small children. The phrase was used from the programme's inception in January 1950. Julia Lang, the original presenter, recalled in 1982: 'The first day it came out inadvertently. I just said it. The next day I didn't. Then there was a flood of letters from children saying "I couldn't listen because I wasn't ready."' (Sometimes she said: 'Then *I'll* begin.') It remained a more or less essential part of the proceedings until the programme was threatened with closure in 1982. I also remember the format phrase: **And when the music stops,** *[Daphne Oxenford or some other]* **will be here to tell you a story . . .**

MEN FROM THE MINISTRY, THE   Edward Taylor, whose brainchild this series was between 1962-77, says: 'We didn't think in terms of catchphrases but I could think of fifty times each, for example, when Deryck Guyler said **Ugly business** or Richard Murdoch **The mind boggles!**' There would also be a touch of rhyming slang from Mildred (Norma Ronald): **Would you Adam-and-Eve it?**

MERRY GO ROUND   Each of the three services took it in turn to be featured in this programme from 1943 to 1948 and the shows were mainly written and performed by men and women in the services. The navy edition which revolved around *HMS Waterlogged* eventually turned into *Waterlogged Spa*; the army edition became *Stand Easy*; and the air force edition, *Much Binding in the Marsh*. Then there were other versions called *Middle East* and *Mediterranean Merry Go Round*.

Sub-Lieutenant Eric 'Heartthrob' Barker (b.1912) starred in the navy version. **Carry on smokin!** was his favourite command to others; to himself: **Steady, Barker!** This last phrase was also carried over to his other show, *Just Fancy*, and became the title of his autobiography in 1956. In that book, he wrote of the phrase: 'It could be used on so many occasions . . . it almost passed into the language. Also each time it was quoted it gave me the all-vital personal publicity . . . I have had letters from those who have said it helped them to cure a lifelong habit of swearing, as they were able to use it instead. One old lady who shared a flat with an awkward sister at Cheltenham said they had been in danger of drifting apart, but that now, lo! when they reached a point when it seemed neither could endure the bickering a moment longer, they both said, "Steady, Barker!" and it cleared the air. I also learned it was sent as a naval signal from a C-in-C to a ship whose gunfire was a little wide of the mark.'

The navy version also gave rise to Commander High-Price (Jon Pertwee) and his saying **Hush, keep it dark!** based on the wartime security slogan (which had not been forgotten by 1983 when Anthony Beaumont-Dark, Tory candidate in the General Election, campaigned successfully under the slogan 'Keep It Dark'.) Richard Gray, as the gravelly-voiced Baron Waterlogged of Waterlogged Spa, came out with **Ullo, cock! 'Ow's yerself?**

Dabra, dabra! (followed by stuttering) was the hallmark of Weatherby Wett (Jon Pertwee) who later became Commander Weatherby in *The Navy Lark*. Pertwee would also say, as a very inefficent character, **The efficiency's the ticket** and portrayed Svenson, a Norwegian stoker, whose cod Norwegian (based on close scrutiny of wartime news broadcasts) always ended up with the words: **Eyaydon, yauden, yaydon, negidicrop dibombit!**

Flying Officer Kite, the ex-RAF officer, complete with handlebar moustache and varsity accent was played by Humphrey Lestocq (who later hosted the children's TV series *Whirligig* and used to say **Goody, goody, gumdrops!**) Lestocq recalled (1980): 'When the show started, I'd just left the RAF. I was madly air-force — "Whacko!" "Good-o!" "Bang-on!" . . . all that sort of thing — and this really fascinated Eric Barker. So he went away and found this character for me.' After many a 'Wizard prang!' Eric Barker would slap Kite down in some way, but Kite would only roar: **Oh, I say, I rather care for that, hahaha-haa-ha!** The producer, Leslie Bridgmont, once commented: 'When we introduced the character we worked out this pay-off very carefully . . . the rhythm of the laugh, for instance, had to be exactly the same each time. It is this inexorable sameness that establishes a phrase.'

In *Mediterranean Merry Go Round*, Jon Pertwee played a Devonshire bugler at Plymouth Barracks who eventually became a postman in Waterlogged Spa — not to mention thirteenth trombonist in the Spa Symphony Orchestra. At one concert he became bored with the slow movement of a symphony and broke into 'Tiger Rag'. When Eric Barker remonstrated with him, he said: 'Ah, me old darling, but it tore 'em through, didn't it?' Barker: 'Well, er, yes . . .' Postman: 'Well, **what does it matter what you do as long as you tear 'em up?**'

MRS DALE'S DIARY   Ellis Powell as the original eponymous heroine of the gentle, long-running soap opera (1948-69) confided to her diary about her doctor husband: **I'm worried about Jim!** Although she may not have spoken the phrase very often, it was essential in parodies of the programme. Her successor in the part, Jessie Matthews, once had the line: 'I'm afraid one thing's never going to change: I shall always worry about you, Jim.'

MONDAY NIGHT AT EIGHT (Originally SEVEN) As a way of covering up a mistake that was *not* deliberate this radio magazine contributed an expression in c1938: **Did you spot this week's deliberate mistake?** Ronnie Waldman had taken over as deviser of the 'Puzzle Corner' part of the programme which was presented by Lionel Gamlin. 'Through my oversight a mistake crept into "Puzzle Corner" one night,' Waldman recalled in 1954' 'and when Broadcasting House was besieged by telephone callers putting us right, Harry Pepper (the producer) concluded that such "listener participation" was worth exploiting as a regular thing. "Let's always put in a mistake," he suggested.'

Waldman revived the idea when he himself presented 'Puzzle Corner' as a part of *Kaleidoscope* on BBC TV in the early 1950s and the expression has continued to be used as a joke phrase covering ineptitude.

Jack Warner also had a spot on the radio programme from time to time. Whether it was on this show or another, I don't know, but he came up with **I didn't oughter 'ave it!** (or 'You didn't oughter . . .') Warner recounted the occasion he was leaving Broadcasting house in London with Richard Murdoch: 'I had to step over the legs of a couple of fellows who were sitting in the sunshine with their backs against the wall eating their lunches from paper bags. As we passed, I heard one say to the other, "I don't know what my old woman has given me for dinner today but I didn't oughter 'ave et it." I remarked to Dickie, "If that isn't a cue for a song, I don't know what is!" It provided me with my first catch-phrase to be picked out by members of the public.'

On another occasion he did a monologue about a wheel-tapper who won the pools and still referred to his old calling in a mixed Cockney and Mayfair drawl. Hence his reference to **Up and down the railway lines** emerged distinctively as something like 'Hup hand dahn the rawlaway lanes'.

Was it also from this show that the line **Put a penny on the drum** came? or perhaps it was *Variety Bandbox?* Anyway, it was said by Clay Keyes, an American. Members of the orchestra had to guess musical riddles sent in by listeners, failing which they paid a forfeit which went to charity, e.g.: 'Where did the salt and vinegar go?' Musical answer: 'All over the pla(i)ce.'

MY WORD   The long-running quiz (from the late 50s on) had a felicitous opening for a while when Jack Longland was the chairman: **"My Word" is a word game played by people whose business is words.**

NAVY LARK, THE   **Left hand down a bit!** — Leslie Phillips doing a spot of navigating (Jon Pertwee: 'Left hand down it is, sir!'). The series ran from the 1960s into the 70s.

P.C.49   The somewhat silly ass constable (played by Brian Reece) whose name was Archibald Berkeley Willoughby appeared in programmes from 1946. His exclamation was: **Oh, my Sunday helmet!**

QUEEN, THE   Queen Elizabeth II (b.1926) has had a regular spot on radio each Christmas Day since 1952 and latterly on TV. Her father had quite naturally spoken the words 'The Queen and I' in his broadcasts but something in the Queen's drawling delivery turned her version into a joke catchphrase — **My husband and I.** It first appeared during her second Christmas broadcast (made from New Zealand in 1953 — 'My husband and I left London a month ago' — but still survived in 1962: 'My husband and I are greatly looking forward to visiting New Zealand and Australia in the new Year.' By 1967, the phrase had become 'Prince Philip and I.' At a Silver Wedding banquet in 1972, the Queen allowed herself a little joke: 'I think on this occasion I may be forgiven for saying "My husband and I".'

SHOW WITH TEN LEGS, THE **I'll do anything for the money** (accompanied by the ring of a cash register) seemed to me to have all the makings of a good catchphrase even if, owing to the obscurity of its placing on Radio 2 in 1979, this phrase from Eli Woods could never take off.

TAKE IT FROM HERE (in which **anything can happen and probably will . . .**) was first broadcast on 23 March 1948 and ran for many years. It was based on highly-literate scripts by Frank Muir and Denis Norden. Among the phrases that came out of it (with comments by Muir):

Black mark, Bentley — Jimmy Edwards referring to Dick Bentley. Frank Muir comments that the phrase arose from the use of 'black mark!' by James Robertson Justice in Peter Ustinov's film of *Vice Versa*.

Clumsy clot Jim using a hangover from RAF wartime slang.

Gently Bentley Jim to Dick.

Greetings, gentlefolk Jim's greeting. When speaking to a convention of opticians he was able to begin, 'Greetings, focal gents.'

Learn a trade A much-repeated phrase of Old Wal from the Buildings (Wallas Eaton). 'We're very proud of Jim back in the Buildings', he would say (of Jimmy Edwards), but he was always exhorting Jim to come on home and learn a trade so that at least when he was out of work he would know what sort of work he was out of. His farewell cry: **Back to the buildings!**

A mauve one Frank Muir adds: 'This is the genuine article — a meaningless phrase, first used by Jimmy Edwards when selecting a wine-gum and given such a risible inflection ("a *mauve* one") that Denis Norden and I worked it into a vast number of shows thereafter to describe (for example) a stamp, a businessman's face, a suit, etc. This is almost a perfect catchphrase in that it was not imposed upon the listeners but chosen by them to be a catchphrase.'

Jimmy Edwards recalled an occasion in May 1952 when, as Rector of Aberdeen University, he went to Buckingham Palace. A courtier remarked that Jim's academic robe was magnificent but that he should do a swap with the Dean of

Westminster, who was also present. When Jim asked why, the courtier replied, 'His is a *mauve* one!'

Oh, Mavis Dick Bentley, the poet.

Oh, Ron! / Yes, Eth? The immortal exchange between June Whitfield as Eth and Dick Bentley as the gormless Ron in 'The Glums' segment of the show. A stock phrase originally rather than a catchphrase but it became popular because of Eth's rising inflexion and Ron's flat response.

That was a good one, was it not? Jimmy Edwards commending one of his own jokes.

Ullo, ullo, ullo, what's this? Jimmy Edwards as Pa Glum (usually interrupting his son Ron who was after a kiss from fiancée Eth): 'It was not meant to be a catchphrase but as Pa Glum always said it on his entrance – and it was so useful a phrase in everyday life – it caught on.' It also, of course, echoes the traditional inquiry of a policeman on encountering something suspicious.

Wake up at the back there 'This was a line I always used in writing Jim's schoolmaster acts. It was technically very useful in breaking up his first line and getting audience attention.'

Bob Monkhouse adds: 'Jimmy Edwards's roaring admonition had everything I felt a gilt-edged catchphrase should have. It was perfectly in character and it arose naturally from Jimmy's actual wrath with a sullen audience. It was short, funny in any setting and *useful* – the kind of all-purpose joke-saving line beloved of comedians who hate to hear a subtle gag go down in silence.'

Jim: They laughed at Suez, but he went right ahead and built his canal – wake up at the back there!

What a ghastly name 'A useful (albeit meaningless) line which could always be given to Jimmy when somebody else mentioned a name. In fact I suppose it was quite a funny, deflating way to react.'

TODAY The breakfast-show which has run in various forms since 1957 has frequently been signed off by John Timpson with the customary **And a very good morning to you!** His **Ho-ho!** after reading a newspaper misprint or ambiguous headline became a feature. An ingredient in the show in the early 1970s was a gardening spot in which Frank Hennig would interview veteran expert Fred Streeter (d.1975). Streeter would sign-off by saying **Cheerio, Frank – cheerio, everybody!**

TOYTOWN   A popular ingredient of *Children's Hour* for many years was the dramatisation of S. Hulme Beaman's 'Toytown' stories. **It is disgraceful – it ought not to be allowed!** (Mr Grouser, played by Ralph de Rohan) and the bleatings of **Laaaa-rry the Laaa-amb!** (played by Derek McCulloch) became famous expressions.

TWENTY QUESTIONS   In this radio quiz which ran from 1947 to the mid-70s, a mystery voice – most memorably Norman Hackforth's – would inform listeners in advance about the object the panellists would try to identify by asking no more than twenty questions. '**And the next object is** the Odour in the Larder . . .' Hackforth would say in his deep, fruity rendition.

WEEK ENDING . . .   From its first broadcast just prior to the 1970 General Election, Radio 4's weekly satirical show has featured comic predictions of forthcoming news events introduced by the phrase **And now here is next week's news . . .** and closed by **And that is the end of next week's news.** In about 1977 there was introduced a ritual exchange of views by pub bores discussing the week's news (played by David Jason and Bill Wallis). Their phrases **This is it!** followed by **Makes you think!** had a brief vogue.

WORLD AT ONE, THE   From 1965, when the programme started, to his death in 1975, the breathless William Hardcastle bestrode this Radio 4 news and current affairs show – the nearest any British broadcaster has come to being an American-style news personality. Almost impossible to reproduce in print, his introduction went (after the Greenwich pips): **The Wooooorld at One! The news headlines this Tuesday lunchtime!** Then: **This is William Hardcastle** (on one occasion he almost said 'William Whitelaw') **and later in today's World at One . . .**

For other radio programmes see IT'S THAT MAN AGAIN; THE HIGHLY-ESTEEMED GOON SHOW; RAISING THE LAUGHS; ROUND AND BEYOND OUR KEN; and BIG-HEARTED ARTHUR, THAT'S ME.

THE FLEET'S LIT UP

The most famous British broadcasting boob of all came from Lieutenant-Commander Tommy Woodrooffe (1899-1978), a leading BBC radio commentator of the 1930s. On the night of 20 May 1937, he was due to give a fifteen minute description of the 'illumination' of the Fleet on the night of the Coronation Naval Review at Spithead. What he said, in a commentary that was faded out after less than four minutes, was this:

'At the present moment, **the** whole **Fleet's lit up.** When I say "lit up", I mean lit up by fairy lamps. We've forgotten the whole Royal Review. We've forgotten the Royal Review. The whole thing is lit up by fairy lamps. It's fantastic. It isn't the Fleet at all. It's just . . . it's fairy land. The whole Fleet is in fairy land. Now, if you'll follow me through . . . if you don't mind . . . the next few moments . . . you'll find the Fleet doing odd things.

'At the present moment, the *New York* opposite me . . . is lit out . . . and when I say "The Fleet is lit up . . . in lamps" . . . I mean she's outlined, the whole ship's outlined, in little lamps . . . *[Long pause]* I'm sorry, I was telling some people to shut up talking. What I mean is this, the whole Fleet is lit up with fairy lamps and each ship is outlined. Now as far as I can see it's about, I suppose I can see down about five or six miles . . . ships are all lit up . . . they're outlined . . . the whole lot . . . even destroyers are outlined . . . In the old days, you know, destroyers used to be outlined by a little kind of pyramid of light . . . and nowadays destroyers are lit up by . . . they outline themselves.

'In a second or two, we're going to fire a rocket and we're going to fire all sorts of things. And — you can't possibly see them — but you'll hear them going off and you may hear my reactions when I see them go . . . because, um, I'm going to try and tell you what they look like as they go off.

But at the moment, there's a whole huge Fleet here . . . the thing we saw this afternoon — this colossal Fleet — lit up by lights and the whole thing is in fairy land. It isn't true! It isn't here!

[The lights are switched off] 'And, as I say it, it's gone, it's gone, there's no Fleet! It's disappeared! No magician who ever could have waved his wand could have waved it with more acumen than he has now at the present moment. The Fleet's gone! It's disappeared! . . . I'm trying to give you, ladies and gentlemen . . . the Fleet's gone, it's disappeared.

'I was talking to you in the middle of this damn — in the middle of this Fleet. And what's happened is the Fleet's gone, disappeared and gone. We had a hundred, two hundred, warships all around us a second ago and now they've gone. At a signal by the morse code — at a signal by the Fleet flagship which I'm in now — they've gone . . . they've disappeared. There's nothing between us and heaven. There's nothing at all . . .'

Eventually, an announcer said: 'The broadcast from Spithead is now at an end. It is eleven minutes to eleven, and we will take you back to the broadcast from the Carlton Hotel Dance Band.'

That familiar BBC figure, A. Spokesman, commented later: 'We regret that the commentary was unsatisfactory and for that reason it was curtailed.' Naturally, many listeners concluded that Woodrooffe himself had been 'lit up' as the result of too much hospitality from his former shipmates on board HMS *Nelson*. But he denied this. 'I had a kind of nervous blackout. I had been working too hard and my mind just went blank.' He told the *News Chronicle:* 'I was so overcome by the occasion that I literally burst into tears . . . I found I could say no more.'

The phrase became so famous that it was used as the title of a musical at the London Hippodrome starring Frances Day and produced by George Black in 1938. Bud Flanagan had a song with the title 'The Fleet's Lit Up'.

The BBC took a kindly view and the incident did not put paid to Woodrooffe's broadcasting career. In 1938-9 he was the sole commentator for the FA Cup Final, the Grand

National and the Derby. Commentating on the Cup Final, he declared in the closing minutes: 'If there's a goal scored now I'll eat my hat.' There, was and he did. When war broke out he returned to the navy and did little broadcasting after 1939.

IT'S THAT MAN AGAIN

It is appropriate that *ITMA*, the radio programme which included more catchphrases per square minute than any other, before or since, should have had as it's title an acronym based on a catchphrase. **It's that man again!** was a late 1930s expression, often used in newspaper headlines, for Adolf Hitler, who was always bursting into the news with some territorial claim or other. During the Second World War, Winston Churchill often spoke of 'that man' in private conversation.

ITMA was first broadcast in July 1939 and ran until January 1949, when its star Tommy Handley died.

What did the show consist of? There would be a knock on the famous *ITMA* door, a character would engage in a little

banter with Tommy Handley, the catchphrase would be delivered (often receiving a giant ovation), and then the next one would be wheeled in. Given this format, it is not easy now to appreciate why the show was so popular. But the laughter undoubtedly took people's minds off the war and the programmes brought together the whole country, fostering a family feeling and a sense of sharing which in itself encouraged the spread of catchphrases. The writing is not to everybody's taste nowadays (it relied heavily on feeble puns) but Tommy Handley's brisk, cheerful personality was the magic ingredient which held the proceedings together.

Characters came and went over the years, the cast fluctuated, and catchphrases changed. But here are a mere fifty or so:

Ah, there you are!

Ain't it a shame, eh? Ain't it a shame?   Spoken by Carleton Hobbs as the nameless man who told banal tales ('I waited for hours in the fish queue . . . and a man took my plaice') and always prefaced and concluded them with 'Ain't it a shame?'

After you, Claude / No, after you, Cecil!   One of the most enduring *ITMA* phrases, this was spoken originally by Horace Percival and Jack Train playing two over-polite handymen, Cecil and Claude respectively. It still survives as an admirable way of overcoming social awkwardness in such matters as deciding who should go through a door first.

As if I cared . . .   Sam Fairfechan (Hugh Morton) would say, 'Good morning, how are you today?' and immediately add 'As if I cared.' The character derived his name from Llanfairfechan, the seaside resort in North Wales, where Ted Kavanagh, *ITMA*'s scriptwriter, resided when the BBC Variety Department was evacuated to nearby Bangor during the early part of the Second World War.

Boss, boss, sumpin' terrible's happened   Spoken in a gangster-like drawl by Sam Scram (Sydney Keith), Handley's American henchman.

But I'm all right now   Sophie Tuckshop (Hattie Jacques) was always stuffing herself and giggling and pretending to suffer. But then, with a squeal, she would say this.

Can I do you now, sir? One of the great catchphrases of all time. Said by Mrs Mopp (Dorothy Summers), the hoarse-voiced charlady or 'Corporation Cleanser', when entering the office of Tommy Handley, as the Mayor. Curiously, the first time Mrs Mopp used the phrase (on 10 October 1940) she said: 'Can I do *for* you now, sir?' This was soon replaced by the more familiar emphases of 'Can I *do* you *now*, sir?' that can still be heard in use today. Bob Monkhouse recalls Dorothy Summers saying: 'Oh, I do wish people wouldn't expect me to be only Mrs Mopp. That awful char. I never wanted to say it in the first place. I think it was rather distasteful.' She seems to have been the only person to detect any awful meaning in it.

can I do you now, sir?

Concentrated cacophony Deryck Guyler's archetypical scouser, Frisby Dyke, found this a bit hard to understand. After a burst of noisy music:

> *Handley:* Never in the whole of my three hundred *ITMA*s have I ever heard such a piece of concentrated cacophony.
> *Frisby Dyke:* What's 'concentrated cacophony?'

Don't forget the diver Of all the many *ITMA* phrases, this one surely has the most interesting origin. Spoken by Horace Percival as The Diver, it was derived from memories Handley had of an actual man who used to dive off the pier at New Brighton some time after the First World War. 'Don't forget the diver, sir, don't forget the diver,' he would say, collecting money. 'Every penny makes the water warmer, sir — every penny makes the water warmer.'

The radio character first appeared in 1940 and no lift went down for the next few years without somebody using the Diver's main catchphrase — or another one, **I'm going down now, sir** (see over).

From various accounts sent to me in 1978 by people who remembered the original, I have compiled this eye-witness description of the diver: 'I thought him very brave. Although tough-looking, he was not so young, only had one leg, and used to dive from a great height as passengers left the ferry boat from Liverpool. He would stand poised, first, and call to them as they waited for the gangway to go down: "Don't forget the diver — I rely entirely on your generosity." His assistant held a fishing net on a pole across from the pier to the jetty where the passengers popped in their contributions. Often he had a very small "Catch". After diving he would climb the vertical steps to the pier ready for the next boat in. He was encased in what looked like a black rubber diving suit and helmet and was, I think, a war casualty. Although he was made famous later by *ITMA* as a figure of fun, I never saw him smile.'

But who was the original diver? Following a mention of my original catchphrases book in *The Listener*, James Gashram wrote (in the edition of 21 August 1980): 'My grandfather McMaster, who came from a farm near the small village of Rathmullen, in Co. Donegal, knew Michael Shaughnessy, the one-legged ex-soldier, in the late 1890s, before he left for the Boer War and the fighting that cost him his leg. About 1910, Shaughnessy, then married to a Chester girl, settled in Bebington on the Wirral peninsula and worked for some years as an odd-job carpenter. Then he hit on the idea of exploiting the swimming he had learned as a child on the beaches of Donegal. He even built a crude "changing hut" for himself in the cross-girders of the pier at New Brighton.

'Before the internal combustion engine, Shaughnessy used to get a lift every weekday from Bebington to New Brighton in a horse-drawn breadcart owned by the Bromborough firm of Bernard Hughes. The driver of that cart, apparently, was always envious of the "easy" money Shaughnessy got at New Brighton — sometimes up to two pounds a day in the summer — and would invariably say to him on the return to Bebington: "Don't forget the driver." Shaughnessy rarely did forget. It was many years later, some time in the early 1930s, that, remembering the phrase so well, he adapted it to his own purposes by changing it to "Don't forget the diver", and shouted it to the people arriving from Liverpool. My grandfather survived until March 1938 and met Shaughnessy several times in Birkenhead — he was well known in pubs there for his habit of placing his wooden crutch on a bar counter and refusing to move it until he needed its help.'

As for 'I'm going down now, sir', I am told that bomber pilots in the Second World War would use this phrase from The Diver when about to make a descent. From the VE-Day edition:

EFFECTS: KNOCKING
Handley: Who's that knocking on the tank?
The Diver: Don't forget the diver, sir — don't forget the diver.
Handley: Lumme, it's Deepend Dan. Listen, as the war's over, what are you doing?
The Diver: I'm going down now, sir.
EFFECTS: BUBBLES

Down, Upsey!   Joan Harben as a fast-talking character, to her dog.

Ever so   The 'Ever So' girls.

Friday!   Any remark ending with the word — or one sounding like it — would bring the response 'Friday?' and the counter-response 'Friday!'

Good morning . . . Nice day!   Exchange between Handley and Clarence Wright as the commercial traveller who never seemed to sell anything.

Wright: Good morning!
Handley: Good morning!
Wright: Nice day!
Handley: Very!

He's a great guy!

I always do my best for all my gentlemen   Mrs Lola Tickle (Maurice Denham) appeared within six weeks of the start of the show in 1939. As office charlady to Mr ITMA (Handley), she was the precursor by a full year of Mrs Mopp.

I'd do anything for the wife

I don't mind if I do   The immortal reply of Colonel Chin-strap (Jack Train) whenever a drink was so much as hinted at. The idea first appeared in 1940-1 in the form 'Thanks, I will!' The Colonel was based on an elderly friend of John Snagge's — a typical ex-Indian army type, well pleased with himself. The phrase had been in existence before, of course. *Punch* carried a cartoon in 1880 with the following caption:

> *Porter:* Virginia Water!
> *Bibulous old gentleman (seated in railway carriage):* Gin and water! I don't mind if I do!

ITMA, however, secured the phrase a place in the language, as the Colonel doggedly turned every hint of liquid refreshment into an offer:

> *Handley:* Hello, what's this group? King John signing the Magna Carta at Runnymede?
> *Chinstrap:* Rum and mead, sir? I don't mind if I do!

I go — I come back!   Said in a hoarse whisper by Ali Oop (Horace Percival), the saucy postcard vendor. First used in the summer of 1940.

I'll 'ave to ask me Dad   The point of this phrase was that it was spoken by a character who sounded about a hundred years old. He was called the Ancient Mark Time. Randolph Churchill, speaking at a general election meeting in 1945, was heckled with the remark, 'He'll have to ask *his* Dad!'

I'll forget my own name in a minute   The nameless man from the Ministry (Horace Percival).

It's being so cheerful as keeps me going   Said by Mona Lott (Joan Harben), the gloomy laundrywoman. When told to keep her pecker up by Handley, she would reply, 'I always do, sir, it's being so cheerful . . .' Her family was always running into bad luck, so she had plenty upon which to exercise her cheerfulness.

It's me noives!   Lefty (Jack Train).

I wish I had as many shillings   Said by Handley in response to remarks such as 'Now I have a million eggs . . .' This was a conscious borrowing from Jimmy Learmouth, a northern comedian from Handley's youth.

Lovely grub, lovely grub Said by George Gorge (Fred Yule) — 'The greediest man ever to have two ration books'. He used to say it smacking his lips, whereas Charles Hill, the Radio Doctor, would sometimes say it without smacking his lips.

Mine's a persico Said by Jack Train as Funf: 'I think it's positively persico!'

Missed him!

**Mr Handley . . .
Mr Handley!**
Miss Hotchkiss.

Most irregular, most irregular! Fusspot (Jack Train), the Civil Servant.

Nobody tells me nothing (or 'Nobody tells no one nothing') Dan Dungeon, the gloomy scouser (Deryck Guyler).

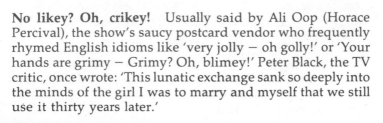

No cups outside! Said in an Ulster accent by Ruby Rockcake (Mary O'Farrell) — reflecting her early upbringing in a railway refreshment room

No likey? Oh, crikey! Usually said by Ali Oop (Horace Percival), the show's saucy postcard vendor who frequently rhymed English idioms like 'very jolly — oh golly!' or 'Your hands are grimy — Grimy? Oh, blimey!' Peter Black, the TV critic, once wrote: 'This lunatic exchange sank so deeply into the minds of the girl I was to marry and myself that we still use it thirty years later.'

Nothing at all, nothing at all! Signor So-So (Dino Galvani), an Italian murdering the English language.

Handley: Now, have you anything to say before you go?
So-So: Notting at all, notting at all!

Now, now, come, come, don't dilly-dally! Charley Come-Come.

Och man, you're daft! (followed by a laugh 'like a tinkling bell, rippling up the scale') − Molly Weir as Tattie MacKintosh. In his book *Sometime Never*, Wilfred Pickles gave an elaborate account of how the phrase got into the programme. According to his rather showbiz version, 'Tommy Handley was having a joke at Molly's expense during a break in rehearsal, when she exclaimed, "Och man, you're daft!" Tommy's eyes flashed. He pointed ecstatically at Molly, "We're going to use that!"'

Molly herself says this is far-fetched. 'Ted Kavanagh, the writer, simply put it in as a Scots expression.' Indeed, when she later joined *Life with the Lyons*, Molly was kitted out with the inevitable, 'Och, Mr Lyon!'

Open the door, Richard! A line from the song, first sung in Britain on *ITMA*.

Smile, please − watch the birdie! From the traditional photographer's instruction.

That's my boy!

This is Funf speaking! Spoken sideways into a glass tumbler by Jack Train, this phrase was 'the embodiment of the nation's spy neurosis' (according to the producer, Francis Worsley). The first time Funf appeared was in the second edition of the show on 26 September 1939, just after the outbreak of war. Initially, he said, 'Dees ees Foonf, your favourite shpy!' Jack Train recalled that, when Worsley was searching for a good name to call the spy, he overheard his six-year-old son, Roger, trying to count in German: 'Ein, zwei, drei, vier, funf' − and that's where he always got stuck. Train himself had been to see Akim Tamiroff in a film and was doing impersonations of him in a pub when Worsley came over and said, 'I want you for the spy.' Train spoke into a beer glass and Worsley decided Funf must be on the telephone.

Funf always uttered threats of dire disasters, at which Tommy Handley would laugh — just as the nation subsequently did at the broadcast snidery of Lord Haw-Haw, the traitorous William Joyce. For a while it became a craze always to start phone conversations with the words.

T.T.F.N. ('Ta-ta for now') The farewell of Mrs Mopp (Dorothy Summers) after having presented her weekly gift (**I brought this for you, sir!**) to Mayor Handley. During the war quite a few people died with this phrase on their lips. Still heard today.

Vicky verky Norman (Fred Yule): 'High time you was here, sir. They're fair frantic — or vicky verky!'

Vous pouvez cracher *ITMA* did a skit on pre-war Radio Luxembourg and called it 'Radio Fakenburg'. 'Ici Radio Fakenburg,' the announcer would say, 'mesdames et messieurs, défense de cracher' (no spitting). Each episode would end: 'Mesdames et messieurs, vous pouvez cracher!'

Wait till I tell the boys! Character with no name.

Well, for evermore! A character played by Sydney Keith.

Well, I'll go to the foot of our stairs! An old northern expression used by Handley.

What a common boy!

What is . . . . . . , Papa? The girl, Naive, would ask such questions as 'What *is* kissing, Papa?'

What me? — in my state of health? Charles Atlas (Fred Yule).

BIG-HEARTED ARTHUR, THAT'S ME

Arthur Askey (1900-82) had a good claim to be the father of the radio catchphrase. He had such a profusion of phrases from *Band Waggon* onwards that he may be said to have popularized the notion that broadcast comedians should have catchphrases. 'There had been radio comedians before this who used catchphrases, like Sandy Powell, but ours was the first show which really made a thing of them,' Arthur said. 'I was the one who was on the air most and kept banging them in.'

Band Waggon was really the first comedy show specifically tailored for radio — as opposed to one made up of variety acts. The basic format was that of a magazine — but the best-remembered segment is that in which Arthur shared a flat with Richard Murdoch (b.1907) on the top of Broadcasting House in London — they were, after all, supposed to be 'resident' comedians.

A catchphrase that stayed with Arthur for the rest of his life was spoken in the first edition of *Band Waggon* broadcast on 5 January 1938: **Big-hearted Arthur, that's me!** 'I have always used this expression,' Arthur told me when we had a long chat on the subject in 1979, 'even when I was at school. When playing cricket, you know, if the ball was hit to the boundary and nobody would go and fetch it, I would, saying "Big-hearted Arthur, that's me!"'

Another early coinage was **Hello, playmates!** though, as Arthur pointed out, this was originally **Hello, folks!** When he used 'Hello, folks' in the first broadcast of *Band Waggon*, he received a phone call from Tommy Handley telling him to lay off as Handley considered it to be *his* catchphrase. Askey coined 'Hello, playmates' instead and Handley continued to use 'Hello, folks' throughout *ITMA*, after which the Goons took up the cry and gave it a strangulated delivery. Harry Secombe extended this to **Hello, folks, and what about the workers?** and Eric Morecambe gave it a sexual connotation by referring to **a touch of hello folks and what about the workers!**

Askey's third most illustrious phrase was: **Ay thang yew!** — a distinctive pronunciation of 'I thank you!' picked up from the cry of London bus conductors. 'I didn't know I was saying it till people started to shout it at me.' Later, it became the title of one of Arthur's films.

Other *Band Waggon* coinages include:

That's tantamount to a rebuff

I don't suppose it'll matter — as when Askey and Murdoch were stirring a giant Christmas pudding in the bath — 'Will it leave a mark? Oh, I don't suppose it'll matter.'

Light the blue touchpaper and retire immediately — the firework instruction was first used on a Guy Fawkes night broadcast and subsequently when withdrawing from any confrontation with Mrs Bagwash.

Proper humdrum

Serve that lady with a crusty loaf! 'Why I said that, I've no idea,' Arthur said. 'It came out of the blue when some woman was laughing very loud in the studio audience. Perhaps it goes back to the days when I used to do the shopping for my mum in Liverpool and picked it up then.'

It'll be all right with a bit of doing up Arthur, clearing out the flat at the top of Broadcasting House: 'Shall we throw this out? No, it'll be all right with a bit of doing up.'

Don't be filthy!

Happy days! – sighed by Askey and Murdoch in unison when reminiscing about their early days in the flat.

You silly little man! As, for example:

> *Murdoch (instructing Arthur how to court Nausea Bagwash, with whom he was supposed to be in love):* You say, 'Darling Nausea, your lips are like petals . . .'
>
> *Askey:* Nausea, darling, your lips are like petals. Bicycle petals.
>
> *Murdoch:* No, no, no, you silly little man!

Doesn't it make you want to spit! Arthur was rapped over the knuckles for introducing this 'unpleasant' expression: '(Sir John) Reith (the Director-General of the BBC) thought it a bit vulgar but I was in the driving seat. The show was so popular that he couldn't fire me. I suppose I said it all the more!'

Old Nasty! A reference to Hitler (nasty/Nazi), in particular from the edition broadcast on 30 September 1939. (Arthur claimed, in similar vein, to have coined the epithet 'Aunty' for the BBC. I am not a hundred per cent sure that he did – but at least it's feasible.)

What would you do, chums? A regular feature of *Band Waggon* was a tale told by the actor Syd Walker (1887-1945) in the character of a junkman. He would pose some everyday dilemma and end with the query – or some variation upon it: 'What would you do, chums?' (also the title of a film in 1939).

In a radio series called *Hello Playmates!* the catchphrase **Speak as you find, that's my motto!** was not spoken by

Arthur — and thereby hangs a tale. Bob Monkhouse (who wrote the show with Denis Goodwin) recalls Mrs Purvis, the studio cleaner, and Nola, her stubbornly unmarried daughter: 'They were a truly marvellous pair of characters who sprang into life fully-blossomed in our first script for the show. They were played by Irene Handl as the mother, forever foisting her undesirable offspring on every male as a perfect bride, and Pat Coombs as the curiously self-composed Nola, whose smug excuse for the appalling insults she hurled was, "Well, speak as you find, that's my motto". We put it in because it amused Denis. Someone he knew, a relative, said it.' In 1955 *Hello Playmates!* won the *Daily Mail* Radio Award for the year's top show and this catchphrase was inscribed on the presentation silver microphone — which was rather odd considering that the show's star, Arthur Askey, had never uttered it.

When Arthur moved to television in the early 1950s his first series was called *Before Your Very Eyes*. Indeed, he was one of the first comedians to address the viewer through the camera in an intimate way rather than just to do a variety turn addressed as if to a larger theatre audience. Arthur registered the title in conversation with the BBC's Ronnie Waldman even before he had been given the series. When he had got it, he would emphasise the 'live' nature of the event by saying it was taking place **Here and now, before your very eyes!**

RAISING THE LAUGHS

Comedian Ted Ray (1909-77) started out as Nedlo the Gipsy Violinist, served his apprenticeship on the halls and achieved enduring fame as one of Britain's great radio comedians. His programme *Ray's a Laugh* ran from 1949 until 1960. In it Ted played a version of himself, married to a stage-wife, Kitty Bluett, and surrounded by a sea of comic characters, played by some of the leading character actors and actresses of the time, some — like Peter Sellers and Dick Emery — on their way to greater fame.

The first of Ted Ray's catchphrases comes, however, from a radio series for the troops after the Second World War — *Calling All Forces*. Ted was the star host and Bob Monkhouse and Denis Goodwin teamed up to script the comedy sequences. In the first show, broadcast live at noon on Sunday 3 December 1950, the guests were Jimmy Edwards, Jean Kent, then a major British film star, and Freddie Mills, the world light heavyweight boxing champion. Mills — departing from his script — told of one punch he had received when he had lowered his boxing gloves. He added, quite seriously: 'My trainer nearly fainted when he saw me drop 'em. I didn't mean to drop 'em.' Ted Ray heard a ripple of laughter as the audience perceived a double meaning and immediately responded: **You should use stronger elastic!** The roar of laughter this line provoked sent Monkhouse and Goodwin hurrying backstage to augment the script for a Napoleon and Josephine sketch. They gave Jean Kent an extra line — 'I have only flimsy defences against your passionate advances and I can't even keep them up!' — so that Ray, as Napoleon, could repeat his line. This he did. The laughter and applause stopped the show for a full minute and the two young writers, both aged twenty-one, were severely reprimanded by the Director of Variety, for 'circumnavigating the censor'.

By mid-week, however, the phrase had caught on. A cartoon appeared in the *Daily Sketch* depicting Clement Attlee, the Prime Minister, in drag, tripped up by a pair of bloomers around his ankles bearing the unlikely phrase, 'The National Health Act'. A chirpy Winston Churchill (Leader of the Opposition) leaned out of a Broadcasting House window, calling, 'Caught you with your plans down, Clem! You should use stronger elastic!'

On *Calling All Forces* the following Sunday it was Googie Withers as a Hollywood film star graduating from cheap two-reelers to stardom who found herself feeding Ted Ray with the line: 'I finally walked out of those crummy shorts!' Every pretty girl from Diana Dors ('I've got a lot of bare-faced cheek, haven't I?') to a fledgling Marilyn Monroe (in Britain on a Bob Hope troop show) gave Ted the cue for his celebrated reply.

After two years of varying the feedlines with tireless but sometimes dogged invention, Monkhouse and Goodwin dropped the gag. Bob Monkhouse at Kempton Park seven years later heard it as an automatic answer to the cry: 'They're off!' Ted Ray kept it in his stage act for several years, pretending to find a frilly pair of panties on the stage after a female performer had made her exit. As he eyed the knickers, some wit in the audience usually beat him to it — 'She should have used stronger elastic, Ted!' 'So should your mother,' Ted would fire back. 'Then you wouldn't be here!'

Bob Monkhouse added to the above account (1980): 'In my partnership with Denis Goodwin I must confess to the deliberate confecting of catchphrases. Also from *Calling All Forces* came **Where did you learn to kiss like that?** But it was what we called a "vehicle phrase", not really constructed to catch on but to carry a fresh joke each week. It really only existed within the confines of the show.'

Ted Ray himself recalled the most famous *Ray's a Laugh* catchphrase in his book *Raising the Laughs*. It occurred in sketches between 'Mrs Hoskin' (played by Bob Pearson) and 'Ivy' (Ted Ray): 'George Inns (the producer) agreed that the climax of their original conversation should be the mention of a mystical "Dr Hardcastle" whom Ivy secretly adored. We had absolutely no inkling of how warmly the listening millions were to take our new voices to their heart; but from the moment Bob, in his new role, had spoken the words, "I sent for young Dr Hardcastle," and we heard Ivy's excited little intake of breath, followed by, **He's loo-vely, Mrs Hardcastle . . . he's loo-oo-vely!** a new phrase had come into being.'

Mrs Hoskin would also say, famously, **'Ee, it was agony, Ivy!** — however, it has been suggested that this expression had earlier origins in music hall.

I can remember people in the mid-1950s saying **Jennifer** in a meaningful way. This appears to have grown out of an exchange between a little girl (again played by Bob Pearson) and Ted Ray:

Jennifer: Hello:
George: Why, it's a little girl. What's your name?
Jennifer: Jen-ni-fer!

Other phrases from the show include:

I love that gag! The American (sometimes known as 'Al K. Traz') played by Peter Sellers.

Shut your mouth, Soppy! was said by a character called 'Soppy' (played by Peter Sellers using his Bluebottle voice).

If you haven't been to Manchester, you haven't lived! As true today as when it was uttered regularly by Tommy Trafford (Graham Stark).

Mastermind! 'Now don't you take that tone of voice with me, Mastermind!' – an expression of Mrs Easy, the home-help, played inevitably by Patricia Hayes (c1954).

Stop it, you sauce box! Crystal Jellybottom, a charlady, played by Peter Sellers.

Not until after six o'clock! – the Mayfair Girl, played with an affected drawl, by Patricia Hayes.

Char-har-lie! / 'Allo, what do you want, Ingrid? – an exchange between Pat Hayes and Fred Yule.

Are you going to pardon me? Mr Muggs (Charles Hawtrey).

I've lost all my faith in human nature! Charles Leno as 'Dear old Dad'.

Do you mind? Sidney Mincing (Kenneth Connor) appeared in a different situation each week. Mincing was usually some sort of unhelpful, downbeat shop assistant and was introduced thus:

> *Ted Ray (in furniture store):* What's this contemptuous looking lamp-standard with a weird looking shade?
> *Mincing:* Do you mind? My name is Sidney Mincing and I happen to be the proprietor of this dishpans, frying pans and Peter Pans (as it's all on the Never-never) emporium. What can I do for you?

Lover boy! Pat Coombs as Ursula.

Ray, Ray, step into my office a minute, Ray! Mr Trumble (Laidman Browne) (c1960).

When Ray died one other catchphrase from the radio show was recalled: **You've got a big red conk!**

THE HIGHLY-ESTEEMED GOON SHOW

The Goons — Peter Sellers, Harry Secombe and Spike Milligan — first appeared in a BBC radio show called *Crazy People* in May 1951. At that time Michael Bentine was also of their number. *The Goon Show* proper (later known as *The Goons*) ran from 1952-60, with one extra programme in 1972, and numerous re-runs.

The humour was zany, often taking basic music-hall jokes and giving them further infusions of surrealism. The cast of three did almost all the funny voices, though Harry Secombe concentrated on the main character Neddie Seagoon. Catchphrases abounded:

And there's more where that came from   Sometimes said by Major Denis Bloodnok (Peter Sellers) and occasionally by Wallace Greenslade (a BBC staff announcer who, like his colleague John Snagge, let down what was left of his hair on the show.) Perhaps also by Moriarty?

And this is where the story really begins . . .

Brandy-y-y-y!   Accompanied by the sound of rushing footsteps, the show's beloved way of getting anybody out of a situation that was proving too much for him.

Damn clever these Chinese   A Second World War phrase taken up from time to time by the Goons.

Dreaded 'lergy
(pronounced 'lurgy')

Have a gorilla   Neddie Seagoon's way of offering a cigarette, to which the reply might be: 'No, thank you, I'm trying to give them up' or 'No, thanks, I only smoke baboons!'

Hello dere!   Eccles (Spike Milligan). Or simply **Hullooo!**

Hello, Jim!   (pronounced 'jeem' and/or sung) Jim Spriggs (Spike Milligan).

He's fallen in the water   Little Jim (Spike Milligan):

> *Voice:* Oh, dear children — look what's happened to Uncle Harry!
> *Little Jim (helpfully, in simple sing-song voice):* He's fallen in the wa-ter!

Hern, hern   'An encapsulation of the American language' — the American noise made by Harry Secombe as 'Lootenant Hern-hern'.

He's very good, you know!

I do not like this game!   Bluebottle (Peter Sellers):

> *Seagoon:* Now, Bluebottle, take this stick of dynamite.
> *Bluebottle:* No, I do not like this game!

I seen 'im!   Cyril (Peter Sellers).

It's all in the mind, you know   Convincing explanation of anything heard in the show — often said as a final word by Wallace Greenslade

I've been sponned   Oddly, this phrase does not actually occur in the episode called 'The Spon Plague' broadcast in March 1958, but I clearly remember running around saying it at school. The symptoms of sponning included bare knees — of which we had quite a few in those days. In 'Tales of Men's Shirts', however, Sellers' 'Mate' character is clobbered and says: 'Ow! I've been sponned from the film of the same name' and proceeds to write his memoirs, 'How I was sponned in action'.

Needle, nardle, noo!

Only in the mating season   The Goons' response to the traditional chatting-up line 'Do you come here often?'

Rhubarb!   The heroic cry, further popularized by the Goons.

Sapristi!   (as in 'Sapristi nuckoes', etc.) Count Jim Moriarty

(Spike Milligan) using a fairly traditional exclamation of surprise — a corruption of the French 'sacristi'. Others will remember it being said by Corporal Trenet, friend of 'Luck of the Legion' in the boys' paper *Eagle*, also in the 1950s.

Shut up, Eccles!   Said by Seagoon, repeated by Eccles, then taken up by everyone.

Time for you OBE, Neddie!   Captain Hercules Grytpype-Thynne (Peter Sellers) to Seagoon.

Well, hello there! (blows raspberry) Seagoon — (and Secombe in many non-Goon contexts, too.)

Yackabakaka!   Count Jim Moriarty (Spike Milligan) — as in 'Stopppp! Ferma yackabakaka le Pune!'

Ying-tong-iddle-i-po!   All-purpose phrase, most notably incorporated in the 'The Ying Tong Song'.

You can't get the wood, you know!   Said by Minnie Bannister or Henry Crun.

You dirty rotten swine, you!   Bluebottle (after being visited by some punishment or disaster). Also: **You have deaded me!**

You gotta go oww!   Moriarty.

You silly twisted boy!   Usually addressed to Neddie Seagoon.

Whatwhatwhatwhat!   (with a rising inflection) Neddie Seagoon.

BEYOND AND ROUND
THE HORNE

Kenneth Horne (1900-69) was a bald, benign and urbane figure who had little show business air about him. He was not a stand-up comedian. It just seemed as if he had drifted into the radio studio on his way back from a busy life elsewhere as a company director (and until ill-health forced him to choose broadcasting in favour of business, this was usually the case).

Horne first came to fame in the post-war years when he appeared with the similarly likeable and urbane Richard Murdoch in the air-force edition of *Merry-Go-Round*. In time

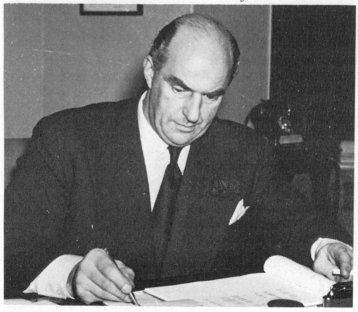

this turned into *Much Binding in the Marsh* which incorporated the following regular phraseology:

Did I ever tell you about the time I was in Sidi Barrani?
Horne to Murdoch, by way of introduction to a boring anecdote.

Not a word to Bessie!   Horne, referring to his fictional wife

Good old Charlieee!   − Murdoch interjection resulting from the birth of Prince Charles (1948).

Read any good books lately?   Murdoch's way of changing the subject:

> *Horne:* One of the nicest sandwiches I've ever had. What was in it, Murdoch?
> *Murdoch:* Well, there was − er − have you read any good books lately?
> *Horne:* I thought it tasted something like that.

(An old phrase of course. It had also been used in *Band Waggon*.)

Oh, jolly D!   (short for 'jolly decent') was said by Maurice Denham as Dudley Davenport. This character would also cry: **Oh, I say, I am a fool!** A Methodist minister in Brighton once advertised it as the title of a sermon. (Ken Platt later used the shorter, 'Oh, I am a fool!')

Oh, what 'ave I sayed?   'I've always wanted to see Stewart Grainger in the flesh, Oh! what 'ave I sayed?' − Maurice Denham as Ivy Placket.

Good morning, sir! Was there something?   Sam Costa's entry line, reflecting his role as a kind of batman to Horne and Murdoch

Emily and her twinges!   Sam Costa would make his exit referring to this lady and her problem.

And I always get the tip-up seat   A correspondent tells me that Costa, feeling hard done by, would go into an incomprehensible muttering, finishing up with this phrase. It became a family catchphrase in one household − used by anyone who thought he was being put upon.

Sir, I have an idea! ('You haven't, Murdoch' — 'Yes, I have . . .') Murdoch to Horne.

These sets take a long time to warm up Horne. Indeed, they did in the days before the valve was replaced by the transistor.

From 1954, Horne presided over a radio programme called *Beyond Our Ken*. This was basically a sketch show, scripted by Eric Merriman and Barry Took, and performed by some able supporting actors. One of these was Kenneth Williams who created a professional countryman figure with a loam-rich voice (perhaps based on Ralph Wightman or A.G. Street) called Arthur Fallowfield who appeared in an *Any Questions* spoof. **I think the answer lies in the soil** was his watchword. He also had the honest lament: **I'm looking for someone to love.** Williams also played an ancient gentleman who when asked how long he'd been doing anything would reply forthrightly: **Thirty-five years!**

In the same show, Hugh Paddick played Cecil Snaith, a caricature hush-voiced BBC outside broadcast commentator. After describing some disaster in which he had figured, Snaith would say: **And with that, I return you to the studio!** Horne suggested the line.

Paddick and Williams played two frightfully correct types who would greet each other with: **Hello, Rodney! / Hello, Charles!**

More or less the same team manifested itself from 1964 in *Round the Horne* — this time with somewhat broader and zanier scripts by Marty Feldman and Barry Took. Took told me: 'Marty and I went all out to avoid catchphrases but the cast kept pencilling them in. Eventually we gave up the unequal struggle!' The new approach was typified by the introduction of two stock figures, the gay ex-chorus boys Julian and Sandy. **Oh hello, I'm Julian and this is my friend, Sandy** was how Hugh Paddick would refer to Kenneth Williams. From their first appearance they larded their speech with bits of camp *parlare* (talk) from the *omipalomi* (homosexual) sub culture of actors and dancers. Fantabulosa! One of their incarnations was as film producers:

> *Sandy:* Mr Horne, we are in the forefront of your Nouvelle Vague. **That's your actual French.**

Julian: It means we are of the New Wave.
Sandy: And very nice it looks on you, too.

(Peter Cook claims to have launched 'your actual' as a turn of phrase, however). **Ooh, bold! Very bold!** was their standard exclamation.

Betty Marsden played Lady Beatrice Counterblast (née Clissold) and would say **Many, many times!** (originally in answer to a query as to how often she'd been married.) When the phrase was used in all seriousness in *The Sound of Music* during the run of the radio show, Barry Took recalls, the theatre audience fell about. Spasm, Lady Counterblast's butler (played by Kenneth Williams) would wail **We be doomed, we all be doomed** − a line shared with the John Laurie character in TV's *Dad's Army* who would exclaim: 'Doomed I am, doomed!')

Williams would occasionally heckle **Oh, get on with it!** to fellow cast members.

The announcer, Douglas Smith, would conclude the show with: **You have either been listening to − or have just missed − "Beyond Our Ken"!**

YOU AIN'T HEARD
NOTHING YET

Not many catchphrases have come out of the cinema because the medium lacks the regularity to impress the words on audiences. However, one or two emerge when performers regularly say certain things in a series of films (like Gary Cooper's **yup!** and **nope!** and Clark Gable's **I love ya!**) or where lines of dialogue have become especially famous for a particular reason.

Before the coming of sound it was possible for a catchphrase to emerge from its use as a subtitle. In *A Fool There Was* (1914), Theda Bara 'spoke' the subtitle **Kiss me, my fool** and this was taken up as a fad expression. Similarly Jacqueline Logan 'said' **Harness my zebras** in Cecil B. De Mille's 1925 *King of Kings*. This became a fad expression for 'let's leave' or as a way of expressing amazement — 'Well, harness my zebras!' Stock subtitles like **Comes the dawn** and **Meanwhile back at the ranch** rapidly acquired cliché status.

Then came sound:

You ain't heard nothin' yet!   Al Jolson (1886-1950) not only ad-libbed a line for the first full-length talking picture, *The Jazz Singer* (1927), he also provided a slogan for the coming age of the sound cinema. Michael Freedland described what happened in his biography of Jolson: 'The original idea was that *The Jazz Singer* would be a completely silent picture with just Jolson's songs and the occasional snatch of the background music . . . There were sub-titles for the picture . . . so no one was terribly concerned when Jolson started ad-libbing in front of the cameras . . . All was ready for Jolson to go into his first big featured number, "Toot, Toot Tootsie Goo'-bye". But Alan Crosland, the director, had never worked with Jolson before. Just as he gave the signal for everything to roll, Al got into the spirit of the thing. "Wait a minute, wait a minute," he cried. "You ain't heard nothin' yet. Wait a minute I tell yer . . . you wanna hear 'Toot Tot Tootsie'? All right, hold on." . . . No screen playwright could ever have put those words in a script and got away with it. But the mikes were switched on, the film and Jolson were in motion and those sentences were preserved for posterity.'

The recording makes it clear that Jolson did not add 'folks' at the end of his mighty line, as both the Bartlett and Oxford dictionaries of quotations make out.

Elementary, my dear Watson The Sherlock Holmes catchphrase appears nowhere in the writings of Sir Arthur Conan Doyle (1859-1930) though the great detective does exclaim 'Elementary' to Dr Watson in *The Memoirs of Sherlock Holmes* ('The Crooked Man') (1894). Conan Doyle brought out his last Holmes book in 1927. His son Adrian (in collaboration with John Dickson Carr) was one of those who used the phrase in follow-up stories – as have adapters of the stories in film and broadcast versions. In the 1929 film *The Return of Sherlock Holmes* – the first with sound – the final lines of dialogue are:

Watson: Amazing, Holmes!
Holmes: Elementary, my dear Watson, elementary.

And so we say farewell . . . The travelogues made by James A. Fitzpatrick (b.1902) were a supporting feature of cinema programmes from 1929 onwards. With the advent of sound, the commentaries to 'Fitzpatrick Traveltalks' became noted for their parting words, summed up by the phrase 'And so we say farewell . . .':

'And it's from this paradise of the Canadian Rockies that we reluctantly say farewell to beautiful Banff . . .'
'And as the midnight sun lingers on the skyline of the city, we most reluctantly say farewell to Stockholm, Venice of the North . . .'
'With the picturesque harbour indelibly fixed in our memory, it is time to conclude our visit and reluctantly say farewell to Hong Kong, the hub of the Orient . . .'

Frank Muir and Denis Norden's notable parody of the genre — 'Balham — Gateway to the South' — first written for radio c1948 and later performed on disc by Peter Sellers (1958) accordingly contained the words: 'And so we say farewell to the historic borough . . .'

Another cliché phrase of the travelogue was **The sun sinks slowly in the West . . .**

You dirty rat!   James Cagney (b.1899) never said the words put into his mouth by countless impressionists. In *Blonde Crazy* (1931) he did, however, call someone a 'dirty, double-crossing rat' — which, I suppose, amounts to much the same thing.

I want to be alone   Greta Garbo (b.1905) claimed that what she said was 'I want to be *let* alone' i.e. she wanted privacy rather than solitude. Oddly, as Alexander Walker observes in his book *Sex in the Movies* (1968):

> Nowhere in anything she said, either in the lengthy interviews she gave in her early Hollywood days when she was perfectly approachable, or in the statements snatched on-the-run from the publicity-shy fugitive she later became has it been possible to find the famous phrase, 'I want to be alone'. What one can find, in abundance later on, is 'Why don't you let me alone?' and even 'I want to be left alone,' but neither is redolent of any more exotic order of being than a harassed celebrity. Yet the world prefers to believe the mythical and much more mysterious catch-phrase utterance.

What complicates the issue is that Garbo herself used the lines several times — in character. For example, in the 1929 silent *The Single Standard* she gives the brush-off to a stranger, while up comes the subtitle: 'I am walking alone because I want to be alone.' And, as the ageing ballerina who loses her nerve and flees back to her suite in *Grand Hotel* (1932), she actually says it. Walker calls this 'an excellent example of art borrowing its effects from a myth that was reality for millions of people.'

The phrase was obviously well-established by 1935 when Groucho Marx spoke it in *A Night at the Opera*. Garbo herself said 'Go to bed, little father, we want to be alone' in *Ninotch-*

ka (1939). So, it is not surprising that the myth has taken such a firm hold — particularly since Garbo became a virtual recluse for the second half of her life.

When Howard Dietz, the lyric writer and MGM promotions executive, died in 1983 it was suggested that he had had a hand in launching the phrase as a publicity gimmick.

Me, Tarzan — you, Jane! A box-office sensation of 1932 was the first sound Tarzan film — *Tarzan the Ape Man*. It spawned a long-running series and starred Johnny Weissmuller, an ex-US swimming champion, as Tarzan, and Maureen O'Sullivan as Jane. At one point the ape man whisks Jane away to his tree-top abode and indulges in some elementary conversation with her: thumping his chest he says 'Tarzan!'; pointing at her he says 'Jane!' — so, in fact, he does not say the catchphrase commonly associated with him, though perhaps he does in later films. Interestingly, this great moment of movie dialogue was written by the British playwright and actor, Ivor Novello. In the original novel *Tarzan of the Apes* (1914) by Edgar Rice Burroughs the line does not occur — not least because, in the jungle, Tarzan and Jane are only able to communicate by writing notes to each other.

Come up and see me some time Mae West (1892-1980) had a notable stage hit on Broadway with her play *Diamond Lil* (first performed 9 April 1928). When she appeared in the 1933 film version entitled *She Done Him Wrong*, what she said to a very young Cary Grant (playing a coy undercover policeman) was:

> You know I always did like a man in uniform. And that one fits you grand. Why don't you come up some time and see me? I'm home every evening.

As a catchphrase, the words have been rearranged to make them easier to say. That is how W.C. Fields says them *to* Mae West in the film *My Little Chickadee* (1939) and she herself took to saying them in the rearranged version, too.

Beulah, peel me a grape — a phrase of dismissive unconcern, was first uttered by Mae West to a black maid in the film *I'm No Angel* (1933) after a male admirer has stormed out on her.

Here's another fine mess you've gotten me into   (and variations upon the same). The anguished cry of Oliver Hardy to Stan Laurel which managed to register itself as a catchphrase with the public from the 1930s on because there were sufficient Laurel and Hardy films to establish it.

The things I've done for England   In Alexander Korda's *The Private Life of Henry VIII* (1933), Charles Laughton as the king says this just before getting into bed with one of his brides. In 1979, Prince Charles sampled curried snake meat in Hong Kong and declared, 'Boy, the things I do for England.'

That's all, folks!   became the concluding line of *Merry Melodies*, the Warner Bros cartoon series, from 1930.

What's up, Doc?   The characteristic inquiry of Bugs Bunny, the cartoon character, in the series which ran from 1937-63. A phrase subsequently used as the title of a film starring Barbra Streisand and Ryan O'Neal.

Come with me to the Casbah   — a line forever associated with the film *Algiers* (1938) and its star, Charles Boyer. He is supposed to have said it to Hedy Lamarr. Boyer impersonators used it, the film was laughed at because of it, but nowhere is it said in the film. It was just a Hollywood legend that grew up. Boyer himself denied he had ever said it and thought it had all been started by a press agent.

Let's put on a show!   A staple line in the Mickey Rooney-Judy Garland movies of the late 1930s and early 1940s was something to the effect: 'Hey! I've got it! Why don't we put on a show?' The line took several forms. Another was **Let's do the show right here (in the barn)!** In *Babes in Arms* (1939) — the first of the series — Rooney and Garland play the teenage children of retired vaudeville-players who decide to put on a big show of their own. They do not, however, actually say any of these lines, although they do express their determination to 'put on a show'. In whatever form, the line became a film cliché, now recalled only with amused affection.

We have ways (and means) of making you talk   The cliché threat of an evil inquisitor to his victim appears to have started with 1930s Hollywood villains and then been applied to Nazis from the Second World War onwards.

Leslie Halliwell traced the earlier use to Douglas Dumbrille as the evil Mohammed Khan in *Lives of a Bengal Lancer* (1935). He says: 'We have ways of making *men* talk.'

A typical Nazi use can be found in the British film *Odette* (1950) in which the French Resistance worker (Anna Neagle) is threatened with unmentioned nastiness by one of her captors. Says she, more than once: 'I have nothing to say.' Says he: 'We have ways and means of making you talk.' After a little meaningful stoking of a fire with a poker, he urges her on with: 'We have ways and means to make a woman talk.'

Later, used in a caricature sense, the phrase saw further action in TV programmes like *Rowan and Martin's Laugh-In*. Frank Muir presented a comedy series for London Weekend Television with the title *We Have Ways of Making You Laugh* (1968).

I'm a ba-a-a-ad boy! Lou Costello (1906-59) of Abbott and Costello fame would occasionally exclaim this in the various films they made together.

Play it again, Sam As is widely-known nowadays, nowhere in *Casablanca* (1942) does Humphrey Bogart — or anyone else — say these words to Dooley Wilson, the night club pianist and reluctant performer of the sentimental song 'As Time Goes By'. At one point, Ingrid Bergman, as Ilsa, does have this exchange with him:

> *Ilsa:* Play it once, Sam, for old time's sake.
> *Sam:* Ah don't know what you mean, Miss Ilsa.
> *Ilsa:* Play it, Sam. Play 'As Time Goes By'.

Later, Bogart (as Rick) also tries to get Sam to play it:

> *Rick:* Of all the gin joints in all the towns in all the world, she walks into mine! What's that you're playing?
> *Sam:* Oh, just a little something of my own.
> *Rick:* Well, stop it. You know what I want to hear.
> *Sam:* No, I don't.
> *Rick:* You played it for her, and you can play it for me.
> *Sam:* Well, I don't think I can remember it.
> *Rick:* If she can stand it, I can. Play it.

But, what the hell, if people think it should have been said, then why not! By the time Woody Allen's film homage to

Bogart — *Play It Again, Sam* — came along in 1972, the catch-phrase was well-established.

From *Casablanca* also came **Here's looking at you, kid** — a quotation turned into a catchphrase by Bogart imperson-ators — and, in a manner of speaking, **Drop the gun, Louis.** Alistair Cooke writing in *Six Men* remarked of Humphrey Bogart: 'He gave currency to another phrase with which the small fry of the English-speaking world brought the neigh-bourhood sneak to heel; "Drop the gun, Looey!"' Quite how Bogart did this, Cooke does not reveal. We have Bogart's word for it; 'I never said "Drop the gun, Louie"' (quoted in Ezra Goodman, *Bogey: the Good-bad Guy*.)

It's just another of those lines that people would like to have heard spoken but which never were. At the end of *Casablanca* what Bogart says to Claude Rains (playing Captain Louis Renault) is: 'Not so fast, Louis.' Ironically, it is Renault who says: 'Put that gun down.'

If you want anything, just whistle This catchphrase is not a direct quotation from a film. It is Lauren Bacall who says to Humphrey Bogart (and not, as is sometimes suggested, the other way round) in *To Have and Have Not* (1945):

> You know you don't have to act with me, Steve. You don't have to say anything, and you don't have to do anything. Not a thing. Oh, maybe just whistle. You know how to whistle, don't you, Steve? You just put your lips together and blow.

A man's gotta do, what a man's gotta do Partridge dates this as a catchphrase from c1945. The only reference I have is to the Alan Ladd film *Shane* (1953) which was based on a Jack Shaeffer novel. Having watched the film through, I have to report that Ladd does not say the line. He says: 'A man has to be what he is, Joey'. A woman character notes: 'Shane did what he had to do.' Perhaps the phrase was used as a promotional slogan for the film.

That's the way it crumbles, cookie-wise Bartlett describes 'That's the way the cookie crumbles' as an anonymous phrase from the 1950s. It was, however, given a memorable twist in Billy Wilder's film *The Apartment* (1960). The main characters make much play with the business jargon use of the suffix '-wise', as in 'promotion-wise' and 'gracious-living-wise'. Then Miss Kubelik (Shirley MacLaine) says to C.C. Baxter (Jack Lemmon): 'Why can't I ever fall in love with somebody nice like you?' Replies Baxter: 'Yeah, well, that's the way it crumbles, cookie-wise.'

A martini — shaken, not stirred This example of would-be sophistication became a running in joke in the immensely popular James Bond films of the 1960s and 70s. Without reading all Ian Fleming's Bond novels over again I can't swear for sure that the line was an invention of the screenwriters and not his, but I think so.

However, the idea stems from the very first Bond novel, *Casino Royale* (1953), in which Bond orders a cocktail of his own devising. It consists of one dry Martini 'in a deep champagne goblet', three measures of Gordon's gin, one of vodka — 'made with grain instead of potatoes' — and half a measure of Kina Lillet. 'Shake it very well until it's ice-cold'. Bond justifies this fussiness a page or two later: 'I take a ridiculous pleasure in what I eat and drink. It comes partly from being a bachelor, but mostly from a habit of taking a lot of trouble over details. It's very pernickety and old-maidish really, but when I'm working I generally have to eat my meals alone and it makes them more interesting when one takes trouble.'

This characteristic was aped by the writers of the first Bond story to be filmed — *Dr No* (1962). A West Indian servant brings Bond a vodka and Martini and says: 'Martini like you said, sir, — and not stirred'. Dr No also mentions the fad, though the words are not spoken by Bond. In the third film, *Goldfinger* (1964), Bond (played by Sean Connery) does get to say 'A Martini, shaken, not stirred' (he needs a drink after escaping a laser death-ray) and there are references to the phrase in *You Only Live Twice* (1967) and *On Her Majesty's Secret Service* (1969), among others.

The phrase was employed and played with in the numerous parodies of the Bond phenomenon on film, TV and radio, though — curiously enough — it is a piece of absolute nonsense. According to an expert, shaking a dry Martini 'turns it from something crystal-clear into a dreary frosted drink. It should be stirred quickly with ice in a jug.'

It's all part of life's rich pageant Not originally a film phrase — but here goes: Peter Sellers as Inspector Clouseau has just fallen into a fountain in *A Shot in the Dark* (1964) when Elke Sommer commiserates with him: 'You'll catch your death of pneumonia'. Playing it phlegmatically as always, Clouseau replies: 'It's all part of life's rich pageant.'

The origin of this happy phrase — sometimes the words 'pattern' or 'tapestry' are substituted for 'pageant' — was the subject of inquiry by Michael Watts of the *Sunday Express* in 1982. The earliest citation he came up with was from a record called 'The Game's Mistress' written and performed by

Arthur Marshall (b.1910) in the 1930s. The monologue concludes: 'Never mind, dear — laugh it off, laugh it off. It's all part of life's rich pageant.'

I'm going to make him an offer he can't refuse   In 1969, Mario Puzo (b.1920) published his novel about the Mafia called *The Godfather*. It gave to the language a new expression. Johnny Fontane, a singer, desperately wants a part in a movie and goes to see the 'godfather', Don Corleone, seeking help. All the contracts have been signed and there is no chance of the studio chief changing his mind. Still, the godfather promises Fontane he will get him the part, explaining: 'He's a businessman. I'll make him an offer he can't refuse.'

In the 1971 film this exchange was turned into the following dialogue: 'In a month from now this Hollywood big shot's going to give you what you want.' 'Too late, they start shooting in a week.' (Marlon Brando, with his mouth stuffed full of orange peel or cotton or something): 'I'm going to make him an offer he can't refuse.'

Yowsir, yowsir, yowsir   The 1969 film *They Shoot Horses Don't They?* (from Horace McCoy's 1935 novel — the title using what I presume is an old Western expression of exhaustion) portrayed a dance marathon contest of the Depression years. Appropriately, it highlighted the 'yowser, yowser' cry (meaning 'yes, sir') originated in the 1930s by the orchestra leader and entertainer, Ben Bernie.

Let's get outta here!   A survey of 150 features made in the US between 1938-74 and shown on British television revealed that the cry 'Let's get outta here!' was used once in 84% of them and more than once in 17%.

May the Force be with you   A delicious piece of hokum from *Star Wars* (1977) and others in the series was the benediction: 'May the Force be with you.' At one point Alec Guinness explains what it means: 'The Force is what gives the Jedi its power. It's an energy field created by all living things. It surrounds us, it penetrates us, it binds the galaxy together.'

The valediction turned up in Cornwall a short while after the film was released in Britain — as a police recruiting slogan.

E.T., phone home The pathetic cry of the extra-terrestrial creature in Steven Spielberg's 1982 film was exploited here and there. British Telecom advertisements replied: 'Give us time, E.T., give us time.'

AND NOW, A WORD
FROM OUR SPONSOR

It is possible for advertising slogans to become catchphrases, but these are mostly dealt with in the second part of this book. However, here are some lines which derive from advertising but which do not quite have the force of full-blooded slogans. In most cases they are incidental phrases which somehow caught the public fancy.

Barry Day, President of McCann & Co., the advertising agency, comments on the catchphrase aspect of his business: 'It occurs to me that *most* of the truly memorable and mind-nagging lines came in the early days of commercial TV in the UK. I suspect that's because early TV was very self-consciously a moving version of print advertising, which had always depended very heavily on the slogan or pay-off line. And just about everything was sung. But from the 1960s there was the revival of the catchphrase type of slogan along the lines of the radio programme ones of the war years. Again, you were consciously trying to create popularity. You *hoped* the comics would take them up and make them part of the language (as opposed to the accidental and usually rude borrowings of slogans like "Can *you* tell Stork from butter?" etc.) Examples of the "planted" lines would include "I'm only here for the beer" and "Nice one, Cyril".'

Didjavagoodweekend? ('No, I forgot the Aerogard.') Aerogard, the Australian insect repellent, used this exchange in advertising during the early 1980s. The phrase, said with a strong Aussie accent, passed into the language Down Under — not least because it was a useful thing for people to say in conversation.

Gercha! Not the most positive of advertising lines, but a distinctive advertising idea from a TV campaign for Courage Best Bitter in the UK, c1980. Various grim-faced beer drinkers sat around in an East End pub and shouted it out in breaks in the music. Dave Trott, the copywriter responsible for using the word, suggested it derives from the expression, 'Get out of it, you.' This is supported by Partridge (1937). The O.E.D. *Supplement* has 'Get away/along with you'. The line got into the commercial from a song composed by the singers Chas and Dave who originally pronounced it 'Wooertcha'. Subsequently they introduced the line **Rabbit, rabbit** to promote the same beer — in emulation of talkative women who interrupt the pleasures of the drinking process. ('Rabbit and port' is rhyming slang for 'talk')

It's b'ootiful. Really b'ootiful! Bernard Matthews promoting his Golden Norfolk self-basting turkeys in a Norfolk burr (and wearing a Norfolk suit) on TV ads in the UK from 1980.

My little perforations 'You have to admit,' said Roy Hudd in 1977, 'that any business which allows a catchphrase to turn you into a household name, buy you a house in the country and gives a certain amount of financial security to you and your family, has to be crazy.' He was referring to the line from his Lyons Quick Brew Tea commercials: 'It's not me, ma'am, it's me little perforations' (i.e. the holes in the tea-bag which let the flavour through).

Keynsham — that's K-E-Y-N-S-H-A-M . . . Listeners to Radio Luxembourg in the 1950s and 60s will remember the rolling, deep West Country accent of Horace Batchelor (1898-1977) who promoted a method of winning the football pools and was said, at his death, to have netted £12 million for his clients. He would say: 'Good evening, friends. This is Horace Bachelor at the microphone— the inventor of the famous infra-draw method for the Treble Chance. I have myself, with my own coupon entries, won 1,012 first Treble Chance top dividends. And my ingenious method can help you to win also. Don't send any — just your name and address.'

Then came the high-spot of his ads: 'Send now to Horace Batchelor, Dept 1, Keynsham — that's K-E-Y-N-S-H-A-M, Bristol'

Nice 'ere, innit? 1976: on a balcony in Venice, a ravishing girl sips Campari and then shatters the atmosphere by saying in a Cockney flame-thrower voice, 'Nice 'ere, innit?' In the follow-up ad, a smoothy asks the same girl, 'Were you truly wafted here from Paradise?' She: '**Nah, Luton Airport.**' These nothing phrases, spoken in an all-to-memorable way, were crafted by copywriter Terry Howard and let fall by Lorraine Chase. Campari sales soared by 35% in a single year. Lorraine went on to record a single called 'It's Nice 'ere, innit?' (1979) and a girl group called Cats UK recorded 'Luton Airport' the same year. Next step was for the Lorraine character to be written into a TV sit. com. called The Other 'Arf (from 1980).

Nice one, Cyril! This is a classic instance of a phrase from advertising being taken up by the public, turned into a catchphrase, and then as suddenly dropped. Its origins were quite soon forgotten. The saying caught the imagination of TV viewers in a 1972 advertisement for Wonderloaf. Two bakers were shown wearing T-shirts labelled 'Nottingham' and 'Liverpool' respectively. 'All our local bakers reckon they can taste a Wonderloaf and tell you who baked it,' a voice-over commentary explained. 'It was oven—baked at one of our local bakeries.' The following exchange then took place between the bakers:

> *Liverpool:* Leeds? High Wycombe? It's one of Cyril's. mmm. Good texture, nice colour, very fresh . . .
> *Nottingham:* Cyril . . . I think it's one of Frank's down at Luton . . . it's definitely saying Newcastle to me . . .'

The voice-over then intervened: 'The truth is, they can't say it for sure. But we can say, —

> *Nottingham:* Nice one, Cyril!

As a phrase, why did 'Nice one, Cyril' catch on? It had a sibilant ease, it was fun to say. More importantly, it could be used in any number of situations, not least sexual ones. In 1973, the phrase was taken up by Tottenham Hotspur supporters of the footballer Cyril Knowles. They even recorded a song about him which went:

Nice one, Cyril
Nice one, son.
Nice one, Cyril,
Let's have another one.

Comedian Cyril Fletcher used it as the title of his 1978 auto-biography. The following year the word 'Cyril' was observed added to the first kilometre signpost outside a seaside resort in the South of France. Shortly afterwards, the phrase disappeared almost completely from use.

THIS SPORTING LIFE

Sport is clearly a branch of entertainment — or, at least, broadcasting has made it so:

Back to square one   meaning to go 'back to the beginning', this expression gained currency from the 1930s onwards through its use by radio football commentators in the UK. *Radio Times* used to print a plan of the football field divided into numbered squares, to which commentators would refer: 'Cresswell's going to make it — FIVE — There it goes, slap into the middle of the goal — SEVEN — Cann's header there — EIGHT — The ball comes out to Britton. Britton manoeuvres. The centre goes right in — BACK TO EIGHT — Comes on to Marshall — SIX . . .' — an extract from the commentary on the 1933 Cup Final between Everton and Manchester City. The idea had been abandoned by 1938, but the phrase lives on.

Bewdy, Newk!   Translated from the Australian, this means 'A beauty, Newcombe' — i.e. the tennis-player, John Newcombe. As is described elsewhere in the book, **Life. Be In It** was the slogan of a campaign which began in the State of Victoria and then spread across Australia in the late 1970s, aimed at getting people involved with healthy activities like tennis. One TV commercial showed 'Norm', a fat chairbound sportsman watching Newcombe and cheering him on with this phrase.

I am the greatest   Vocal athlete Muhammad Ali, originally Cassius Clay (b.1942), first became World Heavyweight boxing champion in 1964. As part of a vigorous campaign to wear down his opponent, Sonny Liston, in advance — which even included the launch of an LP record of abusive humour — Ali admitted that he copied his 'I am the greatest . . . I am the prettiest' routine from a wrestler called Gorgeous George

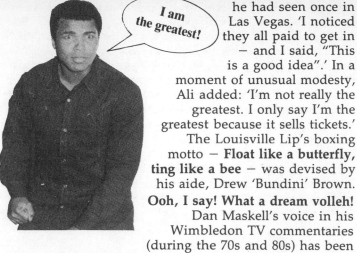

I am the greatest!

he had seen once in Las Vegas. 'I noticed they all paid to get in – and I said, "This is a good idea".' In a moment of unusual modesty, Ali added: 'I'm not really the greatest. I only say I'm the greatest because it sells tickets.'

The Louisville Lip's boxing motto – **Float like a butterfly, ting like a bee** – was devised by his aide, Drew 'Bundini' Brown.

Ooh, I say! What a dream volleh! Dan Maskell's voice in his Wimbledon TV commentaries (during the 70s and 80s) has been as much a part of the sporting atmosphere as, say, Peter O'Sullevan's in horse racing.

Say-hey! Willie Mays (b.1931) the American baseball player was known during the early 50s as Say Hey Willie or the Say Hey Kid from his frequent use of this expression.

Up and under! is a Rugby football term for a short, high kick which sends the ball high in the air enabling the kicker and his team-mates to run forward and regain possession of the ball. But to British TV viewers it is inseparably linked to Rugby league commentator Eddie Waring (b.1909). He broadcast commentaries for twenty years up to his retirement in 1981. His other expressions included **E's a grand lad** and **An early bath** (for a player being sent off early). He commented: 'I think making comments is part and parcel of what it's all about. In a cup tie between Leeds and Wakefield, Don Fox missed a goal under the posts and a cry went up, because it meant they'd lost the match. And during the cheering, and jeering, I just said, **Poor lad.** His brother, Neil Fox, called him all the names under the sun, but when he rang home, obviously in tears, his sister and mother said, "Well, don't worry, you've got all the sympathy of the village, because Eddie Waring said, 'Poor lad'. We all felt sorry for you and we all cried."'

Up there, Cazaly!   Roy Cazaly (1893-1963) was an Australian Rules footballer who played for the South Melbourne team from 1921 and formed a 'ruck' combination with 'Skeeter' Fleiter and Mark Tandy i.e. they were players who worked together but did not have fixed positions. According to *The Australian Dictionary of Biography:* 'Though only 5ft 11ins. and 12½ stone, Cazaly was a brilliant high-mark; he daily practised leaping for a ball suspended from the roof of a shed at his home. He could mark and turn in mid-air, land and in a few strides send forward a long accurate drop-kick or stab-pass. Fleiter's constant cry 'Up there, Cazaly!' was taken up by the crowds. It entered the Australian idiom, was used by infantrymen in North Africa in World War II and became part of folk-lore.' The phrase was also incorporated in a song.

YOU GIVE US 20 MINUTES, WE'LL GIVE YOU THE WORLD

More than one all-news radio station in the US has used the slogan **You give us 20 minutes, we'll give you the world.** I first came across it in Philadelphia in 1972. (Ten years later, the TV satellite news channel was declaring: 'Give us *18* minutes and we'll give you the world.') But, particularly in the 1930s and 40s, American radio could attract devotees for much longer periods than twenty minutes . . .

Individual broadcasters had their catchphrases. Comedian Jerry Lester popularized **George** as a way of saying 'extraordinary!' Arthur Godfrey favoured **clunkhead** to describe a stupid person. Arnold Stang launched the sarcastic expression *big* **deal!** Bob Hope popularized the forces' **hubba bubba** — a spoken wolf-whistle — and Don Rickles **dum dum** for a stupid person. Baseball commentator Red Barber popularized the Southern expression **sitting in the catbird seat,** meaning 'sitting pretty'. Red Skelton played Junior, the Mean Widdle Kid, with his admission of mischief: **I dood it!** Fanny Brice as Baby Snooks asked **Why-y-y-y, daddy?** In other cases it was the show, rather than the performer, that produced the catchphrases:

CAMEL CARAVAN, THE   The late 1940s variety show featured Jimmy Durante and others. One of the singers was customarily introduced by MC Gary Moore thus: **And now her nibs, Miss Georgia Gibbs!** Florence Haslop as the sexpot 'Hotbreath Houlihan' popularized **C'mere, big boy!**

FIBBER McGEE AND MOLLY **Somebody bawl for Beulah?** was the cry of Beulah, the cheery, black housemaid, who was a supporting character in this series but went on to have her own radio show — *Beulah* — and TV series in the period 1944–54. Five people played her over the years — originally she was played by a white man. Also **On the con-positively-trary!** and **Love that man!** (after laughing uproariously at one of Fibber McGee's jokes).

From the same show came wife Molly's response to jokes: **T'aint funny, McGee!** and next door neighbour Gildersleeve's **You're a hard man, McGee!**

GANGBUSTERS   This series ran from c.1945–57 and used to begin with the sound of screeching tires, machine guns and police sirens, followed by the announcement: '**Gangbusters!** With the cooperation of leading law enforcement officials of the United States. Gangbusters presents facts in the relentless war of the police on the underworld, authentic case histories that show the never ending activity of the police in their work of protecting our citizens.' Hence the American slang expression 'to come on like gangbusters' — meaning to perform in a striking manner.

GRAND OLD OPRE   The Nashville country and western venue was featured in broadcasts until 1957. At one time it featured an MC known as the Duke of Paducah (Whitey Ford). His catchphrase was **I'm goin' back to the wagon, boys, these shoes are killin' me!**

LONE RANGER, THE   'Who *was* that masked man?'

'A fiery horse with the speed of light, a cloud of dust, and a hearty **Hi-yo, Silver!** The Lone Ranger! With his faithful Indian companion, Tonto, the daring and resourceful masked rider of the plains led the fight for law and order in the early western United States. Nowhere in the pages of history can one find a greater champion of justice. **Return with us now to those thrilling days of yesteryear** . . . from out of the past come the thundering hoofbeats of the great horse Silver. The Lone Ranger rides again!'

'Come on, Silver! Let's go, big fellow! Hi-yo, Silver, away!'

The above was more or less the introduction to the masked Lone Ranger and his horse, Silver, in the various American radio, TV and cinema accounts of their exploits, accompanied, of course, by Rossini's 'William Tell' overture.

Groucho Marx used to say that George Seaton (the first

Lone Ranger on radio from 1933) invented the call 'Hi-yo, Silver!' because he was unable to whistle for his horse. It does indeed seem probable that the phrase was coined by Seaton and not by Fran Striker, the chief scriptwriter in the early days.

The Lone Ranger's Indian friend, Tonto, wrestled meanwhile with such lines as **Him bad man, kemo sabe!** ('Kemos sabe' — whichever way you spell it — is supposed to have meant 'trusty scout' and was derived from the name of a boys' camp at Mullet Lake, Michigan, in 1911.)

MARCH OF TIME, THE   Sponsored by *Time* magazine, this was a radio newsreel that ran for fourteen years from 1931. It presented the stories of the day in dramatised form and was narrated by a serious personage known as 'The Voice of Time'. The narrator's farewell words were: **Time . . . marches on!** Later, on-the-spot reports and actuality were incorporated, especially during the Second World War.

SUPERMAN   The comic-strip hero, Superman, was the brainchild of a teenage science fiction addict, Jerry Siegel, in 1933. Five years later, Superman appeared on the cover of

No 1 of *Action Comics*. In 1940, he took to the radio airwaves on the Mutual Network with Clayton 'Bud' Collyer as the journalist, Clark Kent, who can turn into the Man of Steel whenever he is in a tight spot: 'This looks like a job for . . . Superman! Now, off with these clothes! **Up, up and awa-a-a-ay!**' After appearing in film cartoons, Superman finally appeared as a live-action hero on the screen in 1948 with a 15-episode serial.

It was from the radio series, however, that the exciting phrases came:

Announcer: Kellogg's Pep . . . the super-delicious cereal . . . presents . . . *The Adventures of Superman!* Faster than a speeding bullet! *(Ricochet)* More powerful than a locomotive! *(Locomotive roar)* Able to leap tall buildings at a single bound! *(Rushing wind)* Look! Up in the sky!
Voice 1: **It's a bird!**
Voice 2 (female): **It's a plane!**
Voice 3: **It's Superman!**
Announcer: Yes, it's Superman — a strange visitor from another planet, who came to earth with powers and abilities far beyond those of mortal men. Superman! — who can change the course of mighty rivers, bend steel with his bare hands, and who — disguised as Clark Kent, mild-mannered reporter for a great metropolitan newspaper — fights **a never-ending battle for truth, justice, and the American way.**

TOWN HALL TONIGHT   Comedian Fred Allen had a feature on this programme called 'Allen's Alley' (from 1942). Incorporated in it was the catchphrase of 'Senator Claghorn' from the Deep South after making some feeble pun: **That's a joke, son!**

THANK YOU,
MUSIC LOVERS

The American musician Spike Jones (1911-1964) specialized in comedy arrangements on radio, records and films from the late 1930s onwards. After massacring some well-known piece of music like 'The Dance of the Hours' he would come on and say: **Thank you, music-lovers!**

This section presents some catchphrases that have come to us from music and/or records:

Go, man, go was a term of encouragement originally shouted at jazz musicians (in the 1940s). Then it took on wider use. At the beginning of the number 'It's Too Darn Hot' in Cole Porter's *Kiss Me Kate* (film version, 1953) a dancer cries: 'Go, girl, go'.

TV newscaster Walter Cronkite reverted famously to 'Go, baby, go!' while describing the launch of Apollo XI in 1969 and this form became fairly standard at rocket and missile departures. *Time* magazine (29 November 1982) reported it being shouted at a test firing of a Pershing II missile. **Crazy, man, crazy** originated at about the same time, but perhaps better suited rock n'roll usage rather than the earlier bop.

See you later, alligator Note how a phrase develops: according to Flexner, 'See you later', as a form of farewell, entered American speech in the 1870s. By the 1930s it had some 'jive' use with the addition of 'alligator'. To this was further added: 'In a while, crocodile.'

This exchange became known to a wider public through the song 'See You Later, Alligator' sung by Bill Haley and his Comets in the film *Rock Around the Clock* (1956). Princess Margaret and her set became keen users of the phrase.

The next step was for the front and back of the expression

to be dropped, leaving simply 'lay-tuh' as a form of farewell . . .

Hoots man, there's a moose loose about this house (and **It's a braw bricht moonlicht nicht**)   were cod Scotticisms spoken during breaks in the music on the immensely successful disc 'Hoots Mon' — a hit (17 weeks at No 1) for Lord Rockingham's XI in 1958. There is dispute among Scots as to the meaning of the phrase 'hoots mon' — it may mean 'Goodness, man!' or (if you accept that a 'hoot' is a 'dram') 'Have a dram!' Less memorable phrases were included in the follow-up record 'Wee Tom' (1959): 'Wee Tom and a wee brown coo/ Tom said boo and the coo said moo' and 'Wee Tom and a wee brown coo/ Both got the flu, ta—ta the noo'.

Slow, slow, quick, quick, slow   Dance tempo spoken by Victor Sylvester (1902-78), ballroom dance instructor and orchestra leader, on radio and TV from the 1950s. His sign-off was something to the effect: **Goodbye everyone, everywhere** (appropriate because of his broadcasts on BBC World Service.)

Goodness gracious me   This was the key phrase in Peter Sellers's Indian doctor impersonation which all citizens of the subcontinent rushed to emulate. It first occurred in a song called 'Goodness gracious me' recorded by Sellers and Sophia Loren in 1960 and based on their characters in the film of Shaw's *The Millionairess* (1960).

Yeah, yeah, yeah   In August 1963, the Beatles released a single called 'She Loves You' which was in the UK charts for 31 weeks and was for 14 years Britain's all-time best-selling 45 rpm record. The repeated phrase 'Yeah, yeah, yeah' (a Liverpudlian version of the American corruption — since the 1920s — of 'yes') became a hallmark of the Beatles.
    Some of the spadework had been done by the non-Liverpudlian singer Helen Shapiro who had a hit in September 1961 with 'Walking Back to Happiness' which included the refrain 'Whoop Bah Oh Yeah Yeah'.

It's only rock 'n roll   was the title of a Mick Jagger/Keith Richard composition in 1974. The phrase entered the language. In a 1983 newspaper interview, Tim Rice was quoted as saying: 'It would be nice if [the musical *Blondel*] is a success but I won't be upset if it isn't. It is only rock 'n roll after all and it doesn't really matter a hoot.'

Nice legs, shame about the face was the title of a briefly popular song performed by The Monks in 1979. However, the title introduced a format phrase, which reappeared, for example, in a take-off by TV's *Not the Nine O'Clock News* team: 'Nice video, shame about the song' and in a slogan for Hofmeister lager: 'Great lager, shame about the . . .' (both in 1982).

DO NOT ADJUST
YOUR SET

In the early years of British television, particularly in the late 1940s and early 50s, technical breakdowns were a common feature of the day's viewing. The BBC's caption **Normal service will be resumed as soon as possible** became a familiar sight. As standards improved, this tended to be replaced by the more temporary 'There is a fault — **do not adjust your set**'. The latter phrase was used as the title of a children's comedy series in 1968, devised in part by some of the future Monty Python team.

This section is devoted to TV series that originated in the UK:

ALL GAS AND GAITERS (BBC) Pauline Devaney and Edwin Apps, who scripted this late 60s series about clerical folk, remembered (in 1979): 'Derek Nimmo who played Noot, the Bishop's chaplain, was always asking for a catch-phrase and we always resisted the suggestion until one day a neighbour who was a pillar of the church, discussing something over the garden wall, said "Moses!" and we wrote it into the script. Derek leapt on it and thereafter used it with such frequency that we eventually got a notice to the effect that it was time the writers stopped putting in "Moses" whenever they couldn't think of anything funny!' Usually remembered, I think, as **Oh, Moses!**

The comic actor Robertson Hare (1891–1979) appeared as the archdeacon and inevitably his own personal catch-phrases were hard to keep down. **Oh, calamity!** stemmed from an Aldwych farce of long ago — perhaps one in which this much put-upon little man had lost his trousers — but even he was unable to remember which one. His other

characteristic utterance was **Indubitably!** He called his autobiography *Yours Indubitably*.

ALL YOUR OWN (BBC)   Showcase of the 1950s for young
viewers who had some interesting hobby and could be seen
to enjoy themselves doing it. Introduced by an avuncular
Huw Wheldon. At the close of the programme he would look
forward to the next edition and say: **Whatever else it will be,
it will be well and truly − all your own!**

ARE YOU BEING SERVED? (BBC)   The lilting cry of Mr
Humphries (John Inman), the lighter-than-air menswear
salesman of Grace Bros store, was **I'm free!** (1974−)

ARMY GAME, THE (Granada)   Quite the most popular
catchphrase of the late 1950s was **I only arsked!** Bernard
Bresslaw played a large, gormless army private − 'Popeye'
Popplewell − from 1957-62 and this was his response
whenever anyone put him down. The phrase occurred in the
very first episode and a story is told of the day when the
Army Game team first realised it had a potential catchphrase
on its hands. It is said that Milo Lewis, the director, was
rehearsing a scene in which the lads from Hut 29 found that
although they had been moved to a new camp they had not
escaped from the clutches of their sergeant-major (William
Hartnell). 'Quite a reunion!' he commented, walking into the
hut. 'Can we bring girls?' the Bresslaw character inquired.
'No, you can't,' replied the sergeant-major. 'I only arsked!'
said Popeye.

At this point, Milo Lewis is said to have exclaimed excited-
ly, 'We've got a catchphrase!' The others chorused, 'You
mean . . .?' 'Yes,' replied Lewis, 'Can we bring girls!'

A feature film entitled *I Only Arsked* was made in 1958.

In the same show, Alfie Bass as Excused Boots Bisley was
wont to exclaim philosophically: **Still . . . ne'er mind, eh?**

BILLY BUNTER (BBC)   The famous fat boy from Frank
Richards's Greyfriars School stories was recreated memorably on TV by Gerald Campion in several series between
1952-62. He gave a memorably metallic ring to the phrases **I
say, you fellows! Oh, crikey!** and **Yaroooo!**

The Indian schoolboy, Hurree Jamset Ram (known as
Inky), had a format phrase **the . . . -fulness is terrific**, as in

'the rottenfulness is terrific' or as in this example from one of the original stories by Richards (*The Magnet* No 401, October 1915):

> (Inky:) 'Are we not in a state of warfulness?'
> Bob Cherry chuckled: 'The warfulness is terrific, as terrific as your variety of the English language, Inky.'

BOOTSIE AND SNUDGE (Granada)   Sergeant Major Claud Snudge (Bill Fraser) with hand anticipating a tip: **I'll be leaving you now, sir!** in this spin-off from *The Army Game* (1960-2).

BOYS FROM THE BLACKSTUFF, THE (BBC)   Alan Bleasdale's drama series about unemployment in Liverpool, first shown in 1982, introduced the character of Yosser Hughes. His plea **Gi' us a job, I could do that** became a nationally known catchphrase in no time at all, not least because of its political ramifications. It was chanted by football crowds in Liverpool and printed on T-shirts with Yosser confronting Prime Minister Thatcher.

COOL FOR CATS (ABC)   This late 1950s pop show was introduced by Kent Walton. At the end of the show he would spin round in his chair and say 'Happy Monday, Tuesday — **see you Wednesday!**' But someone tells me it was **See you Friday!** I think the confusion comes about because Walton was also famous for his all-in wrestling commentaries on Wednesdays and Saturdays. Hence on Saturday he would say 'See you Wednesday' and on Wednesday 'See you Saturday.' Obviously, he had a sign-off that could be adapted to any day of the week, whatever the show.

CRACKERJACK (BBC)   Right from this programme's 1955 inception, with Eamonn Andrews as presenter, the children in the studio audience of this show had only to hear the word 'Crackerjack' for them to scream back **Crackerjack!** This use has almost nothing to do with the American meaning of the word — 'Excellent!' — or its use as the name of a brand of pop corn and peanuts. It's just a noise.

DAD'S ARMY (BBC)   Right from the very first episode transmitted in July 1968, Captain Mainwaring (Arthur Lowe)

was apt to exclaim: **Stupid boy!** to Private Pike (Ian Lavender). When Lowe died in 1982, the *Daily Mail* reported: 'The Captain did try to go unrecognised in private life, but found it increasingly difficult. Often people would come up to him in the street or in restaurants and ask him to say "Stupid boy!" just once.'

In the Home Guard platoon from the Second World War, the elderly Lance-Corporal Jones (Clive Dunn) would request **Permission to speak, sir!**, shout **Don't panic!** and remark **They don't like it up 'em.** John Laurie as Private Fraser (a Scots undertaker when out of uniform) would wail **We're doomed** or **Doomed I am, doomed.** John Le Mesurier as Sergeant Wilson would quietly inquire **Excuse me, sir, d'you think that's wise?** and Arnold Ridley as Private Godfrey **May I spend a penny?**

DIXON OF DOCK GREEN (BBC)   Accompanied by a shaky salute to the helmet, PC George Dixon (Jack Warner) would bid us **Evening all!** and sometimes caution us with a **Mind how you go!** (1955-76).

DR WHO (BBC) This science fiction series has given rise to numerous beasties since its inception in 1963 but none more successful than the Daleks (who arrived in 1964) — mobile pepper-pots whose metallic voices barked out **Exterminate, exterminate!** as they set about doing so with ray guns. Much imitated by children.

FALL AND RISE OF REGINALD PERRIN, THE (BBC) 'C.J.', the boss, (John Barron) would frequently muse: **I didn't get where I am today . . .** (1976—80).

FAWLTY TOWERS (BBC) Manuel the Spanish waiter (played by Andrew Sachs) would ask **¿Que?** (Spanish for 'what?') But then, as Basil Fawlty (John Cleese) would explain: 'You'll have to excuse him — he comes from Barcelona' (1975-9).

FLOWERPOT MEN, THE Current in 1954, this short programme for very young children is indelibly printed on the minds of a generation. Bill and Ben, the little men made out of flowerpots, conversed in a kind of Goonish language (devised and performed by Peter Hawkins) as they pottered about a potting shed at the bottom of someone's garden. A little weed kept watch and had only one word to say and that was a high-pitched **Weed!**

GAME FOR A LAUGH (LWT) A rapid success, early on Saturday evenings, from 1981 onwards, this was a show with elements of *Candid Camera* (and several others) as it persuaded members of the public to take part in stunts both in and out of the studio. The title — being an extension of 'I'm game for . . . (anything)' was much repeated by the presenters of the show, as in 'let's see if so-and-so is **game for a laugh . . .**' Jeremy Beadle would say, with all the confidence of a used car dealer **trust me!** The programme was billed as **the show where the people are the stars**. The presenters would intone the catchphrase **You'll be watching us, watching you, watching us, watching you.**

GOLDEN SHOT, THE (ATV) Bob Monkhouse, once compère of the long-running quiz show explained (1979) how the phrase **Bernie, the bolt!** came into being: 'I dislike the notion of a conscientiously created catchphrase. The best, it appears to me, have been born spontaneously and have survived because of their multiple applications. This one broke all my own rules. Lew Grade had bought the Swiss-German TV success *The Golden Shot*. Jackie Rae, the original host, had to repeat one line eight times in each show — the word of instruction to the technician to load the dangerous crossbow and simultaneously warn the studio of the fact that the weapon was armed. He said: "Heinz, the bolt!"

'When I took over in 1967 I increased the number of times he would have to load the crossbows from eight to fifteen. But a lucky chance saved me from finding 57 ways of saying Heinz. Heinz went home. He stayed long enough to train an ATV technician, Derek Young. I said, "'Derek, the bolt' sounds lousy. Let's make it alliterative. What's funny and begins with B?" Colin Clews, the producer, favoured Basil. I liked Bartholomew. We were reckoning without the man himself. Derek liked Derek. "Well, you think of a name that begins with B and won't embarrass you," I said. And Bernie it became. I found out later that his wife liked it. Certainly the audience did. Only blokes called Bernie grew to loathe it. Thousands of letters were addressed simply to "Bernie the Bolt, ITV".'

(The phrase stayed the same even when Derek was replaced by another technician.) 'I spoke the magic three little words for the last time on 13 April 1975. At a conservative estimate, I said them on network TV no less than 2,500 times. On a May night in 1979 I found written in the dust on my car outside a Nottingham cabaret club: "BERNIE THE BOLT LIVES!"'

At one time, viewers watching the programme at home could ring in and instruct the operator to aim the gun. Hence: **Left a bit, — stop! Down a bit, — stop! Up a bit, — stop! Fire!**

GOOD OLD DAYS, THE (BBC) Old-time music hall from the Leeds Palace of Varieties was a long-running TV favourite from 1953-83. As its chairman, Leonard Sachs has reproduced what presumably were standard late Victorian mannerisms. Before banging his gavel to bring on the next act, he would describe **your own, your very own** artistes with alluring alliteration. The programme would conclude with the audience (all in period costume) joining in a sing-song:

'To conclude, we assemble the entire company, ladies and gentlemen — the entire company, the orchestra, but this time, ladies and gentlemen, **chiefly yourselves!**

GROVE FAMILY, THE (BBC)   The first British soap opera — or something approaching it — told of a suburban family and ran for three years from 1953. The irritable Grandma Grove (Nancy Roberts) would demand: **I want me tea!**

HI-DE-HI (BBC)   The spirit of the traditional holiday camp cry **Is everybody happy?** was recreated in this popular series (1980-). The title comes from a song which was taken up in the Second World War, particularly by army instructors greeting their troops. Hence, the exchange **Hi-di-hi! / Ho-de-ho!**

JUKE BOX JURY   Pop record jury programme (adapted from the US radio/TV show devised by Peter Potter), in which host David Jacobs would invite comment on newly-released records of the 60s. **I like the beat** was a frequent critical comment. He would then invite the panellists to vote: **Will it be a hit [ping!] . . . or a miss [honk!]**

KENNY EVERETT TELEVISION SHOW, THE (BBC)   Following more than one incarnation on ITV, Kenny Everett's 'zany' (he hates the word) TV show arrived at the BBC in 1981 and fairly rapidly established a catchphrase: **it's all done in the best possible taste!** This was spoken by Kenny (with beard) playing a large-breasted Hollywood actress being 'interviewed' by a cardboard cut-out Michael Parkinson. She was explaining how she justified playing in some forthcoming film with less than award-winning potential. According to co-scriptwriter Barry Cryer this was never intended to be Dolly Parton. He had heard these very words said in an interview by an American actress whose name he has since forgotten. (In *Time* magazine for 20 July 1981, I came across John Derek, director of *Tarzan the Ape Man* declaring almost the same thing: 'The sacrifice scene was done in the finest of taste — taste the Pope would applaud.')

As an illustration of how a catchphrase is soon seized on by the media, I noted that in the *Scottish Daily Express* of 28 April 1982 there were two separate stories with the headlines: 'Pia . . . in the best possible taste' and 'Spicy Geraldine

. . . in the best possible taste.' Wills Tobacco began to promote Three Castles brand with 'in the best possible taste'.

LOVE THY NEIGHBOUR (Thames)   Jacko: **I'll have a half!** (from the early 70s mixed race comedy series.)

MASTERMIND (BBC)   From *The Times* (8 November 1977): 'For proof of how Magnus Magnusson's television programme *Mastermind* is catching on, I would refer you to this story sent in by a reader from London NW6. He was accosted by a small lad, asking for a penny for the guy. On being asked if he knew who Guy Fawkes was, the lad replied with engaging honesty: **Pass**.' The word has been used by participants in the quiz when they do not know the answer to a question and wish to move on to the next so as not to waste valuable time. In 1981, London Transport advertisements showed an empty studio chair with the query 'How can you save money on bus fares?' The answer was 'Correct. The London Bus pass' — which would be rather lost on anyone unfamiliar with the programme. **I've started so I'll finish** also fascinated people. Chairman Magnusson would say it if one of his questions was interrupted for reasons of time.

MISS WORLD CONTEST, THE (BBC/Thames)   Eric Morley founded the Miss World beauty contest in 1951. He assured himself a small measure of fame each year by announcing the winners: **I'll give you the results in reverse order** i.e. No 3, No 2, No 1. This is sometimes referred to as 'giving the results in Miss World order'.

MONTY PYTHON'S FLYING CIRCUS (BBC)   Like most graduate comedy shows of the 1960s and 70s, *Monty Python* rather frowned upon the use of catchphrases as something belonging to another type of show business. However **Naughty bits!** from a lecture on parts of the body from the second series caught on as a euphemism for the genitals. John Cleese's **And now for something completely different . . .** was a stock phrase and used as the title of the team's first cinema feature. Monty Python thus deprived radio and TV presenters of a useful phrase. When I introduced Radio 4's *Today* programme at breakfast-time in the mid-70s, I regretted this. After all, if you are introducing a certain type of magazine programme there's not much else you can say to link together an interview with the Prime Minister and an item about talking budgerigars.

Wink-wink, nudge-nudge, say no more! also caught on in a

naughty bits!

big way following Eric Idle's use of the words as the prurient character who accosted people with remarks like 'Is your wife a goer, then? Eh? Eh?' I also rather enjoyed Graham Chapman's bossy military character who would interrupt sketches with deep-voiced cries of **Silly!** and occasionally **So-rry!** The show was first aired 1969-74.

MUPPET SHOW, THE (ATV) Miss Piggy, the porcine vamp and Kermit-crusher, would say **Kissy, kissy!** though perhaps her catchphrases were more visual — the prima-donna-ish toss of the hair and the thwacks she would aim at Kermit (1976-80).

NOT SO MUCH A PROGRAMME, MORE A WAY OF LIFE (BBC) Not really a catchphrase in itself, the title of this late-night satire-plus-chat show (1964) nevertheless encouraged the use of the verbal formula **not so much a . . . more a . . .**

OH NO, IT'S SELWYN FROGGIT! (Yorkshire) Bill Maynard in the cheerful title role of this mid-70s series would exclaim **Magic!** about almost anything he encountered.

ON THE BUSES (LWT) The Inspector (Stephen Lewis) would say **I hate you, Butler!** to Stan Butler (Reg Varney) (1970-5).

OPPORTUNITY KNOCKS (ABC/Thames) Talent contest (1956-77). Hughie Greene always seemed to be saying **I mean**

that most sincerely, friends when he compèred this show. However, Mike Yarwood claimed to have invented this precise formulation for his impersonation of Greene. A case of art imitating art perhaps. Introducing contestants, he would say; **For − − of − −, opportunity knocks! It's make-your-mind-up-time** meant that the point had been reached when viewers had to decide which was the best act in the contest.

PRISONER, THE (ATV) First shown in 1967, Patrick McGoohan's unusual series about a man at odds with a '1984' world − political prisoner Number Six − acquired a cult following in the late 1970s. The Six of One Appreciation Society had 2,000 members in 1982 and took its name from **six of one** a catchphrase of the series. The Prisoner would also declare: **I'm not a number, I'm a free man!**

Q (BBC) Spike Milligan's various 'Q' series have been rich in potential catchphrases, none of which may be said to have caught on. However, I rather liked one of them − **A tree fell on him!** as in:

Q. Are you Jewish?
A. No, a tree fell on me.

However, it seems that Milligan had used this on earlier occasions. *Q8* (in 1979) had a running gag: **There's a cheque in the post**.   Another phrase **There's a lot of it about** was used as the title of a Milligan series in 1982.

QUATERMASS EXPERIMENT, THE (BBC) The first in a series of science fiction drama series (1953) held viewers enthralled with the tale of a British astronaut who returned from a space trip and began turning into a plant. Eventually he holed up in the Poets' Corner of Westminster Abbey and covered it with waving fronds. Although the phrase was not used in the programme it gave rise to the expression − still to be heard in 1983 − **it looks like something out of Quatermass**, used to describe any peculiar but especially rambling and leafy specimen.

RAG TRADE, THE (BBC/LWT) This programme had the unusual though not unique experience of running on BBC from 1961-65 and then being revived on London Weekend

Television from 1977. Miriam Karlin in her best flame-thrower voice as Paddy, the cockney shop stewardess, would shout **Everybody out!**

SATURDAY NIGHT OUT (BBC) A series of Outside Broadcast specials was put out in 1956/7 at seven o'clock on a Saturday night. There was, even then, a dated bit of hokum at the start: an unseen figure would pick up the ringing telephone next to an in-tray labelled 'MAN WITH THE MIKE' and say: **Outside Broadcasts? — we're starting now. Stand by!** The OB vans would be seen racing off to some 'live' location to cover events — as the billing had it — **as they happen, when they happen, and where they happen**.

SOME MOTHERS DO 'AVE 'EM (BBC) **Ooh, Betty!** became a key phrase for impersonators of the accident-prone Frank Spencer (Michael Crawford) in this series which ran 1974-9.

SOOTY (BBC) Harry Corbett's little bear puppet first appeared on TV screens in 1952 and has been there ever since — latterly on Thames TV with Harry's son Matthew putting his hand up the back. Sooty was mute, so Harry did all the talking. The magic spell for conjuring tricks was **Izzy-wizzy, let's get busy!** The programme invariably ended with Sooty squirting water at, or throwing a custard pie in, Harry's face ('Ooh, 'e's a scamp, 'e is really!') Harry would then intone the famous farewell in his flat Lancashire vowels: **Bye-bye, everyone, bye-bye!**

STEPTOE AND SON (BBC) The younger Steptoe (Harry H. Corbett) would shout **You dirty old man!** at his father (Wilfred Brambell) (1964-73).

SYKES (BBC) From the 50s to the 70s, in numerous episodes of the adventures of Eric Sykes and his stage sister, Hattie Jacques, she would exclaim: **Oh, Eric!**

TAKE YOUR PICK (Associated Rediffusion) Contestants in this old ITV quiz which ran for almost twenty years from 1955 were given the option of opening a numbered box (which might contain anything from air-tickets to Ena Sharples's hairnet) or accepting a sum of money which might turn out to be worth more — or less — than what was in the box. The studio audience would chant their advice — usually, **Open the box!**

When Michael Miles, **your quiz inquisitor**, died it was said that his funeral was interrupted by the congregation shouting 'Open the box! Open the box!'

THANK YOUR LUCKY STARS (ABC)   **I'll give it foive** was a real rarity — a catchphrase launched by a member of the public. Not that Janice Nicholls, a Brum girl conscripted on to the 'Spin-a-Disc' panel of ABC's pop show in c1963, could avoid a peculiar form of celebrity for long. Awarding points to newly-released records in her local dialect and declaring (as if in mitigation of some awful vocal performance) 'But **I like the backing!**' she became a minor celebrity herself. She even made a record called 'I'll Give It Five' (coupled with 'The Wednesbury Madison') . . . of which almost everyone declared they'd give it minus five.

She was only 16, had just left school and was working as a junior clerk/telephonist in a local factory at the time. She was soon meeting 'all the stars except Elvis' and became the pin-up of three ships, a submarine and a fire station. Janice told me in 1980: 'I think it was just the accent really. It's different to a Brummy. It's a broad Black Country accent, y'know. I think it must have took the fancy of a lot of people. So they just kept asking me to go back and it ended up being three years before I finished.'

THAT WAS THE WEEK THAT WAS (BBC)   After satirical attacks, David Frost pretended conciliation by saying **Seriously, though, he's doing a grand job!** I can remember it being seized on by clergymen and others (1962-3) but Ned Sherrin, the producer, claims that the phrase was used no more than half a dozen times altogether.

The title of the show — suggested by John Bird in emulation of the slogan 'That's Shell-That Was' — also gave a format phrase to the language: **That was the . . . that was**.

TILL DEATH US DO PART (BBC)   Alf Garnett (Warren Mitchell) would say **Silly old moo!** or, simply, **Silly moo!** to his wife (Dandy Nichols) — a euphemism for 'cow'. Dandy Nichols says that people used to call it out to her in the street affectionately, nonetheless. The series ran 1964-74.

TONIGHT (BBC)   The stock concluding phrase of the original BBC TV early evening magazine (1957-65) was **And the next** *Tonight* **will be tomorrow night, good night!** Cliff Michelmore, who used to say it, commented (1979): 'The combined brains of Alasdair Milne, Donald Baverstock, myself and three others were employed to come up with the phrase. There were at least ten others tried and permed. At least we cared . . .!'

TRAINING DOGS THE WOODHOUSE WAY (BBC)   If proof were needed that life can begin at seventy it was provided by Barbara Woodhouse (b.1910) who, after much badgering, persuaded BBC TV to let her introduce a series of programmes about training dogs — and, more importantly, their handlers. She immediately (1980) became a national figure of the eccentric kind the British like to have from time to time and also found fame in the US. Her authoritative delivery of such commands as **Ssssit!** and **Walkies!** were widely imitated. However, by December 1981 she was telling a newspaper that she was going to retreat from the public eye a fraction: 'It's just that I'm getting tired of people saying "Walkies!" to me wherever I go. Even in a village of 300 inhabitants in Queensland.'

TWO RONNIES, THE (BBC)   In their long-running comedy series from the 70s onwards, Ronnie Corbett and Ronnie Barker gently poked fun at the clichés of TV presentation with such phrases as **And in a packed programme tonight . . .** and **it's goodnight from me / And it's goodnight from him!**

UNIVERSITY CHALLENGE (Granada) Ultra-smooth chairman Bamber Gascoigne, has been starting off rounds in this quick-fire quiz between university and college teams by saying **Here's your starter for ten (and no conferring)** (1962-).

WHEELTAPPERS AND SHUNTERS SOCIAL CLUB, THE (Granada)   **Give order — thank you please!** was Colin Crompton's injunction to members of this mythical working men's club (1974/7). 'I had been including the club chairman character in my variety act for some years,' Colin said in 1979, 'before Johnny Hamp of Granada suggested that we build a sketch round it for inclusion in the stage version of *The*

Comedians. This led to *Wheeltappers*. Like most successful catchphrases it was manufactured. It has been used by club concert chairmen for years — and still is. I suppose it was the exaggerated accent and facial expression which helped it "catch on".'

Then there was: **On behalf of the committee-ee!** Colin said: 'Letters by the score told me my catchphrases were a schoolteachers' nightmare. And we had so many children outside the house, shouting them out, that we were forced to move to a quieter neighbourhood! Although it is several years since the last programme was transmitted, the phrases have remained popular and I'm flattered that most impressionists include them in their acts.'

ERIC AND ERNIE

The long-running double-act of comedians Eric Morecambe (1926-84) and Ernie Wise (b.1925) began on the variety stage, went through a period on ITV, and finally achieved the status of national institution on BBC TV from the late 1960s to the late 1970s. Then, once more, they returned to ITV. The essence of their cross-talk has been the inconsequentiality of Eric's zany interruptions to the relatively 'straight' Ern's somewhat irritable posturings:

Just watch it, that's all!   Eric admonishes little Ern by grabbing him by the lapels.

Pardon?   Eric's inconsequential query, not necessarily seeking to elicit something he has failed to hear.

You can't see the join   Eric to Ernie concerning his (presumed) hair-piece. Ernie recalled (1979) the origin of this: 'We once shared digs in Chiswick with an American acrobat who had a toupee which − like all toupees − was perfectly obvious as such. We would whisper to each other, out of the side of our mouths, "You can hardly see the join!"'

Short, fat, hairy legs   Applied by Eric to Ernie's in contrast to his own long, elegant legs. Ernie says that this emerged, like most of their catchphrases, during rehearsals − particularly during their spell with ATV. I have encountered people who refer to short trousers which reveal hairy legs as 'Morecambes'.

I'll smash your face in!   Eric's threat.

Good evening, young sir!   Eric's customary greeting to any young girl.

I'm no mug!   According to Ernie, a catchphrase used 'years ago' by Eric and himself.

Let's be honest!

Arsenal!

I just said that!   (all Eric)

What do you think of it [the show] so far? — Rubbish!   Eric's customary inquiry of audiences animate or inanimate. He says he got the idea from his family and it was first put into a famous sketch between Antony and Cleopatra (featuring Glenda Jackson) in 1971. Eric recalled (1980); 'I said it during rehearsals in a sketch with a ventriloquist's dummy. It got such a laugh that we kept it in . . . but it's bounced back on me more than once. When I was a director of Luton Town I dreaded going to see away games. If we were down at half time, home fans would shout up to me, "What do you think of it so far?"'

It reminds me of the ventriloquist Saveen who worked with a girl doll called Daisy May and an actual dog — which sometimes seemed as if it were speaking. It would bark **Rrrrr!** and Saveen would say **Stop it!** I think it said 'Rubbish!' too.

This boy's a fool!   Eric of Ernie.

This play what I have wrote   − from the long-running joke that Ernie is capable of writing plays (in which guest stars can perform on the show).

There's no answer to that!   Eric's standard innuendo-laden response to such comments as:

> *Casanova (Frank Finlay):* I'll be perfectly frank with you − I have a long felt want.

And not forgetting: Ernie's unchanging introduction **Good evening, ladies and gentlemen, and welcome to the show!** and Janet Webb's **Thank you for watching my little show here tonight. Goodnight . . . and I love you all!** During series of *The Morecambe and Wise Show* on BBC TV in the early 1970s, buxom actress Janet Webb (1930-83) would appear at the end of every show, in which she had played no other part, and momentarily upstage Eric and Ernie by flinging her arms out wide and intoning these words in a diminutive voice.

See also under ACTIONS SPEAK LOUDER THAN and HELLO, GOOD EVENING AND WELCOME.

ACTIONS SPEAK
LOUDER THAN

Along with their verbal catchphrases, Morecambe and Wise, like certain other entertainers, had a host of visual trade-marks:

  the 'throttling' of Eric, which appears to happen as he goes through the gap in a theatre curtain but is, of course, self-inflicted;

  the imaginary stone which thuds into a paperbag held out by Eric to catch it;

  Eric's skew-whiff spectacles, hooked over one ear and under the other;

  the rapid hand-slaps administered by Eric on the back of his own neck;

  Eric's two-handed slap of Ernie's cheeks;

  the shoulder hug;

  Eric's judo-hold under Ernie's chin, accompanied by the line **Get out of that!** ('We were in a summer season at Morecambe with Alma Cogan in 1961 when that first arose,' Ernie recalls precisely);

  the characteristic hornpipe dance, with hands alternately behind head and bottom, while Eric and Ernie lope in deliberate emulation of Groucho Marx.

From other entertainers and shows one recalls other bits of body language which are every bit as memorable as verbal catchphrases:

Harry Worth (b.1920) standing on one leg alongside a shop window, raising the other with an arm outstretched, to make it look as though he's doing the splits in mid-air. Imitated by kids everywhere following its use during the opening titles of his 60s comedy series.

Bruce Forsyth opening shows with his impression of Rodin's Thinker — clenched fist on brow, in mock contemplation.

John Cleese's funny walk from *Monty Python's Flying Circus* — done by a bowler-hatted civil servant, legs jutting out at right angles to the body and then brought in from the side;

the thumbs up gesture (and **Aaayh!**) frequently done by Henry Winkler as The Fonz in *Happy Days* (US TV 1974-);

the rapid three, two, one finger count used by compère Ted Rodgers in ITV's *3-2-1* quiz (from the late 70s) — about the only comprehensible part of the show;

Max Wall's loping walk, with bottom out-pushed, as Professor Walloffski.

HELLO THERE, RECORD-LOVERS EVERYWHERE

The disc jockeys of British radio — once described by D.G. Bridson as 'the wriggling ponces of the spoken word' — did not emerge in full flood until the 1960s. Along with their musical jingles they also developed what you might call 'verbal jingles' — any number of verbal tics, mannerisms and identity tags:

JIMMY SAVILE OBE (b.1926)   After dance-hall exposure, Savile began his broadcasting career with Radio Luxembourg in the 1950s. **How's about that then, guys and gals?** started then. Another of his identifying marks has been the phrase **As it happens**. He used it as the title of his autobiography in 1974. However, when the book came out in paperback it had been changed to *Love is an Uphill Thing* because (or so it was suggested) the word 'love' in a title ensured extra sales.

ROGER MOFFATT (b.1927)   Before the BBC really began to use disc jockeys in the modern sense of the word, there were just one or two 'introducers' of live music or record programmes who developed distinctive ways. Roger Moffatt was a staff announcer in Manchester with the necessary plummy voice for reading the news and doing announcements. He also had a long and fruitful relationship with the BBC Northern Dance Orchestra (originally Northern Variety Orchestra) from the mid-50s to the mid-60s. After some dazzlingly impressive instrumental number he would be inclined to inquire: **Well, how about about that then?**

Introducing a programme called *Make Way for Music* (broadcast simultaneously on radio and TV) he would say:

Wherever you are, whoever you are, why not make way for music?

ALAN FREEMAN (b.c1927)   When Al 'Fluff' Freeman took over the BBC Light Programme's *Pick of the Pops* in 1962 he devised a cheery greeting: **Hi there pop-pickers!** His farewell routine – **All right? Right! Stay bright!** was inter-cut with the music of 'At the Sign of the Swingin' Cymbal' and incorporated Al's 'All right' Australianism. Ann Todd, the actress, helped 'Fluff' develop this tic. They were making arrangements to meet over the phone. Al signed off by saying: 'All right – Right!' and hung up. Ann Todd rang him back and asked: 'What was that you said?' Fluff couldn't remember until he happened to say it again. Ann said: 'You ought to use that.' Another of his verbal mannerisms, not cultivated originally, has been **Not arf!**

JACK JACKSON (1906-78)   Former band-leader Jackson created a form of inter-cutting pop music with extracts from comedy records. His greeting: **Hello there, record-lovers everywhere, and welcome to the show** was well-established by 1976.

TONY BLACKBURN (b.1943)   The first voice on Radio 1 in 1967, Blackburn has not really had a catchphrase of his own, though he did have a recording of a dog he called Arnold which went 'Woof-woof!' – which amounts to much the same thing, I suppose. It was more his verbal tics that stood out: **There you go!** (at the end of a record – though someone wrote to the *Guardian* suggesting this referred to yet another listener switching off) and a toothy, idiosyncratic rendition of the word **Sensational!** These were not really remarked upon until the late 1970s, however.

DAVE CASH (b.19— —)   gave added impetus to a quintessential 1960s expression during his time with BBC Radio 1. He would play a brief tape of a babyish voice saying: **Groovy baby!** Referred to as Microbe, the baby was in fact the son of a BBC producer, Pat Doody. As a result, 'Groovy baby' stickers were much in demand c1967-8 and Blue Mink incorporated 'Microbe' saying his phrase on a record.

KEITH SKUES (b.1939)   Radio 1 DJ 'Cardboard Shoes' who later went into commercial radio began with Forces Broadcasting. When compèring *Family Favourites* in Germany (1959-60) he developed a format phrase: **Talking about . . . which we weren't . . . !**

JIMMY YOUNG (b.1923)   One-time crooner Jimmy Young became an unlikely recruit to BBC Radio 1 as disc jockey in the late 1960s and became hugely popular with the morning housewife audience. His recipe spot was heralded by a jingle extolling the merits of 'Home Cooking' and also by the chipmunk-voiced Raymondo asking **What's the recipe to-day, Jim?** Jim would then recite the ingredients for Cabbage and Custard Surprise, or some such delicacy, after which Raymondo would intone **And this is what you do!** Jim would also chat to listeners on the telephone, which he would refer to in curious Euro-lingo as **sur le telephoneo**. In the early 70s

he took his show on a tour of European capitals to mark Britain's entry to the EEC — i.e. **sur le continong**. This foreshadowed his move to Radio 2 in the mid-70s when he became involved with current affairs subjects and more or less dropped his catchphrases. These, in their heyday, were great fun. He would begin with a routine like this: '**Morning all!** I hope you're all leaping about to your entire satisfaction, especially those sur le contynont . . . and **Orft we jolly well go!**' He would frequently have recourse to **You see!** and **Where is it all leading us, I ask myself?** before concluding with **B.F.N.** — **'bye for now!** (perhaps harking back to *ITMA's* 'T.T.F.N.!')

TERRY WOGAN (b.1938)   Terry's term for physical jerks — **The Fight on Flab** —was used by him for a while on his Radio 2 programme in the early 70s. Terry's language is a wonderfully rich amalgam of idiom, allusion and blarney. Out of the many passing fancies he has dallied with, the word **Banjaxed** lingered a little longer than others. This is an Irishism, meaning broken, smashed, out of order, reduced to the condition of a pig's breakfast.

ED STEWART (b.1941)   A young cockney lad intoned the greeting **'Ello darlin'!** into Ed 'Stewpot' Stewart's tape-recorder when he was visiting a hospital for Radio 1's *Junior Choice* in about 1971. The tape was played countless times thereafter as a kind of verbal jingle but the identity of the speaker was never discovered. Ed said (1979): 'I didn't play back the tape for three or four months and in any case I hadn't made a note of the speaker's name — so I've no idea who, or where, the phrase came from.'

Ed also used a falsetto **Morning!** and **byeee!** on *Junior Choice* from about 1971 onwards, echoing the way his young listeners might have uttered these greetings.

AS SEEN ON TV

Like the Hollywood film, the American TV series has strayed far beyond its native shores. Sold and shown all over the world, programmes like *Dallas* and *I Love Lucy* are a powerful form of cultural colonialism. Only a few series seem to have been restricted to the domestic audience.

Dates shown below are for origination and do not take account of re-runs. Most series were shown in the UK and elsewhere fractionally later:

ADDAMS FAMILY, THE   The comedy series based on the macabre Charles Addams cartoon characters (1964-6) included Lurch, the butler, who would say sepulchrily: **You rang?** To the disembodied hand called Thing would be said: **Thank you, Thing!**

ALDRICH FAMILY, THE   A TV version of the long-running radio sit.com. was broadcast 1949-53 and used the same, famous introduction: **Henry! Henry Aldrich! / Coming, Mother!**

ALICE   Polly Holliday as Flo, the Southern-born, man-hungry waitress, had a wonderful catchphrase during her time with this sit.com. (1976-80): **Kiss my grits!** She went on to have her own series, *Flo*.

AMOS AND ANDY   When the long-running radio series of the 1930s and 40s was transferred to TV (1951/3) black actors had to be found to play the characters originally portrayed by whites. The catchphrases were carried over intact, however: '**Holy mackerel, Andy!** We's all got to stick together in dis heah thing ... remember, we is brothers in that great fraternity, the Mystic Knights of the Sea.' Plus: **I'se regusted**; **Check and double check** and **Now ain't dat sump'n?**

BATMAN Batman and Robin were characters created by Bob Kane and featured in comic books for over thirty years before being portrayed by Adam West and Burt Ward in a filmed series for TV (1966-8). The putting of the prefix **Holy . . !** to any exclamation was a hallmark of the programme — 'Holy flypaper!' — 'Holy cow!' — 'Holy schizophrenia!' etc. Also used were **Quick thinking, Batman** — a typically crawling remark from sidekick Robin — and **Boy wonder!** — Batman's commendation in return. The visual subtitles 'Pow!' 'Biff!' 'Thwack!' 'Crunch!' 'Rakkk!' 'Ooofff!' and 'Bonk!' could also be said to be a kind of catchphrase.

CANDID CAMERA Allen Funt translated his practical joke radio programme *Candid Microphone* to TV and it ran from 1948-78 (there was a homegrown British version.) On revealing to members of the public that they had been hoaxed, he would cry: **Smile, you're on Candid Camera!**

CISCO KID, THE The popular Western film series (1950-6) featured Leo Carrillo as the Kid's fat old sidekick, Pancho. In fractured English this Mexican character would say such things as **'Ceesco? Let's went!** The shereef. He ees getting closer!'

DALLAS The hero-villain, J.R. Ewing (played by Larry Hagman), of the top-rated soap opera about oil-folk was shot in the cliff-hanging last episode of the programme's 1979-80 season. For reasons which are not entirely clear, the question of who had inflicted this far from mortal wound caused a sensation in the US and the UK. Consequently, the first episode of the next series attracted 53.3% of the American viewing audience, the highest-ever rating. All those who had posed the question **Who shot J.R.?** or sported bumper-stickers declaring **I hate J.R.** discovered that the guilty party was a jilted lover.

DRAGNET The TV series was made between 1951-8 and revived in 1967-9. It was largely the creation of Jack Webb (1920-82) who produced, directed and starred. As police Sergeant Joe Friday he had a deadpan style which was much parodied. The show first appeared on radio in 1949 and was said to draw its stories from actual cases dealt with by the Los Angeles police — hence the famous announcement: 'Ladies and gentlemen, the story you are about to hear is true. **Only the names have been changed to protect the innocent**.'

The signature tune was almost a catchphrase in itself — 'Dum-de-dum-dum'. Joe Friday had a staccato style of questioning: **Just the facts, ma'am** or **All we want is the facts, ma'am**. And to add to the list of memorable phrases, here is the opening narration from a typical TV episode:

Ladies and gentlemen, the story you are about to see is true, the names have been changed to protect the innocent . . . **This is the city**. Everything in it is one way or the other. There's no middle ground — narrow alleys, broad highways; mansions on the hill, shacks in the gulleys; people who work for a living and people who steal. These are the ones that cause me trouble. **I'm a cop**. It was Monday April 17. We were working the day-watch on a forgery detail. My partner: Frank Smith. The boss is Captain Welch. **My name's Friday** . . .

FAME   A spin-off from the feature film, this (1982-) series about students at the High School of Performing Arts in New York began each episode with dance teacher Lydia Grant (Debbie Allen) warning: **You've got big dreams. You want fame. Well, fame costs, and right here's where you start paying** . . .

FLIP WILSON SHOW, THE   Wilson was host of a comedy variety hour (1970-4) and famous for a wide-eyed saying **The Devil made me do it!**

FORD SHOW, THE   This musical variety show ran 1956-61 and featured Tennessee Ernie Ford's homespun catch-phrases, including: **Bless your pea-pickin' hearts!**

GEORGE GOBEL SHOW, THE   'Lonesome George' Gobel hosted a comedy variety show (1954-60) in which he made famous little sayings like **Well, I'll be a dirty bird!** (an expression of self-effacing surprise meaning the same as 'Well, I'm a so-and-so, aren't I?') and **You don't hardly get those no more**.

GOLDBERGS, THE   Gertrude Berg played Molly Goldberg in a Jewish sit.com. transferred to TV (1949-54) after twenty years on radio. Molly would gossip with a neighbour, attracting her attention with: **Yoo-hoo, Mrs Bloom**.

GOOD TIMES   A spin-off via *Maude* of *All in the Family*, this series (1974-9) featured James Evans Jr. (J.J.) (played by Jimmie Walker) — a young black teenager in Chicago whose catchphrase was **Dy-No-Mite**.

GUNSMOKE   Matt Dillon's side-kick in this Western series during the years 1955-64 was Chester Goode (Dennis Weaver). His limping walk and twangy **Misster Dillon!** were much imitated.

HAVE GUN, WILL TRAVEL   The title of this Western (1957-63) became a format phrase capable of much variation. Originally on the calling card of a hired gun — '**Have gun, will travel** . . . wire Paladin, San Francisco' — the phrase turned up as graffiti ('Have pill, will') and even as the UK title of another TV series (1981) *Have Girls, Will Travel* (known as *The American Girls* in the US.)

HAWAII FIVE-O   Hawaiian police series (1968-80). On making an arrest, Det. Steve McGarrett (Jack Lord) would say to Det. 'Danno' Williams (James MacArthur): **Book 'em, Danno!** —adding 'Murder One' if the crime required that charge.

HIGHWAY PATROL   Cop series 1955-9. Chief Dan Matthews (Broderick Crawford) was always bellowing **Ten four** into his radio, signifying agreement to some strategy.

JACKIE GLEASON SHOW, THE (1952-70)   The rotund comic hosted a variety show, leading into the first sketch with **And awa-a-aay we go**. His other catchphrase was **How sweet it is!** and he popularized the word **labonza** for posterior ('a kick in the labonza' etc.)

KAY KYSER'S KOLLEGE OF MUSICAL KNOWLEDGE Bandleader Kyser ran a jokey musical quiz show 1949-54 in which contestants were sometimes required to give a wrong answer, in which case he would say **That's right, you're wrong** or **That's wrong, you're right**, as fitted.

KOJAK   Telly Savalas, as the lollipop-sucking New York police lieutenant who said **Who loves ya, baby?** (1973-7).

KUNG FU   Cult series 1972-5. David Carradine as Kwai Chang Caine would quote: **Remember, the wise man walks always with his head bowed, humble, like the dust**.

LIFE OF RILEY, THE   During Jackie Gleason's time with this sit.com. (1949-50) he developed a stock response to twists of fate: **What a revoltin' development this is!** John Brown playing a smiling undertaker called Digger O'Dell would say: **Guess I'd better by shovelling off . . .**

MORK AND MINDY   Robin Williams played Mork an alien from Ork (1978-81). His goodbye in Orkan — **Na nu, na nu** — caught on briefly.

PERRY COMO SHOW, THE   Towards the end of its run the popular singer's show (1948-63) had a request spot introduced by girl singers warbling: **Letters, we get letters, we get stacks and stacks of letters!**

RAWHIDE   Western series (1959-66) notable for its Frankie Laine theme song over the credits:

> **Move 'em on, head 'em up**, head 'em up, move 'em on, Move 'em on, head 'em up . . . Rawhide!

77 SUNSET STRIP   During his time with this cop show (1958-63), Ed Byrnes as Kookie sang a song called 'Kookie, **Koookie, Lend Me Your Comb**' which became a hit record. The phrase referred to his habit of constantly combing his hair.

SIXTY   FOUR   THOUSAND   DOLLAR   QUESTION, THE   'Ah, that's **the sixty four dollar question**, isn't it?' people will exclaim, when surely they mean the 'sixty four thousand dollar question'? Well, put it down to inflation. *Webster's Dictionary* says that $64 *was* the highest award in a CBS radio quiz called *Take It or Leave It* which ran from 1941-8 and in which the value of the prize doubled every time the contestant got a right answer. That was how the saying entered common parlance — meaning 'the question which would solve all our problems if only we knew the answer to it'. An example of the original use in the mid-1950s is contained in a *Daily Express* article about P.G. Wodehouse written by Rene McColl: '"Wodehouse, Esq.," I observed,

"Could I, to use the vernacular of this our host nation, pop the jolly old 64-dollar question? If you were back in Germany, a prisoner, and you had it all to do again — would you do it?"'

Subsequently, in the US TV version of the show (1955-8), the top prize did go up to $64,000 though, cunningly, when ATV imported the show for British viewers shortly afterwards, the title was simply *The 64,000 Question* or *Challenge*, making no mention of the pounds involved.

STAR TREK   This short-lived science fiction series (1966-9) nevertheless acquired a considerable after-life through countless repeats (not least in the UK) and the activities of 'trekky' fans. It was the series about split-infinity whose introduction proposed **To boldly go where no man has gone before!** Capt. Kirk (William Shatner) would say to Lt. Commander 'Scotty' Scott, the chief engineer, **Beam me up, Scotty!** — which meant transposing body into matter, or some such thing . . .

THIS IS YOUR LIFE   Ralph Edwards hosted the original American TV series from the 1950s in which a subject's life was told after he or she had been taken by surprise. Largely sentimental, the shows were notable for tearful reunions between long-lost relatives. Edwards also hosted the first programme when the BBC took up the idea in 1955. The first UK 'victim' to be hailed with the cry **This is your life** was Eamonn Andrews. He then went on to become the presenter of the long-running series for the BBC and, later, Thames Television. When surprised by Eamonn with his 'big Red Book', the victims hear his Irish drawl intoning something like: 'Fred Pincushion, all-round-entertainer and mass-murderer, this is your loif!' To which the victim all too rarely says: 'Push off!'

TO TELL THE TRUTH   In the American TV game devised by Goodson-Todman Productions and shown from 1956-66, a panel had to decide which of three contestants, all claiming to be a certain person, was telling the truth. After the panellists had interrogated the challenger (and the two impostors) they had to declare which person they thought was the real one. MC Bud Collyer would then say: **Will the real ----- -----, please stand up!** and he or she would do so.

TONIGHT Said with a drawn-out rising inflection on the first word, Ed McMahon's introduction to Johnny Carson on NBC's *Tonight* show (from 1961) has been: (*Drum roll*) ' And now . . . **Here's Johnny!**' It was emulated during Simon Dee's brief reign as chat-show host in Britain during the 1960s. The studio audience joined in the rising inflection of the announcer's **It's Siiiimon Dee!** Jack Nicholson playing a psychopath chopped through a door with an axe and said 'Here's Johnny!' in the film *The Shining* (1981). Guest host Joan Rivers popularized **Can we talk?**

WHAT'S MY LINE Televised on and off since 1950 this Goodson-Todman production was the archetypal TV panel-game. Guessing the jobs of contestants and then donning masks to guess the identity of a visiting celebrity, turned panellists into national figures in the US (and the UK). Attempting to establish the size of an article made by one contestant, Steve Allen formulated the classic inquiry **Is it bigger than a breadbox?**

Would the next challenger sign in please! the chairman would say, inviting the guest maybe to indicate something by the way he or she wrote. Then **a spot of mime for the panel** would be largely mystifying. The chairman, trying to get the contestant to answer 'No' to ten of the panel's questions would score: **And that's three down, seven to go**. If ten was scored: **You've beaten the panel!** In the UK the game ran from 1951-63, with brief revivals in the 70s and 80s.

YOU ARE THERE Originally a radio show, this series of reenactments of historical events ran on American TV from 1953-7 (there was also a British version). The programme's closing lines: 'What sort of a day was it? A day like all days, filled with those events that alter and illuminate our times . . . and **you were there!**'

See also BEAUTIFUL DOWNTOWN BURBANK

BEAUTIFUL DOWNTOWN
BURBANK

A quintessential late 60s sound was the announcer, Gary Owens, with hand cupped to ear, intoning: **This is beautiful downtown Burbank** — an ironic compliment to the area of Los Angeles where NBC TV's studios are located and where *Rowan and Martin's Laugh-In* was recorded. An enormous hit on US television right from its inception in 1967, *Laugh-In* lasted until 1973 and was briefly revived without Rowan and Martin, and with little success, in 1977. It was a brightly-coloured, fast-moving series of sketches and gags, with a wide range of stock characters, linked together by the relaxed charm of Dan Rowan (b.1922) and Dick Martin (b.1923).

For a while, the whole of America was ringing to the programme's catchphrases. The most famous of these was **Sock it to me!** spoken by the English actress Judy Carne (b.1939) who became known as the Sock-It-To-Me Girl. She would appear and chant the phrase until — ever unsuspecting — something dreadful would happen to her. She would be drenched with a bucket of water, hit on the head, fall through trap doors, get blown up or even find herself shot from a cannon.

The phrase 'to sock it to someone' originally meant 'to put something bluntly' (and was used as such by Mark Twain). Negro jazz musicians gave it a sexual meaning, as in 'I'd like to sock it to her'.

The precise way in which this old phrase came to be adopted by *Laugh-In* was described to me by Judy Carne in 1980: 'George Schlatter, the producer, had had great success in America with a show starring Ernie Kovacs in the 1950s. The wife on that show used to get a pie in the face every week and got enormous sympathy mail as a result. So George

wanted a spot where an actress would have *horrendous* things done to her each week — a sort of "Perils of Pauline" thing — and then find a catchphrase to fit it.'

In the summer of 1967, Aretha Franklin had a hit record with 'Respect' which featured a chorus repeating 'Sock it to me' over and over very rapidly. The previous year there had been a disc called 'Sock it to 'em, J.B.' by Rex Garvin with Mighty Craven, and in February 1967 an LP entitled 'Sock it to me, baby' had come from Mitch Ryder and the Detroit Wheels. But Aretha Franklin's record was where the *Laugh-In* catchphrase came from. 'George came up with the idea of making it literal. I said, "Well, it should be cockney." He said, "How far are you prepared to go?" And I said, "I'll do anything for a laugh. If I'm safe I don't mind what you do to me."

'It all happened very, very fast . . . in about three weeks we were No 1 with 50 million people watching. The sayings caught on at exactly the same time as the show did . . . It had a dirty connotation and it was also very clean and was great for the kids. That's why I think that it took off the way it did — because it appealed to everyone at one level or another.'

On being known as the Sock-It-To-Me Girl: 'It got in the

way for a while. You have to go through a period of living a tag like that down, and proving that you are not just a saying. The main thing is not to identify with it, not to sit about worrying that people think of you as a saying. But better they think of you as a saying than not at all.'

Among the guest artists on the show who spoke her line were John Wayne, Mae West, Jack Lemmon, Jimmy Durante, Marcel Marceau (even) and Richard Nixon. The latter, running for the Presidency, said it on the show broadcast 16 September 1968. He pronounced it perplexedly: 'Sock it to *me*?' And, lo, they finally did.

The next most famous phrase from the show was probably **Verrry interesting . . . but stupid!/but it stinks!** (or some other variant) pronounced in a thick accent by Arte Johnson as a German soldier peering through a potted plant. Judy Carne recalls Arte Johnson arriving at rehearsal one day in a German helmet. The phrase just came out at a script meeting. 'Everyone went mad and it was kept in.'

The third great phrase was **You bet your sweet bippy!** usually spoken by Dick Martin. A foreign delegate at the United Nations once asked an American official in all seriousness: 'I have heard a phrase in your country that I do not understand. What is it you mean by "bippy"?'

Other phrases from the show included:

I didn't know that!   Dick Martin.

I forgot the question!   Goldie Hawn (b.1945) shot to fame as the resident blonde dum-dum of *Laugh-In*, apparently incapable of getting her lines right. In the middle of a quickfire exchange she would giggle and then miaow 'I forgot the question' or **What was the question?** At first her fluffs were a case of misreading cue cards, then they became part of her act. Judy Carne comments: 'Goldie is not a dizzy blonde. She's about as dumb as a fox. She's incredibly bright.'

The Flying Fickle Finger of Fate Award   This was the name of the prize in a mock talent show segment ('Who knows when the Fickle Finger of Fate may beckon *you* to stardom?') 'Fucked by the Fickle Finger of Fate' was a Canadian armed forces expression in the 1930s.)

Is this the party to whom I am speaking? Ernestine, the snobbish, nasal switchboard operator (Lily Tomlin).

That was not very tasteful! was another Lily Tomlin line.

Hi, sports fans! accompanied by the tinkling of bell — Alan Sues as an all-American TV sports presenter.

Look that up in your Funk and Wagnalls! Referring to the American dictionary.

Here come de judge! The old vaudeville catchphrase had a revival when Dewey 'Pigmeat' Markham, a Negro vaudeville veteran, was brought back to take part in a series of blackout sketches to which the build-up was 'Here come de judge!'

> *Judge:* Have you ever been up before me?
> *Defendant:* I don't know — what time do you get up?

In July 1968 both Pigmeat and US vocalist Shorty Long had records of a song called 'Here Come(s) the Judge' in the American and British charts.

And now here's the man with the news of the present — the man to whom the news wouldn't be the news without the news — here's Dickie! Dan Rowan's nonsense introduction to Dick Martin in a segment of the show. A slight echo of 'Here's Johnny (Carson)' at the end.

I don't want to hear about it! Dan Rowan's stock phrase when confronted with Dick Martin endlessly on the look-out for 'action'. Rowan could hardly keep his partner's mind off sex:

> *Rowan (fretting about Martin's frail appearance):* For your own good, you should pick up some weight.
> *Martin:* Shoulda been with me last night. I picked up 118 pounds!
> *Rowan:* I don't want to hear about it . . .
> *Martin:* It was for my own good, too!

I'll drink to that! Dick Martin, giving further currency to a basic North American way of showing agreement.

Is that a chicken joke? Jo Anne Worley.

Say goodnight, Dick / Goodnight, Dick! Rowan and Martin exchange, echoing George Burns and Gracie Allen's famous sign-off:

Burns: **Say goodnight, Gracie.**
Allen: **Goodnight, Gracie!**

And then there are two lines I can't place: **Well, ring my chimes!** and **Irky perky!**

WE DON'T WISH TO KNOW THAT

A failed catchphrase is a contradiction in terms. If a phrase does not catch on it is not a catchphrase. However, here are some phrases which were contrived so that they might take off but lacked some essential ingredient to help them do so. The prominence of Bob Monkhouse in this section is not significant — he just had the courage to remember more than others!

He remembered (1979): 'As a comedian in the early 1950s I had one unique aspect. I was without a catchphrase. Radio producers sympathized and made suggestions. Charlie Chester even offered to give me one. "Every time you score a big laugh," he said, "just remember to dance a little jig and say: **Now there's a beaut if ever there was one!**" I tried it out on a *Variety Ahoy!* down at Portsmouth. I got a big laugh which I killed by suddenly shuffling inexplicably and shouting this catchphrase at the audience who were understandably baffled. So they stopped laughing at once. I politely declined and Charlie, never a comic to waste material, repeated it in his next series until its consistent failure to please drove him to ad-lib another line, a plea for audience response — "Speak to Charlee-ee!" — which proved to be a genuine winner.'

Monkhouse also tried to launch **I said a subtle** when, for some reason, a joke failed. Another trick that Denis Goodwin and he both used if a gag really died, was to give a complicated explanation of the joke, ending with 'That's what the joke means, **and I wish I was dead**.'

Later, at the time of his *Golden Shot* appearances on TV: 'I had the idea that a phrase like **Hang on to your hollyhocks!** would work. During the warm-ups I would tell a joke "I'd been told not to tell" — Lady Chatterley is in bed with a light cold. Through the French windows comes Mellors the gamekeeper, his hands full of hollyhocks, freshly-picked from the garden, to present to her ladyship. She says, "Thank you for the hollyhocks. And I would appreciate your attention for I have never been bed-ridden before." "Haven't you?" says Mellors. "Then hang on to your hollyhocks!" I could then place that phrase anywhere in the show with a hundred per cent certainty of getting a roar of laughter . . . and I waited and waited for the nation to be aware of this phrase. A year later I quietly dropped it . . .'

Ted Ray recalled two failed catchphrases from *Ray's a Laugh* in about 1950: **What about Rovers?** — as in the exchange 'Unlucky? — what about Rovers?' 'Unlucky? — you don't know you're born.' Also: **He's one of Nature's!** — as in Martha about Albert: 'Don't you insult my husband, he's one of Nature's . . .')

Peter Cook remembered (1979) that the exclamation **Funny!** — delivered in a strangulated Dud and Pete voice between himself and Dudley Moore on BBC 2 TV's *Not Only . . . But Also* in the late 60s — caught on with the performers if not with the public at large. I think he may underestimate the extent to which the pronunciation of the word *did* catch on. Later, Fozzy Bear had something similar in *The Muppet Show*, pronouncing the word 'fun-neee!'

Max Bygraves told me that in his 1979 TV series: 'I had Geoff Love keep walking on. He'd get a big laugh and I'd turn to the audience and say **You can't help loving him, can you?** It happened in the studio, but it didn't happen with the public.'

On the *Generation Game* in the early 70s, Bruce Forsyth tried **Tell me — who's to know?** while Larry Grayson tried unsuccessfully to follow Brucie's 'Didn't he do well?' with **What a lot you've got!**

Slogans

All over London the lights flickered in and out, calling on the public to save its body and purse . . . Whatever you're doing, stop it and do something else! Whatever you're buying, pause and buy something different! Be hectored into health and prosperity! Never let up! Never go to sleep! If once you are satisfied, all our wheels will run down. Keep going — and if you can't, Try Nutrax for Nerves!

Dorothy L. Sayers,
Murder Must Advertise

What passes for culture in my head is really a bunch of commercials.

Kurt Vonnegut junior

Slogans

AN INTRODUCTION

This is the age of the slogan. They leap out at us from countless billboards, TV screens, T-shirts, bumper stickers and buttons. Politicians and minorities hector us with them; polishers of diamonds, makers of movies and slicers of bread use them to nudge and cajole. We even wear and bear slogans ourselves to proclaim our beliefs and sexual preferences. They show what we stand for and what we will not stand for.

There is much feeble-minded puffery. There is also much that is lively, arresting and entertaining. Only occasionally do slogans achieve excellence or memorability or touch a popular chord. The following chapters set out to record a thousand or so notable examples, good and bad.

What is a slogan? Richard Usborne defined it as 'a form of words for which memorability has been bought'. Indeed, few of the following phrases would have arisen without bidding. Unlike those phrases from entertainment which spontaneously catch on, the success of these slogans has been engineered and encouraged. In some cases, vast sums of money have been spent to keep them before the public. They rarely contain universal truths or profound insights. They may not be true at all. The distance between a copywriter's fancy and reality can be infinite.

The common denominator is that all these phrases *promote* a product, a cause or an idea.

In strict advertising parlance, the slogan is the phrase which comes at the end of the ad and encapsulates the message. It has been said that it should never comprise more than seven words. The advertiser's devout wish is that the phrase will then continue to buzz around the consumer's head, further enforcing the message. There are, in addition, certain advertising phrases which are generally regarded as slogans because they are associated with specific products.

Good To The Last Drop
Does She . . . Or Doesn't She?
It Beats As It Sweeps As It Cleans

These phrases have the *power* of slogans even if they are not self-sufficient. The days are long gone when a perfect slogan was supposed to name and define a product as well as promising some benefit.

In trying to discover when and where these phrases were first used, together with some indication of how and by whom they were created, I was frequently told that their origins had been lost in the mists of time. Only a few commercial or political organisations have assembled archives recording their promotional activities. Even among those which have, few have bothered to record specifically who coined the phrases which have helped give enduring success or fame to their products.

There are some people in advertising who feel that this is only proper. One creative chief warned: 'If you are going to try and credit individuals with slogans, you are inevitably going to upset an awful lot of people. Slogans tend to evolve by some strange form of osmosis and normally more than one person can genuinely lay claim to having made a contribution.' Indeed, in advertising more than most professions 'success has a hundred fathers and failure is an orphan'. Nevertheless, when it has been possible to get somewhere near the truth it has been thought worthwhile to point a finger.

A further complication is that advertising agencies are for ever splitting up, regrouping under ever more peculiar names – and occasionally they lose accounts in sudden-death situations which erase memories of even the proudest achievements.

All this applies equally, if not more, to slogans carrying a social or political message. These often arise out of a popular mood and are snapped up before anyone has had time to record how they were formulated.

So, inevitably, much of the information here gathered is incomplete. Corrections and suggestions for future editions will be warmly welcomed.

Slogans can be either sharp or blunt instruments, even if it is hard to measure what slogans do to our minds by simplifying issues and purveying propaganda or what they do to our language by relying so heavily on puns, alliteration, rhythm and balance. This book is a celebration of slogans, but one tempered with a certain irreverence. Occasional examples have been included of the way in which slogans have been alluded to or maltreated in other contexts. If manufacturers or even copywriters recoil, they should console themselves with the knowledge that they have contributed something to the language.

At one time everybody seemed to have a slogan. The crisp phrase was refreshing after the torrents of verbiage that characterised early advertising. Now, whether in press ads or on TV, there is a greater emphasis on the visual. One agency creative director comments: 'Slogans have to be brilliant to work, and actually say something rather than merely boast. If all that can be said is a bit of clever puff, we'd rather do without.'

What, then, makes a successful slogan? There is only one test — whether it promotes the product or cause effectively. **Votes For Women** is not notably witty but it achieved its purpose. On the other hand, there are plenty of phrases which have 'caught on' but which have failed to promote the product or the cause.

If the collective noun for the phrases that follow is a 'boast' of slogans, let the boasting begin.

I'D LOVE A
BEER*

The Beer That Made Milwaukee Famous   Schlitz; US, from
c1895. The Jos. Schlitz Brewing Company has its roots in an
operation begun in Milwaukee in 1849. By 1871, the year of
the great Chicago fire, it was a thriving concern. The fire left
Chicago thirsty. The city was desperately short of drinking
water and its breweries had virtually been destroyed. So
Joseph Schlitz floated a shipload of beer down Lake Michigan to refresh his parched neighbours. They liked and remembered the Milwaukee beer long after the crisis passed. It
is not known who coined the phrase but this is the incident
which led to it. The slogan was incorporated in a label and
registered in 1895, and has been in use ever since.

   Claude C. Hopkins, one of advertising's immortals, was
once engaged on a campaign for Schlitz. He was taken on a
tour of the brewery to give him ideas. He saw the malt and
the hops but his enthusiasm for the steam bath, in which the
bottles were washed before being filled with beer, was un-
bounded. As the client was at pains to point out, this method
was standard in all breweries, but Hopkins realised that the
point had never been used in ads before. Hence: **Our Bottles
Are Washed With Live Steam.**

A Double Diamond Works Wonders   Double Diamond;
UK, from 1952. Double alliteration may have something to do
with it, but it was surely the singing of this slogan to the tune
of 'There's a Hole in my Bucket' that made it one of the best
known of all beer slogans. In 1971, a visiting American
copywriter, Ros Levenstein, came up with the phrase **I'm**

* A generic campaign in New Zealand (current 1981) tried to woo people
away from wine-drinking with this slogan.

Only Here For The Beer, which has passed into the language as an inconsequential catchphrase. In September 1971, the Duke of Edinburgh attended a champagne reception at Burghley, 'Don't look at me,' he was quoted as saying, 'I'm only here for the beer.'

For An A1 Nation Beer Is Best   Brewers Society; UK, from 1933. Part of a campaign to restore the pub's status as a social centre and to 'publicize the goodness of beer produced from prime barley and full-flavoured hops':

> On working days
>   or holidays
> On dismal days
>   or jolly days −
> Beer is best.

The temperance variant was: 'Beer is best − left alone'.

Gone For A Burton   Folk-memory suggests that this phrase was originally used in the UK prior to the Second World War to promote a Bass brew known in the trade as 'a Burton' (though, in fact, several ales are brewed in Burton-upon-Trent). However, research has failed to turn up more positive proof. Early in the war, the phrase was adopted as an idiom to describe what had happened to a missing person, presumed dead, especially in the RAF.

Great Stuff This Bass!   Bass; UK, current 1928. A character called 'Bill Sticker' was shown in ads plastering this slogan in various unlikely places.

Guinness Is Good For You   Guinness; UK, from 1929. After 170 years without advertising, Arthur Guinness Son & Company decided to call in the image-makers. Oswald Greene at S.H. Benson initiated some consumer research (unusual in those days) into why people were drinking Guinness. 'We spent an awful lot of time in an awful lot of pubs,' recalled a colleague. Wherever they went they found that people thought Guinness did them good. Greene spotted the potential in this approach, though the slogan was nearly rejected as being too ordinary and not clever enough. The claim also conflicts with the fact that most drinkers drink for social reasons rather than for health.

The slogan has been revived only once since being discontinued c1941 because claims for the health-giving powers of alcohol are frowned upon nowadays. The Advertising Standards Authority says that, technically, Guinness has never fallen foul of it because the 'Good For You' claim has not been made during the Authority's existence, adding: 'It is not certain it would offend.

There is a story Guinness like to tell about the man who questioned the amount of money they spend each year telling him to drink the stuff. 'The only reason I drink Guinness', he said, 'is because it's good for me.'

Ask any British person to give an example of an advertising slogan and he is more than likely to say 'Guinness is good for you'. It is etched on the national consciousness to such an extent that although the slogan has not been used since 1963 people remember it as though they saw it yesterday.

Guinness Gives You Strength first appeared in 1929 as 'Guinness Is So Strengthening' and ran until 1959. It achieved its most memorable form in the 1934 poster by John Gilroy which shows a man carrying an iron girder on his fingertips.

As for **My Goodness, My Guinness**, Dicky Richards, Benson's art director, got the idea of a zoo-keeper chasing a sealion which had stolen his Guinness after he had paid a visit to the circus at Olympia. This led to a whole menagerie of animals being associated with the product between 1935 and 1958 — ostriches, lions, kinkajous and, above all, toucans. These last emerged as the brainchild of Dorothy L.

Sayers, the novelist, who was then a copywriter at Benson's:

> If he can say as you can
> Guinness is good for you,
> How grand to be a Toucan
> Just think what Toucan do.

Give Him/'Em A Guinness marked the removal to J. Walter Thompson of the Guinness account in 1969. Ironically, the form of the slogan had been used by Benson's many years previously to promote Bovril. It was followed by **7 Million Every Day And Still Going Down** in 1971 (which seems quite modest beside the 1955 Coca-Cola jingle **Fifty Million Times A Day**) and the pointed line **I've Never Tried It Because I Don't Like It** in 1973. In addition, there was a string of puns: **Tall, Dark And Have Some; Cool, Calm And Collect It; Hop Squash; Pint Sighs;** and, in Jubilee Year, **We've Poured Through The Reign**. None of these quite rose to the depths, however, of the old Benson's line, **Pour Encourager Les Huîtres**.

Harp Puts Out The Fire Harp Lager; UK, from c1976. Keith Ravenscroft, who coined the phrase at Ayer Barker, is surprised that no one remarked on the detumescent promise inherent in this otherwise successful slogan.

Heineken Refreshes The Parts Other Beers Cannot Reach Heineken Lager; UK, from 1975. 'I wrote the slogan,' says Terry Lovelock, 'during December 1974 at 3 a.m. at the Hotel Marmounia in Marrakesh. After eight weeks of incubation with the agency (Collett, Dickenson, Pearce), it was really a brainstorm. No other lines were written. The trip was to refresh the brain. Expensive, but it worked.' The slogan has

ineken. Refreshes the parts other beers cannot reach.

always been linked to amusing visuals — the 'droop-snoot' of Concorde raised by an infusion of the brew; a piano tuner's ears sharpened; or a policeman's toes refreshed. There has also been a strong topical element: when Chia-Chia, a panda from the London Zoo, was sent off in 1981 to mate with Ling-Ling in Washington, a full-page press ad merely said 'Good Luck Chia-Chia from Heineken', the slogan being understood.

This kind of claim is allowed under the British Code of Advertising Practice, Section 4.2.3.: 'Obvious untruths or exaggerations, intended to catch the eye or amuse, are permissible provided that they are clearly to be seen as humorous or hyperbolic and are not likely to be understood as making literal claims for the advertised product.'

How Do You Feel? I Feel Like A Toohey's Toohey's beer; Australia, current 1980.

It Looks Good, Tastes Good And, By Golly, It *Does* You Good Mackeson; UK, current 1950s. The notion of beer being 'good for you' — a key element in Guinness advertising over the years — was eroded by the rise of consumer and advertising watchdogs. As if to avoid any conflict with the massed ranks of such people, Mackeson revived the slogan in 1981 but substituted a row of dots after 'By Golly . . .

It's What Your Right Arm's For Courage Tavern; UK, current 1972. Although this line became a popular catchphrase it risks being applied to rival products, whereas the earlier **Take Courage** (current 1966) clearly does not.

Probably The Best Lager In The World Carlsberg; UK, from 1973. Even were it not intoned by Orson Welles in the TV ads, the 'probably' inserted into this hyperbole would still fascinate.

AIRLINES

A problem all airlines share is in projecting a distinct image when the nature of the service they offer can differ only in minor respects. They also seem bound to pretend that being thrust through the air at 39,000 feet, in a cramped metal tube, is somehow a glamorous, life-enhancing experience. Here the reassuring slogans and corporate tags are brought into play, though putting **Say Hello To A Brand New World** on the emergency exit of a Pan Am jet hardly puts you at ease, and Air Siam's **We Serve You Better − Not Just A Slogan: A Commitment** seems unduly apologetic.

How far have the airlines succeeded in differentiating themselves? These are the slogans, old and new. To which companies do they apply?

1   I'm Margie. Fly Me
2   You're Going To Like Us
3   A Great Way To Fly
4   We Fly The World The Way The World Wants To Fly
5   The End Of The Plain Plane
6   Ready When You Are
7   The Airline Run By Professionals
8   We Never Forget You Have A Choice
9   We'll Take *More* Care Of You
10 No 1 In Europe
11 When You Got It, Flaunt It
12 Fly The Friendly Skies Of Your Land
13 Doing What We Do Best
14 We Have To Earn Our Wings Every Day
15 The Wings Of Man
16 We Really Move Our Tails For You

ANSWERS

1 National Airlines; US, current c1971. The campaign, also using **I'm Going To Fly You Like You've Never Been Flown Before**, aroused the ire of feminist groups. Later, Wall's Sausages sent up the slogan with **I'm Meaty, Fry Me**.

2 TWA; US, current 1980. In 1967, when TWA hinted that they might be on the point of quitting their New York agency, Foote, Cone & Belding saved its bacon by slipping over to California and buying sole rights to the Jim Webb song 'Up, Up and Away'. They proceeded to incorporate this in the airline's ads as **Up, Up And Away With TWA**.

3 Singapore Airlines; US, current 1980.

4 Pan Am; US, current 1980.

5 Braniff; US, from 1965. Braniff planes were painted in bright colours and the hostesses dressed in Pucci outfits.

6 Delta; US, from 1968.

7 Delta is, too.

8 British Caledonian; UK, current 1981.

9 British Airways; UK, current 1976. Originally **BOAC Takes Good Care Of You (All Over The World)** (from 1948) and adapted when the airline changed its name. Japan Air Lines began to say they would take **Good Care Of You, Too** but were persuaded to drop the line, although they had used **Love At First Flight** a dozen years before BOAC took up the slogan. In its time, BA has ranged from the patriotic **Fly The Flag** to **Try A Little VC 10derness**.

10 British European Airways (before being incorporated with BOAC in BA).

11 Braniff; US, current 1969. Used on ads featuring celebrities like Sonny Liston, Andy Warhol and Joe Namath. Perhaps the line was acquired from the 1967 Mel Brooks movie *The Producers*, where it appears as 'If you got it, baby, flaunt it'.

12 United; US, from 1973. Also **Fly The Friendly Skies Of United**.
13 American Airlines; US, current 1980.
14 Eastern Airlines; US, current 1980.
15 Eastern, too.
16 Continental; US, current 1975. In that year some of the airline's stewardesses threatened to sue over the 'bad taste' it had shown in selecting this slogan.

BLACK POWER

The civil rights struggle in the United States as proclaimed through its slogans

Abolition!   Originally a cry of the white colonists, c1765, demanding the repeal of the British Stamp Act. After repeal in 1766, it was widely applied to the abolition of slavery.

Amistad!   In 1839, fifty-four slaves aboard the Spanish schooner *Amistad* on a voyage from Cuba murdered the captain and three crew members. They ordered the remaining crew to sail to Africa. Instead, they found themselves taken to Long Island and imprisoned. Subsequently, they were freed and returned to Africa. The cry was taken up by militants in the 1960s.

Black Is Beautiful   Martin Luther King junior launched a poster campaign round this slogan in 1967 but Stokely Carmichael had used the phrase at a Memphis civil rights rally in 1966. It may have its origins in The Song of Solomon 1:5: 'I am black, but comely.'

Black Power   An all-purpose slogan encompassing just about anything that people want it to mean, from simple pride in the black race to a threat of violence. The Harlem Congressman Adam Clayton Powell junior said in a baccalaureate address at Howard University in May 1966: 'To demand these God-given rights is to seek black power — what I call audacious power — the power to build black institutions of splendid achievement.' On 6 June, James Meredith, the first black to integrate the University of Mississippi (in 1962), was shot and wounded during a civil rights march. Stokely Carmichael, heading the Student Nonviolent Coordinating Committee, continued the march, during which his contingent first used the shout. Carmichael used the phrase in a speech at Greenwood, Mississippi, the

same 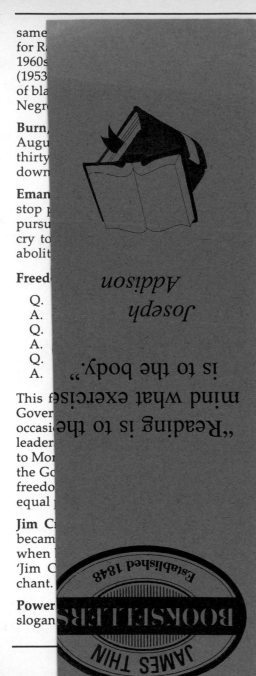 gan by the Congress
for R   was not new in the
1960s   *Simple Takes a Wife*
(1953   ecause just *one* drop
of bla   *ne* drop — you are a
Negr

Burn,   slogan following the
Augu   f Los Angeles when
thirty   tire blocks burned
down

Eman   f 1850 attempted to
stop   allowed owners to
pursu   ionists adopted the
cry to   d a straightforward
abolit

Freed   ack litany went:

Q.
A.
Q.   you want?
A.
Q.
A.

This   etition delivered to
Gover   March 1965. On this
occasi   d other civil rights
leader   e march from Selma
to Mor   e have come to you,
the Go   t we must have our
freedo   vote; we must have
equal   to police brutality.'

Jim C   phrase 'Jim Crow'
becam   s back to the 1730s
when   1835 'Jim Crow' or
'Jim C   ce the early 1960s
chant.

Power   nched fist raised — a
slogan   and publicized as

such by its leader, Bobby Seale, in Oakland, California, July 1969. Also used by other dissident groups, as illustrated by Eldridge Cleaver: 'We say "All Power to the People" — Black Power for Black People, White Power for White People, Brown Power for Brown People, Red Power for Red People, and X Power for any group we've left out.' It was this somewhat generalized view of 'People Power' that John Lennon appeared to promote in the 1971 song 'Power to the People (Right on!)'.

Ten Acres And A Mule   were what was sought by slaves from 1862 onwards. They thought that their masters' plantations would be divided up to their benefit after the Civil War. However, this escalated to **Forty Acres And A Mule** when, in January 1865, General Sherman stated that 'Every family shall have a plot of not more than forty acres of tillable ground' — a promise which had nothing to do with the Federal government. Consequently, this Reconstruction slogan dwindled to **Three Acres And A Cow**. *This* phrase had originated in John Stuart Mill's *Principles of Political Economy* (1848) — 'When the land is cultivated entirely by the spade and no horses are kept, a cow is kept for every three acres of land.' Jesse Collings (1831-1920), a henchman of Joseph Chamberlain in the 1880s, proposed that every smallholder in the UK should have these things. He was an advocate of radical agrarian policies and the smallholding movement. He became known as 'Three Acres And A Cow Collings'. (Noel Coward once described Edith, Osbert and Sacheverell Sitwell as 'two wiseacres and a cow'.)

We Shall Overcome   From a song that became the civil rights anthem of the early 1960s. It originated in pre-Civil-War times, was adapted as a Baptist hymn called 'I'll Overcome Some Day', c1900, by C. Albert Hindley, and first became famous when sung by black workers on a picket line in Charleston, South Carolina, 1946. Pete Seeger and others added verses.

> Oh, deep in my heart, I know that I do believe,
> We shall overcome some day.

In the Spanish Civil War a Republican chant was **¡Venceremos!** which means the same thing.

HEY! WHY DON'T
WE SAY

Lurking in almost every copywriter's mind is a streak of
iconoclasm and bad taste which gets sublimated in the telling of jokes about the lines they would love to have written
about the products if only they had dared:

Hail Jaffa — King Of The Juice

It's What It's Not That Makes It What It Is

Un Oeuf Is As Good As A Feast

Tampax . . . Insofar As (in response to the tampon ad that
said **Modess . . . Because**)

People Are Sticking To Kleenex

Her Cup Runneth Over (suggested by Shirley Polykoff to a
corset manufacturer — 'it took an hour to unsell him')

From Those Wonderful Folks Who Gave You Pearl Harbor (a
suggestion for Panasonic by Jerry Della Femina and used as
the title of a book by him)

And one of Jimmy Carter's aides, keen that the President
should utter as illustrious a phrase as John F. Kennedy's **Ich
Bin Ein Berliner** on a visit to West Germany, suggested he go
to Frankfurt and say . . .

ENEMY EARS ARE
LISTENING

Slogans rained down upon the hapless British as profusely as German bombs during the Second World War. The Ministry of Information, in blunderbuss fashion, fired away with as much material as possible in the hope of hitting something. Some of the slogans were brilliant, others were quite the reverse, and some unofficial phrases joined the propaganda war:

A Bayonet Is A Weapon With A Worker At Each End   Pacifist slogan, 1940.

Be Like Dad, Keep Mum and **Keep Mum, She's Not So Dumb** (illustrated by an elegant un-Mum-like blonde being ogled by representatives of the three services) emanated from the Ministry of Information, c1941. The security theme was paramount in UK and US wartime propaganda. Civilians as well as military personnel were urged not to talk about war-related matters lest the enemy somehow got to hear.

Britain Can Take It   'While the public appreciated due recognition of their resolute qualities, they resented too great an emphasis on the stereotyped image of the Britisher in adversity as a wise-cracking Cockney. They were irritated by propaganda which represented their grim experience as a sort of particularly torrid Rugby match.' (McLaine) Hence the Ministry's abandonment of the slogan 'Britain Can Take It' in December 1940.

Careless Talk Costs Lives   Introduced in mid-1940, this became the most enduring of the security slogans, especially when accompanied by Fougasse cartoons — showing two men in a club, for example, one saying to the other '. . . strictly between four walls' (behind them is a painting through which Hitler's head is peeping), or two women gossiping in front of Hitler wallpaper.

Coughs And Sneezes Spread Diseases A Ministry of Health warning from c1942, coupled with the line 'Trap The Germs In Your Handkerchief'.

Dig For Victory Shortage of foodstuffs was an immediate concern upon the outbreak of war. On 4 October 1939, the Minister of Agriculture, Sir Reginald Dorman Smith, broadcast: 'Half a million more allotments properly worked will

provide potatoes and vegetables that will feed another million adults and one and a half million children for eight months out of twelve ... So, let's get going. Let "Dig For Victory" be the motto of everyone with a garden and of every able-bodied man and woman capable of digging an allotment in their spare time.' As a result, the number of allotments rose from 815,000 in 1939 to 1,400,000 in 1943.

Freedom Is In Peril – Defend It With All Your Might (1939) Selected by George Orwell at the end of the war as an example of a 'futile slogan obviously incapable of stirring strong feelings or being circulated by word of mouth ... One has to take into account the fact that nearly all English people dislike anything that sounds high-flown or boastful. Slogans like **They Shall Not Pass**, or **Better To Die On Your Feet Than Live On Your Knees**, which have thrilled continental nations, seem slightly embarrassing to an Englishman, especially a working man.' 'To which Angus Calder adds: 'It was partly from the de-sensitized prose of most of the British press during the war, from the desertion of subtleties of meaning in favour of slogans, that George Orwell derived the notion of Newspeak, the vocabulary of totalitarianism' in *Nineteen Eighty-Four*.

Go To It In the summer of 1940, the Minister of Supply, Herbert Morrison, called for a voluntary labour force in words that echoed the public mood after Dunkirk. The quotation was used in a campaign run by the S.H. Benson agency (which later indulged in self-parody on behalf of Bovril with **Glow To It** in 1951-2).

Intern The Lot Anti-alien slogan, 1940.

Is Your Journey Really Necessary? First coined in 1939 to discourage evacuated Civil Servants from going home for Christmas. 'From 1941, the question was constantly addressed to all civilians, for, after considering a scheme for rationing on the "points" principle, or to ban all travel without a permit over more than fifty miles, the government had finally decided to rely on voluntary appeals, and on making travel uncomfortable by reducing the number of trains.' (Longmate)

Keep 'Em Flying   Slogan in support of the US Air Force.

Keep It Dark   was a phrase which appeared in more than one formulation, also in verse:

If you've news of our munitions
                    KEEP IT DARK
Ships or planes or troop positions
                    KEEP IT DARK
Lives are lost through conversation
Here's a tip for the duration
When you've private information
                    KEEP IT DARK.

cf. 'Hush, keep it dark' catchphrase. *Shush, Keep It Dark* had been the title of a variety show running in London during September 1940.

'Let Us Go Forward Together'   A direct quotation from Churchill's first speech on becoming Prime Minister (May 1940), presented as such, and used to accompany his picture, in bulldog pose.

Make Do And Mend   A phrase which set the tone for British life during the Second World War and after. Based on the Royal Navy expression for an afternoon free of work and still often used for mending clothes.

Second Front Now   The demand chalked on walls (and supported by the Beaverbrook press) during 1942-3 for an invasion of the European mainland, particularly one in collaboration with the Soviet Union. The Allied military command disagreed and preferred to drive Axis troops out of North Africa and the Mediterranean first. Churchill's argument against a second front was that Britain's resources were fully stretched already.

Walls Have Ears   was the neatest encapsulation of the security theme (the idea goes back beyond 1727, when Jonathan Swift wrote 'Walls have tongues, and hedges ears'). Also, **Tittle Tattle Lost The Battle** and **Keep It Under Your Hat** (US: **Keep It Under Your Stetson**). **Loose Talk Costs Lives** and **Idle Gossip Sinks Ships** were additional US versions of the same theme, together with **The Slip Of A Lip May Sink A Ship** and **Enemy Ears Are Listening**. The only

Don't forget that
walls
have ears!

CARELESS TALK
COSTS LIVES

drawback to these generally clever slogans was that they tended to reinforce the notion that there *were* spies and fifth columnists under every bed even if there were not.

Your Courage, Your Cheerfulness, Your Resolution Will Bring Us Victory   One of the first posters after the outbreak of war, printed in vivid red and white. It caused a bitter outcry from those who resented any implication of 'Them and Us'. The slogan was suggested by A.P. Waterfield, a career Civil Servant at the Ministry of Information. He wanted 'A rallying war-cry that will . . . put us in an offensive mood at once.' *The Times* thundered: 'The insipid and patronizing invocations to which the passer-by is now being treated have a power of exasperation which is all their own. There may be no intrinsic harm in their faint, academic piety, but the implication that the public morale needs this kind of support, or, if it did, that this is the kind of support it would need, is calculated to promote a response which is neither academic nor pious.'

BURN YOUR BRA

If a slogan is judged purely by its effectiveness, **Votes For Women** is a very good slogan. The words may not sparkle, but they achieved their end.

Both Emmeline and Christabel Pankhurst, founders of the Women's Social and Political Union, have described how this particular battle-cry emerged. In October 1905, a large meeting at the Free Trade Hall, Manchester, was due to be addressed by Sir Edward Grey, who was likely to attain ministerial office if the Liberals won the forthcoming general election. The WSPU was thus keen to challenge him in public on his party's attitude to women's suffrage in Britain.

'Good seats were secured for the Free Trade Hall meeting. The question was painted on a banner in large letters, in case it should not be made clear enough by vocal utterance. How should we word it? "Will you give women suffrage?" — we rejected that form, for the word "suffrage"

suggested to some unlettered or jesting folk the idea of suffering. "Let them suffer away!" — we had heard the taunt. We must find another wording and we did! It was so obvious and yet, strange to say, quite new. Our banners bore this terse device: "WILL YOU GIVE VOTES FOR WOMEN?"' The plan had been to let down a banner from the gallery as soon as Sir Edward Grey stood up to speak. Unfortunately, the WSPU failed to obtain the requisite tickets. It had to abandon the large banner and cut out the three words which would fit on a small placard. 'Thus quite accidentally came into existence the slogan of the suffrage movement around the world.'

Alas, Sir Edward Grey did not answer the question, and it took rather more than this slogan — hunger-strikes, suicide, the First World War — before women got the vote in 1918. Other slogans employed were **Deeds, Not Words; Arise! Go Forth And Conquer**; and **The Bill, The Whole Bill, And Nothing But The Bill**. (At a meeting in the Royal Albert Hall, someone boomed 'Votes For Women' down an organ pipe.)

In the US, the Nineteenth Amendment, extending female franchise on a national scale, was ratified in time for the 1920 elections.

The modern Women's Liberation movement, advocating the rights and equality of women and commitment to an alteration in woman's role in society, has given rise, in the US and the UK, to the following slogans, all since c1970:

Burn Your Bra By analogy with burning a draft-card as a protest against the Vietnam War.

Equal Pay for Equal Work Echoing a cry of teachers' organisations in the late nineteenth century.

This Ad Insults Women

A Woman's Right To Choose (US, National Abortion Campaign)

Women Reclaim The Night (or, US, **Take Back The Night**) From the campaign to make it possible for women to go out in the dark without fear of attack or rape.

COMING TO THIS
CINEMA SHORTLY

The promotion of films takes slogan writing into realms of hyperbole seldom encountered in the marketing of political creeds or even consumer goods. The art of the come-on is at its peak in the tags applied to horror movies:

If This One Doesn't Scare You, You're Already Dead *Phantasm 1*

Thank God It's Only A Movie. Please Let It Stay A Movie! *Fleish*

It Takes All Kinds Of Critters To Make Farmer Vincent Fritters *Motel Hell*

Paraquat!. . . Agent Orange!. . . But Nothing Prepared The World For This! *Forest of Fear*

£10,000 If You Die Of Fright! *Macabre*

Can You Survive *The Texas Chain Saw Massacre* . . . It Happened!

They Were Going To Rape Her One By One. She Was Going To Kill Them . . . One By One. *Death Weekend*

It Crawls! It Creeps! It Eats You Alive! Run — Don't Walk From *The Blob*.

Where Your Nightmare Ends *Willard* Begins.

***The Curse Of Frankenstein* Will Haunt You Forever (Please Try Not To Faint).**

The most notorious of all film campaigns is the one for the Howard Hughes production of *The Outlaw* in 1943. As if **The**

Two Great Reasons For Jane Russell's Rise To Stardom (skilfully supported by the Hughes-designed cantilever bra) were not enough in the various pictures of the skimpily clad new star (one version had her reclining with a long whip), the producer attached a smouldering succession of slogans:

Tall . . . Terrific . . . And Trouble!

Who Wouldn't Fight For A Woman Like This?

Mean! Moody! Magnificent!

The Girl With The Summer-Hot Lips . . . And The Winter-Cold Heart

How'd You Like To Tussle With Russell?

Although it is hard to believe, *Julius Caesar* was promoted as **Greater Than *Ivanhoe*** and *Joseph Andrews* got away with **The Epic Love Story In Which Everybody Has A Great Role And A Big Part**. I do know, however, that 'The Book They Said Could Never Be Written Has Become The Movie They Said Could Never Be Filmed' is pure invention that has not appeared on a poster — yet. See how many of the following slogans you can connect with the films they actually advertised.

1 The Greatest Motion Picture Ever Made
2 They're Young . . . They're In Love . . . And They Kill People
3 A Thousand Thrills . . . And Hayley Mills
4 A Lion In Your Lap
5 Like The Act Of Love, This Film Must Be Experienced From Beginning To End
6 Love Means Never Having To Say You're Sorry
7 Love Means Not Having To Say You're Ugly
8 Getting There Is Half the Fun . . . ********** Is All Of It
9 ********** is *Not* A Musical
10 A Completely New Experience Between Men And Women!
11 We Are Not Alone
12 Garbo Talks!
13 Garbo Laughs!
14 God Created Woman — But The Devil Created Brigitte Bardot
15 Gable's Back And Garson's Got Him
16 A Cast Of 125,000
17 If There Were An 11th Commandment, They Would Have Broken That, Too

18 Don't Give Away The Ending. It's The Only One We Have

19 He Treated Her Rough — And She Loved It!

20 When The Hands Point (Straight) Up . . . The Excitement Starts At **********

21 What We've Got Here Is A Failure To Communicate

22 Pray For **********

23 In Space No One Can Hear You Scream

24 Don't Pronounce It — See It!

25 Boy. Do We Need It Now

26 They Had A Date With Fate In . . . **********

27 You'll Believe A Man Can Fly

28 Every Father's Daughter Is A Virgin

29 The Thousands Who Have Read The Book Will Know Why We Will Not Sell Any Children Tickets To See This Picture!

30 **********Is Coming

31 The Story Of A Homosexual Who Married A Nymphomaniac

32 The Motion Picture With Something To Offend Everyone

ANSWERS

1 *Gone with the Wind*
2 *Bonnie and Clyde*
3 *In Search of the Castaways*
4 *Bwana Devil* (first 3-D film)
5 *The Sailor who Fell from Grace with the Sea*
6 *Love Story*
7 *The Abominable Dr Phibes*
8 *Being There*
9 *The Boys in the Band*
10 *The Men* (about paraplegics)
11 *Close Encounters of the Third Kind*
12 *Anna Christie*
13 *Ninotchka*
14 *And God Created Woman*
15 *Adventure*
16 *Ben Hur* (1927 version — origin of the phrase 'Cast of Thousands?)
17 *The Postman Always Rings Twice* (1981 version)
18 *Psycho*
19 *Red Dust*
20 *High Noon*
21 *Cool Hand Luke*
22 *Rosemary's Baby*
23 *Alien*
24 *Phffft/Ninotchka*
25 *That's Entertainment*
26 *Casablanca*
27 *Superman — The Movie*
28 *Goodbye Columbus*
29 *The Grapes of Wrath*
30 *The Birds*
31 *The Music Lovers* (about Tchaikovsky)
32 *The Loved One*

THE CUSTOMER IS
ALWAYS RIGHT

H. Gordon Selfridge (1856-1947) was an American who after a spell with Marshall Field & Co. in Chicago came to Britain and introduced the idea of the monster department store. It was he who said **The Customer Is Always Right** and many another phrase now generally associated with the business of selling through stores. He may have invented the notion of so many **Shopping Days To Christmas** — at least, when he was still in Chicago he sent out an instruction to Marshall Field's heads of departments and assistants: 'The Christmas season has begun and but twenty-three more shopping days remain in which to make our holiday sales record.' The store which he opened in Oxford Street, London, in 1909 gave rise to the slogans **This Famous Store Needs No Name On The Door** (because it had none) and **Complete Satisfaction Or Money Cheerfully Refunded**.

Other shopping slogans in stores . . . and in the home:

Avon Calling!   was first heard in the US in 1886. The first Avon Lady, Mrs P.F.A. Allre, was employed by the firm's founder, D.H. McConnell, to visit and sell cosmetics in the home.

Don't Ask The Price It's A Penny   That great British institution, Marks & Spencer, had its origins in a stall set up in Leeds market in 1884 by a 21-year-old Jewish refugee from Poland, Michael Marks. His slogan has become part of commercial folklore. It was written on a sign over the penny section — not all his goods were that cheap. He simply hit upon the idea of classifying goods according to price.

It's Just A Part Of The Austin Reed Service   became a catchphrase from its inception in 1930 and was devised by

Donald McCullough, the firm's advertising manager (who subsequently found fame as the question-master in the popular BBC radio series, *The Brains Trust*). It was still in use on behalf of the London store in 1950.

Never Knowingly Undersold was formulated by the founder of the John Lewis Partnership, John Spedan Lewis, in about 1920 to express a pricing policy which originated with his father, John Lewis, who first opened a small shop in London's Oxford Street in 1864. The slogan is believed to have been used within the firm before it was given public expression in the 1930s: 'If you can buy more cheaply elsewhere anything you have just bought from us we will refund the difference.' The firm does not regard 'Never Knowingly Undersold' as an advertising device in the generally accepted sense of the word, although it is displayed on the sides of its vehicles and, together with the undertaking set out above, printed on the backs of sales bills. Its main purpose is 'as a discipline upon the Partnership's Central Buyers to insure that the best possible value is offered to customers'. The firm does not advertise its merchandise. Hence, the phrase has an almost mystical significance for the Partnership.

Nothing Over Sixpence The first British Woolworth's opened in 1909 and was described as a 'threepence and sixpence' store, the equivalent of the 'five-and-ten' (cent) stores in the US. Hence the phrase 'Nothing Over Sixpence' arose and endured until the Second World War, when prices could no longer be contained below this limit. A song dating from 1927 includes the lines:

> To Woolworth's, Hobbs and Sutcliffe always go to get their bats,
> Stan Baldwin gets his pipes there, and Winston gets his hats;
> And the Prince would never think of going elsewhere for his spats —
> And there's nothing over sixpence in the stores!

Pile It High, Sell It Cheap Sir John Cohen (1898-1979), founder of Tesco Supermarkets, built his fortune upon this golden rule. In 1963 Tesco was one of the biggest traders to proclaim **We Give Green Shield Stamps**.

The Universal Provider   Whiteley's, first in Westbourne Grove and later in Queensway, introduced department store shopping to London, in 1863. William Whiteley (1831-1907), the self-styled 'Universal Provider', claimed to supply anything from **A Pin To An Elephant**. One morning, as Whiteley described it: 'An eminent pillar of the Church called upon me and said, "Mr Whiteley, I want an elephant." "Certainly, sir. When would you like it?" "Oh, today!" "And where?" "I should like it placed in my stable." "It shall be done!" In four hours a tuskiana was placed in the reverend gentleman's coach-house. Of course, this was a try-on designed to test our resources, and it originated in a bet. The Vicar confessed himself greatly disconcerted because, as he frankly avowed, he did not think we would execute the order. He displayed the utmost anxiety lest I should hold him to the transaction. But I let him down with a small charge for pilotage and food only, at which he confessed himself deeply grateful.'

The World's Largest Store   Macy's New York City. Current 1981.

YES! WE HAVE NO
BANANAS!

Britain became 'banana-conscious' in the early years of the twentieth century following the appointment of Roger Ackerley as chief salesman of Elders & Fyffes, banana importers, in 1898. The phrase **Have A Banana**, never a slogan as such, was popularly interpolated at the end of the first line of the song 'Let's All Go Down The Strand', published in 1904. It had not been put there by the composer but was so successful that later printings of the song always included it. Every time it was sung the phrase reinforced the sales campaign, free of charge.

Other banana songs followed. In 1922, a further Elders & Fyffes campaign benefited from the composition 'Yes, We Have No Bananas' (a remark the composer claimed to have heard from the lips of a Greek fruit-seller). Fyffes cooperated with the music publishers and distributed 10,000 'hands' of bananas to music-sellers with the inscription **Yes! We Have No Bananas! On Sale Here.**

The title of the next song, 'I've Never Seen A Straight Banana' — like the line 'I had a banana/With Lady Diana' from the earlier 'Burlington Bertie from Bow' — underlined the sexual suggestiveness of the product, which no doubt explains some of its popular appeal or at least the humour surrounding it. **Unzipp A Banana** went the whole hog; in 1959, Mather & Crowther launched it in a joint promotion on behalf of the three main UK banana importers.

EVERY HOME SHOULD HAVE ONE

Chases Dirt Old Dutch Cleanser; US, from 1905. The ad showed a Dutch woman with a stick, literally chasing dirt away.

Cleans Round The Bend Harpic lavatory cleaner; UK, from 1930s.

Hasn't Scratched Yet Bon Ami cleanser; US, from c1890, still current 1941.

Hold It Up To The Light, Not A Stain And Shining Bright Surf washing powder; UK, current late 1950s. A line from the 'Mrs Bradshaw' series of TV ads in which the eponymous lady never appeared but her male lodger did. (From the radio *Goon Show* of the same period: 'The BBC — hold it up to the light — not a brain in sight!')

It Beats As It Sweeps As It Cleans Hoover carpet sweepers; US, from 1919, still current 1981. Coined by Gerald Page-Wood of Erwin Wasey in Cleveland, Ohio. 'The Hoover' started as an invention by James Murray Spangler in 1908. It was taken up by William H. Hoover whose company, until that time, manufactured high-grade leather goods, harnesses and horse collars. Spangler's idea was developed to include the principle of carpet vibration to remove dust. This gave 'Hoovers' their exclusive feature — the gentle beating or tapping of the carpet to loosen dirt and grit embedded in it. An agitator bar performed this function, together with strong suction and revolving brushes — giving the Hoover the 'triple action' enshrined in the slogan.

It's A Lot Less Bovver Than a Hover Qualcast Concorde lawn-mower, UK, current 1981. Knocking copy from a maker of cylinder and rotary mowers against hover mowers. Adapted by Hoverspeed, the cross-channel Hovercraft company, who said it was 'much less bovver on a hover'.

$6.25 is all you need pay down to secure a Hoover complete with household cleaning attachments. Now, anyone can afford a Hoover. Have yours delivered today!

It beats rugs gently; sweeps as no broom can; and thoroughly air-cleans — *electrically!* Its handy new air-cleaning tools dust, *dustlessly.* It keeps your home immaculate; saves time, strength, health; makes rugs wear years *longer.* Certainly, it's a Hoover! Delivered to any home upon payment of only $6.25 down! Your Authorized Hoover Dealer will explain our easy purchase plan.

THE HOOVER COMPANY, NORTH CANTON, OHIO
The oldest and largest maker of electric cleaners
The Hoover is also made in Canada, at Hamilton, Ontario

The **HOOVER**
It BEATS... as it Sweeps   as it Cleans

Kills All Known Germs
Domestos household bleach; UK, from 1959.

Omo Adds Brightness To Whiteness Omo washing powder; UK, current late 1950s.

Poor Cold Fred Electricity Council storage heaters; UK, from 1969. A memorable but briefly exposed line from copy written at Hobson Bates by Roger Musgrave. A TV campaign showed 'Fred', who thought that storage heaters would cost hundreds of pounds and thus remained cold until enlightened about them. Musgrave admits he was probably influenced by memories of the old rhyme 'Here lies Fred/Who was alive and is dead'.

See That Hump? The Long Patented Hook & Eye Company; US, from 1891.

Softness Is A Thing Called Comfort Comfort fabric conditioner; UK, current 1981.

Someone's Mother Persil washing powder; UK, current 1940 — a theme carried from posters and press ads on to TV:

What someone's mum really ought to know,
So someone's mum better get to know,
That Persil washes whiter, whiter —
Persil washes whiter.

Also the phrase **What Is A Mum?** featured in a series of TV ads from 1961.

Stronger Than Dirt   Ajax cleanser; US, quoted 1979.

This Is Luxury You Can Afford By Cyril Lord   Cyril Lord carpets; UK, current early 1960s.

Tide's In, Dirt's Out   Tide washing powder; UK, current 1950s. Also 'Get your clothes clean. Not only clean but **Deep Down Clean**, Tide clean

Use Sapolio   Sapolio soap; US, quoted in 1952 as 'once ubiquitous in the USA'. The words **Spotless Town** were also synonymous with Sapolio. They came from rhymes devised by J.K. Fraser, like this one:

> This is the maid of fair renown
> Who scrubs the floors of Spotless Town
> To find a speck when she is through
> Would take a pair of specs or two,
> And her employment isn't slow.
> For she employs SAPOLIO.

'"Spotless Town" (while selling Sapolio by the ton) was parodied in many papers and a syndicated political series ran all over the country. At one time four theatrical companies booked shows called *Spotless Town* . . . and one community changed its name permanently thereto.' (Watkins)

Very **********, Very Sanderson   Sanderson furnishing fabrics and wall-coverings; UK, current 1973. Various celebrities were photographed amid what purported to be their natural surroundings. Among them: Joan Bakewell, Petula Clark, Jilly Cooper, Britt Ekland and Kingsley Amis. I happened to be visiting Mr Amis in his home the day after the first advertisement featuring him had appeared in the colour magazines. I took the opportunity to exclaim 'Very Kingsley Amis, Very Sanderson' as we stepped into his sitting-room. The novelist seemed perturbed at my reaction and was at pains to point out that, although he and the other celebrities had had a room decorated by Sanderson in addition to their fees, the photograph in the ad bore little resemblance to the conditions under which he actually lived (I saw that it did not). He described the wallpaper chosen to reflect his refined tastes as 'superior Indian restaurant'. Alan Coren, writing in *Punch*, warned Alexander Solzhenitsyn, at that time just arrived in the West, that he might find the role of the writer a bit different this side of the Iron Curtain. He would know that he had finally settled in when he heard people declaring 'Very Solzhenitsyn, Very Sanderson'

The Watch Of Railroad Accuracy   Used in watch advertisements by the Hamilton Watch Co.; US, from 1908. The phrase first arose from a testimonial sent to the company by a railroad worker.

The Watch That Made The Dollar Famous   Ingersoll dollar watches; US, from c1892. Soon after the first dollar watch appeared, Mr R.H. Ingersoll was being introduced at some ceremony by a flushed hostess who forgot his name. So she said: 'Oh, the man that made the dollar famous.' Next day, Mr Ingersoll presented the company with its long-lasting slogan.

THE EYES AND EARS
OF THE WORLD

The world of leisure pursuits and communications — records, radio and TV, photography and going to the pictures . . .

Ars Gratia Artis Metro-Goldwyn-Mayer film company; US, from c1916. Howard Dietz, director of publicity and advertising with the original Goldwyn Pictures company, had left Columbia University not long before. When asked to design a trademark, he based it on the university's lion and added the Latin words meaning 'Art for Art's Sake' underneath. The trademark and motto were carried over when Samual Goldwyn retired to make way for the merger of Metropolitan with the interests of Louis B. Mayer. 'Goldwyn Pictures Griddle The Earth' is the probably apocryphal but typical suggestion said to have come from Samuel Goldwyn for a slogan.

Brings The World To The World Gaumont-British cinema newsreel; UK, from the 1930s.

Don't Write — Telegraph Western Union Telegraph Co.; US, from 1920 — though the words first appeared unofficially written up on office windows of various branches in 1917-19.

The Eyes And Ears Of The World Paramount News cinema newsreel; UK, from 1927 to 1957.

Fine Sets These Fergusons Ferguson radio sets; UK, current 1950s.

The Greatest Show On Earth Name given by P.T. Barnum (1810-91) to the circus formed by the merger with his rival, Bailey's; US, from 1881. Still the slogan of what is now

Ringling Bros and Barnum & Bailey Circus. Used as the title of a Cecil B. De Mille circus movie, 1952.

His Master's Voice   One of the best-known trademarks and brand names of the twentieth century. The words have something of the force of a slogan. In 1899, the English painter Francis Barraud approached the Gramophone Company in London to borrow one of their machines so that he could paint his dog, Nipper, listening to it. Nipper was accustomed, in fact, to a *phonograph* but his master thought that the larger horn of the gramophone would make a better picture. Subsequently, the Gramophone Company bought the painting and adapted it as a trademark. In 1901, the Victor Talking Machine Company (slogan **Loud Enough For Dancing**) acquired the American rights. The company later became RCA Victor and took Nipper with them. Nowadays, Britain's EMI owns the trademark in most countries, RCA owns it in North and South America, and JVC owns it in Japan.

The Instrument Of The Immortals   Steinway pianos; US, from 1919. The slogan was coined 'in a flash' by Raymond Rubicam at N.W. Ayer & Son: 'I learned that the piano had been used by practically all the greatest pianists and most of the great composers since Wagner . . . without effort, the phrase formed in my mind . . . when the ad was finished I showed it to Jerry Lauck, the account executive, and by that time I was so enthusiastic about the idea that I urged him to persuade Steinway to use the phrase not just for one but for a whole series . . . Lauck shared my enthusiasm for the idea, but said that Steinway did not believe in "slogans". I remember saying "all right, don't call it a slogan, call it an advertising phrase."' (Watkins)

It's The Lubitsch Touch That Means So Much   Used on posters for films directed by Ernst Lubitsch; US, from c1925.

Let Your Fingers Do The Walking   Yellow Pages (classified telephone directories) from American Telephone & Telegraph Co.; US, current 1960s. Also **Want To Reach 8 Out Of 10 Adults? – Walk This Way**. (UK graffito, quoted 1981: '8 out of 10 buying executives walk this way', to which was added: 'They should loosen their belts.')

More Stars Than There Are In Heaven   MGM studio motto; US, current 1930s. Devised by Howard Dietz.

Say It With Flowers   National Publicity Committee of the Society of American florists; US, from late 1920s. Henry Penn of Boston, Mass., originated the phrase as chairman of the committee. He was discussing the need for such a slogan with Major P.K. O'Keefe, head of an agency. The Major suggested: 'Flowers are words that even a babe can understand' — a line he had found in a poetry book. Mr Penn considered this too long. The Major, agreeing, rejoined: 'Why, you can say it with flowers in so many words.' Mr Penn's hand went bang! on the table. They had found their slogan. (Lambert)

They Come As A Boon And A Blessing To Men,/The Pickwick, The Owl, And The Waverley Pen   Macniven & Cameron Ltd's pens, manufactured in Edinburgh and Birmingham; UK, current c1920. Also **Macniven & Cameron's Pens Are Recommended By 3,050 Newspapers.**

They Laughed When I Sat Down At The Piano, But When I Started To Play!   US School of Music piano tutor; US, from 1925. A classic advertising headline written by John Caples at Ruthrauff & Ryan. The copy underneath includes the following: 'As the last notes of the Moonlight Sonata died away, the room resounded with a sudden roar of applause. I found myself surrounded by excited faces. . . . Men shook my hand — wildly congratulated me — pounded me on the back in their enthusiasm! Everybody was exclaiming with delight — plying me with rapid questions . . . "Jack! Why didn't you tell us you could play like that?" . . . "Where *did* you learn?" And then I explained how for years I had longed to play the piano. "A few months ago," I continued, "I saw an interesting ad for the US School of Music — a new method of learning to play which only costs a few cents a day!"' The ad gave rise to various jokes — 'They laughed when I sat down to play — somebody had taken away the stool' — and Caples also wrote a follow-up: 'They Grinned When The Waiter Spoke To Me In French — But Their Laughter Changed To Amazement At My Reply.'

"Can he really play?" a girl whispered. "Heavens no!" Arthur exclaimed. "He never played a note in his life."

They Laughed When I Sat Down At the Piano But When I Started to Play!—

ARTHUR had just played "The Rosary." The room rang with applause. I decided that this would be a dramatic moment for me to make my debut. To the amazement of all my friends, I strode confidently over to the piano and sat down.

"Jack is up to his old tricks," somebody chuckled. The crowd...

...musician himself were speaking to me—speaking through the medium of music—not in words but in chords. Not in sentences but in exquisite melodies!

A Complete Triumph!

As the last notes of the Moonlight Sonata died away, the room resounded with a sudden roar of applause. I found myself surrounded by recited applause. How my friends carried on! Men...

...the lessons continued they got easier and easier. Before I knew it I was playing all the pieces I liked best. Nothing stopped me. I could play ballads or classical numbers or jazz, all with equal ease. And I never did have any special talent for music!

Play Any Instrument

You too, can... ...teach yourself to be an accomplished home...

The Weekend Starts Here   Associated-Rediffusion TV pop show *Ready, Steady, Go*; UK, current 1964. Transmitted live early on Friday evenings

We Never Closed   Windmill Theatre, London; UK, from Second World War. Vivien Van Damm, the proprietor, coined this slogan for the venerable comedy and strip venue which was the only West End showplace to remain open during the blitz. An obvious variant: 'We Never Clothed'.

You Press The Button — We Do The Rest   Kodak cameras; US, current 1890. 'It was literally edited out of a long piece of copy by George Eastman himself — one of the greatest of advertising ideas.' (Watkins)

You Want The Best Seats, We Have Them   Keith Prowse ticket agency; UK, from 1925.

BUILD UP YOUR
EGO, AMIGO

Build Up Your Ego, Amigo   Adler Elevated Shoes; US, current 1940s. Coined by Shirley Polykoff.

Children's Shoes Have Far To Go   Start-Rite children's shoes; UK, current 1946. The idea of the boy and girl 'twins' walking up the middle of a road between rows of beech trees came to the company's advertising agent as he drove back to London from a meeting at Start-Rite's Norwich offices. He was reminded of the illustration in Kipling's *Just So Stories* of 'the cat who walked by himself' and developed the idea from there — despite many subsequent suggestions from the public that walking down the middle of the road would not enable children, or their shoes, to go very far.

He Who Loves Me, Follows Me   Jesus Jeans; various countries, from 1970. In that year, Maglificio Calzificio Torinese, an Italian clothing manufacturer launched an advertising campaign showing the rear view of a young girl in a tight-fitting pair of the company's new 'Jesus Jeans' cut very short. The slogan echoed the New Testament, as also: **Thou Shalt Have No Other Jeans Before Me**. Later, a spokesman for the company explained (*International Herald Tribune* article, 12 January 1982): 'We were not out looking for a scandal. It's just that it was the late 1960s and Jesus was emerging increasingly as a sort of cult figure. There was the Jesus generation and *Jesus Christ Superstar*. There was this enormous protest, in Italy and around the world, and Jesus looked to a lot of people like the biggest protester ever ... It's funny, we had no trouble in the Mediterranean countries, but the biggest resistance came in the protestant countries, in North America and northern Europe.'

Jesus Jeans eventually were only sold in Italy, Greece and Spain. In Greece, there was a threat of prosecution for 'insulting religion and offending the Christian conscience of the public'. In France complaints of blasphemy and sacrilege flooded in when the slogan 'Qui M'aime me Suive' was tried out, appearing similarly located on a girl's behind in 1982.

I Dreamed I ********** In My Maidenform Bra   Maidenform bras; US, from 1949. A classic ad from the days when bras were not for burning but for dreaming about — if, that

is, women had ever fantasized about being out in their underwear. Evidently, many had and the series, devised by Norman Craig & Kummel, ran for twenty years. Maidenform offered prizes up to $10,000 for dream situations they could utilize in the advertising, in addition to: 'I Dreamed I Took The Bull By The Horns/Went Walking/Stopped The Traffic/ Went To Blazes/Was A Social Butterfly/Rode In A Gondola/ Was Cleopatra . . . In My Maidenform Bra.'

If You Want To Get Ahead, Get A Hat   The Hat Council; UK, quoted 1965.

Looks Even Better On A Man   Tootal shirts; UK, from 1961. A girl was featured wearing an oversize man's shirt.

The Man In The Hathaway Shirt   C.F. Hathaway shirts; US, from 1950. It was the eye-patch on the male model that made David Ogilvy's campaign famous, but people always refer to 'The Man in the Hathaway shirt' as such and the reason is plain — this was the bold headline to the advertisement.

My Bottoms Are Tops   Gloria Vanderbilt jeans by Murjani; US, current 1980.

Next To Myself I Like BVD's Best   BVD's (comfortable, loose-fitting underwear); US, from c1920.

Quality Never Goes Out Of Style   Levi jeans; US, current 1980.

Rael-Brook Toplin, The Shirt You Don't Iron   Rael-Brook shirts; UK, current mid-1960s. That rarity — a slogan created by the manufacturer. Johnny Johnson, who wrote the music for the jingle used in the TV ad, says: 'Harry Rael-Brook would not work through an agency. He came into my office and said, "I want a 30-second jingle." I said, "Oh yes, and what do you want to say?" And he said, "Rael-Brook Toplin, the shirt you don't iron."' And that was that. The jingle consists of this phrase repeated over and over.

Step Out With A Stetson   Hats manufactured by John B. Stetson Co; US, current 1930s.

Triumph Has The Bra For The Way You Are   Triumph foundation garments, swimwear and lingerie; UK, from c1977.

Walk The Barratt Way   Barratt shoes; UK, current early 1940s.

What Becomes A Legend Most?   Blackglama mink; US, current 1976. Headline from a series of press ads showing mink coats being worn by 'legendary' figures including Margot Fonteyn, Martha Graham, Rudolph Nureyev (all three in one ad), Shirley Maclaine and Ethel Merman.

GO NOW,
PAY LATER

Better Yet Connecticut   From the *New York Times*, 22 April 1981: 'Connecticut came forth today with its official slogan . . . It was created by Joseph Roy, a 45-year-old graphic artist . . . "We had thought of 'I Love New York, But Better Yet Connecticut,' but it was too long," said Richard Combs, chairman of the Governor's Vacation Travel Council as he announced at a news conference that Mr Roy's slogan was "the winner of a blockbuster contest."'

'John J. Carson said the slogan would adorn T-shirts and be displayed in banks and on billboards and bumper stickers. Both state officials and Vacation Travel Council members voiced confidence that their slogan could vie in the marketplace with such tourism precursors as **I Love New York, Make It In Massachussetts** and **Virginia Is For Lovers**.

Virginia is for lovers.♥

'Asked to describe the creative process that went into formation of the phrase, Mr Roy replied: "I went to bed thinking about it and when I woke in the morning I had it." The runner-up was "Connecticut Is a Whale of a State."'

I Love New York   New York State Department of Commerce; US, from 1977. Created by Charlie Moss of Wells, Rich, Greene — though maybe he had heard the song 'How about you?' with lyrics by Ralph Freed which includes the line 'I like New York in June'. The campaign began in June 1977 with a commercial which showed various people enjoying themselves in outdoor activities — fishing, horseback riding, camping, and so forth. Each one said something like: 'I'm from New Hampshire, but I love New York,' 'I'm from Cape Cod, but I love New York,' and ended with a funny little man, shown in a camping scene, saying: 'I'm from Brooklyn, but I *looooove* New York.' Since when it has become one of the best known advertising slogans in the world.

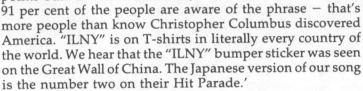

Jane Maas, who supervised the campaign from its inception, points out: 'In New York State, 91 per cent of the people are aware of the phrase — that's more people than know Christopher Columbus discovered America. "ILNY" is on T-shirts in literally every country of the world. We hear that the "ILNY" bumper sticker was seen on the Great Wall of China. The Japanese version of our song is the number two on their Hit Parade.'

As familiar in its abbreviated forms, most often with 'love' replaced by a heart-shape, 'I Love New York' has also been widely copied (as has the use of the heart-shape for 'love'). There is 'I Love Osaka', 'J'aime Paris', and in the US the phrase has been picked up by hundreds of places and pro-ducts, ranging from hotels to hot dogs.

Inter-City Makes The Going Easy, And The Coming Back British Rail; UK, from 1972 (London and South-East Region) and 1975 (Inter-City).

It's So Bracing Skegness (seaside resort in Lincolnshire, promoted along with London & North Eastern Railway com-pany); UK, current 1909. The slogan is inseparable from the accompanying jolly fisherman drawn by John Hassall (1868-1948). Actually, he did not visit Skegness until twenty-eight years after he did the poster. His first visit was when he was made a freeman of the town.

Let The Train Take The Strain British Rail Awayday fares; UK, 1970

SKEGNESS

IS SO BRACING

Queen Elizabeth Slept Here Stately homes and inns; UK, from seventeenth century? Elizabeth I was an inveterate traveller — and guest. By 1888, Jerome K. Jerome was writing in *Three Men In A Boat:* 'She was nuts on public houses, was England's Virgin Queen. There's scarcely a pub of any attractions within ten miles of London that she does not seem to have looked in at, or stopped at, or slept at, some time or other.' In the US: **George Washington Slept Here**.

The Road Of Anthracite The Delaware Lackawanna & Western railroad; US, from 1900. The character of 'Phoebe Snow' was created to promote the idea of cleanliness in travelling on a railroad which used sootless anthracite coal as locomotive fuel. She appeared for half a century and the railroad came to call itself **The Route Of Phoebe Snow**. Her adventures were described in short verses, such as:

> Yes, Phoebe, I
> Can now see why
> The praises of
> This road you cry.
> My gloves are white
> As when last night
> We took the Road
> Of Anthracite.

See America First Great Northern Railway Co; US, from c1914. Variously credited to G. Herb Palin, a leading US slogan writer, and Louis W. Hill Senior, president of the company. The slogan was splashed all over the US and helped turn the tide of travel from the east coast to the west. Hill said he just picked up the phrase from an ad and adopted it as his company's slogan. Perhaps Palin wrote the original?

Sleep Like A Kitten Chesapeake & Ohio Lines; US, from 1933. This slogan appeared with the logo of a kitten tucked up in bed. A vice-president of the company came across a picture entitled 'The Sleepy Cat' in a New York newspaper and asked around the office what phrase best signified sound sleep. Among the suggestions were 'like a top' and 'like a kitten'. The latter was voted the winner.

This Is The Age Of The Train British Rail; UK, from 1980. Somewhat wishful thinking. The public countered with graffiti: 'Yes, it takes an age to catch one' and 'Ours was 104'.

THAT GOOD
MORNING FEELING

The Best To You Each Morning   Kellogg's corn flakes and other brands; US, from 1953.

Breakfast Of Champions   Wheaties; US, current 1950. A series featuring sporting champions showed 'Jackie Robinson — one of the greatest names in baseball . . . this famous Dodger star is a Wheaties man: "A lot of us ball players go for milk, fruit and Wheaties," says Jackie . . . Had *your* Wheaties today?' Kurt Vonnegut used the phrase as the title of a novel, 1973.

Food Shot From Guns   Quaker Puffed Wheat and Puffed Rice; US, current from early 1900s. Claude C. Hopkins: 'I watched the process where the grains were shot from guns. And I coined the phrase. The idea aroused ridicule. One of the greatest food advertisers in the country wrote an article about it. He said that of all the follies evolved in food advertising this certainly was the worst — the idea of appealing to women on "Food Shot From Guns" was the theory of an imbecile. But the theory proved attractive. It was such a curiosity rouser that it proved itself the most successful campaign ever conducted in cereals.'

That 'Good-Morning' Feeling   Welgar Shredded Wheat; UK, current mid-1940s.

Snap! Crackle! Pop!   Kellogg's Rice Krispies; US, from c1928. A version early in the century went 'It Pops! It Snaps! It Crackles!'

Sunny Jim   Force breakfast cereal; US, from c1903. Few people who use the nickname 'Sunny Jim' know that it originated in ads for Force. The Force Food Company was formed in 1901. A London office was established the following year. By 1903, advertising on both sides of the Atlantic was featuring the character called 'Sunny Jim'. He was the invention of two young American girls, a Miss Ficken and Minnie Maud Hanff (usually credited with the phrase), who had submitted a jingle and rough sketch to the company. One of the first jingles was:

> Vigor, Vim, Perfect Trim;
> Force made him, Sunny Jim.

In the 1920s came:

> High o'er the fence leaps Sunny Jim,
> Force is the food that raises him.

In the 1930s Force was advertised on commercial radio broadcasts to the UK from Radios Luxembourg, Lyons and Normandie. In the US, the product has now disappeared from sale but in 1970 the A.C. Fincken Company relaunched it in the UK. When James Callaghan became Prime Minister in 1976 the phrase inevitably became much used (headline from *The Observer*, 18 March 1979: 'Sunny Jim tires of wheeler-dealing'). The name of the cereal was long a gift to jokesters:

A: I can't coax my husband to eat any breakfast.
B: Have you tried Force?
A: Madam, you don't know my husband.

There's A Reason Postum and Post cereals; US, from 1899 to 1924. Charles William Post invented the beverage now known as Postum. This was a vague phrase he used as he explained the merit of the product when it was new. A 1908 ad for Postum Grape-Nuts uses it thus: 'One of Uncle Sam's Navy boys was given up by the doctor. His stomach would not retain food or medicine until a mess-mate suggested Grape-Nuts. On this world-famed food and milk he gained about 40 lb. in four months and got well. It requires no "Expert Chemist" to prove that "THERE'S A REASON" FOR Grape-Nuts.'

They're G-R-Reat! Kellogg's Sugar Frosted Flakes; US, from c1951.

THE GREAT NEW FRONTIER FAIR DEAL SOCIETY

For some US presidents it is not enough to attain the White House. They have to dignify their policies with a resounding label:

'We demand that big business give people a **Square Deal**,' said President Theodore Roosevelt, campaigning in 1901. 'If elected I shall see to it that every man has a Square Deal, no more and no less.'

Woodrow Wilson, campaigning successfully for the presidency in 1912, sought the **New Freedom**, safeguarding the democratic rights of small business against big business, 'a revival of the power of the people'.

'I pledge you, I pledge myself, to a **New Deal** for the American people,' Franklin D. Roosevelt said in a speech to the 1932 Democratic Convention which had just nominated him. The phrase became the keynote of the ensuing election campaign but it was not new — in Britain, Lloyd George had talked of 'A New Deal For Everyone' in 1919.

'Every segment of our population and every individual has a right to expect from this government a **Fair Deal**' — from President Truman's State of the Union message, 1949. Proposals included legislation on civil rights and fair employment practices.

Dwight Eisenhower called for a **Great Crusade** during his successful campaign in 1952.

'We stand today on the edge of a **New Frontier** — the frontier of the 1960s . . . [it] is not a set of challenges. It sums up not what I intend to offer the American people, but what I intend to ask them' — John F. Kennedy, accepting the Democratic nomination in 1960.

After tentatively trying out *his* phrase several times, President Lyndon B. Johnson elevated it to capital letters in a speech at the University of Michigan in May 1964 — 'In your time we have the opportunity to move not only towards the rich society and the powerful society but upward to the **Great Society**.'

In 1967, Governor George Romney put it all in a nutshell: 'There was the New Deal of Franklin Roosevelt, the Fair Deal of Harry Truman, and the ordeal of Lyndon Johnson.'

HAIR CARE

Does She . . . Or Doesn't She?/Only Her Hairdresser Knows For Sure Clairol; US, from 1955. 'This seemingly non-acceptable phrase turned a non-acceptable commodity into the highly respected industry that hair-colouring is today' — the claim of Shirley Polykoff, who coined it. Or did she? In her book entitled *Does She . . . Or Doesn't She?*, Ms Polykoff wonders whether her mother-in-law didn't invent it twenty years before: 'I had just met George . . . when he invited me to Passover dinner in Reading, Pa . . . it was tantamount to a proposal of marriage . . . I could hardly wait to start the drive home to find out how I had done . . . "She (George's mother) says you paint your hair. Well, do you?" I merely scrunched

down on my side of the car. I could hear his mother thinking as she cleared away the dishes: "Zee paint dos huer? Odder zee paint dos nicht?" Freely translated that means, "Does she . . . or doesn't she?"'

When the Clairol account moved to Foote Cone & Belding in the mid-1950s, Shirley Polykoff was assigned to it and suffered the customary creative block that precedes many a great coinage. As she tells it, she was at a party with George, now her husband, when in came a girl with flaming red hair and Shirley P. involuntarily uttered the line.

Next morning she wrote a memo to the head art director, giving two lines to be rejected and the one she wanted accepted to be followed by the phrase 'Only her mother knows for sure!' or 'So natural, only her mother knows for sure'. She felt she might have to change 'mother' to 'hairdresser' so as not to offend beauty salons. First reaction was that the double meaning in the words would have the line rejected out of hand. Indeed, *Life* magazine would not take the ad. But subsequent research at *Life* failed to find a single female staff member who admitted seeing a double-meaning in it, and the phrases were locked into the form they had for the next eighteen years. ('J' underlines the double-meaning implicit in the slogan with this comment from *The Sensuous Woman*: 'Our world has changed. It's no longer a question of "Does she or doesn't she?" We all know she wants to, is about to, or does.' A New York graffito, quoted 1974: 'Only *his* hairdresser knows for sure.')

Then came **Is She . . . Or Isn't She?** Harmony hairspray; UK, current 1980. Not by Shirley Polykoff, but a deliberate echo. 'Harmony has a ultra-fine spray to leave hair softer and more natural. She *is* wearing a hairspray but with Harmony it's so fine you're the only one that knows for sure.'

Going! Going!! Gone!!! Too Late for Herpicide Newbro's Herpicide; US, current from c1900. Coined by Dr Newbro for his dandruff germ remedy. Accompanied by the cartoon logo of a man looking at the hairs coming out on his comb.

Friday Night Is Amami Night Amami hair products; UK, current 1920s. (Presumably this inspired the title of the long-running BBC radio show *Friday Night is Music Night*.)

Is It True . . . Blondes Have More Fun?   Lady Clairol; US, from 1957. Chosen from ten suggestions, including 'Is it true that blondes are never lonesome?' and 'Is it true blondes marry millionaires?', 'Blondes have more fun' entered the language. The TV jingle even became a hit in the USSR c1965. Shirley Polykoff, again.

A Little Dab'll Do Ya   Brylcreem; US, from 1949.

Which Twin Has The Toni?   Toni home perms; US, current 1951. A headline that asks a question, a slogan that contains the brand name, and an idea that was dotty enough to be much copied. The ads featured pairs of identical twins (real ones), who also toured doing promotional work for the product. One had a Toni home perm, the other a more expensive perm – a footnote explained which was which. (During the 1970 UK general election, the Liberal Party produced a poster carrying pictures of Harold Wilson and Edward Heath and the slogan **Which Twin Is The Tory?**)

HAPPY MOTORING

Ask The Man Who Owns One Packard; US, from 1902.
This slogan originated with James Ward Packard, the founder of the company, and appeared for many years in all Packard advertising and sales material. Someone had written
asking for more information about his motors. Packard told
his secretary: 'Tell him that we have no literature
– we aren't that big yet – but if he wants
to know how good an automobile the
Packard is, tell him to ask the man who
owns one.' A 1903 placard is the first
printed evidence of the slogan's use.
It lasted for more than thirty-five years.

**At 60 Miles An Hour The Loudest
Noise In This New Rolls-Royce
Comes From The Electric Clock**
Rolls-Royce; US, from 1958. The
best-known promotional line there
has ever been for an automobile.
It was not devised by some copy-
writing genius but came from a car
test of the 1958 Silver Cloud by the

Technical Editor of *The Motor* magazine. Ogilvy recalls presenting the headline to a senior Rolls-Royce executive in
New York who shook his head sadly and said: 'We really
ought to do something about that damned clock.' Even the
motoring journalist had not been entirely original. A 1907
review of the Silver Ghost in the *The Autocar* stated: 'At
whatever speed the car is driven, the auditory nerves when
driving are troubled by no fuller sound than emanates from
the 8-day clock.'

   R-R originally used **The Best Car In The World** (current
1929, following a description in *The Times*, 1908.)

"At 60 miles an hour the loudest noise in this new Rolls-Royce comes from the electric clock"

The Esso Sign Means Happy Motoring   Esso; UK, current 1950s. The line occurred in the 1950s' 'longest-running jingle', written by David Bernstein at McCann-Erickson.

Eye It − Try It − Buy It!   Chevrolet; US, current 1940.

Fit Dunlop And Be Satisfied   Dunlop tyres; UK, quoted 1925.

The Getaway People   National Benzole; UK, from 1963. Bryan Oakes of London Press Exchange commented: 'They were the jet set, clean-limbed beautiful girls, the gods and goddesses who did exotic things. We used expensive cars − E-type Jaguars and Aston Martins − and the promise was that, if you get this petrol, you're aligning yourself with those wonderful people, midnight drives on the beach and so on. Of course, it's tough luck − you don't happen to have a Jag just yet, or a girl like that, but any day now . . .' (Pearson)

Go Well – Go Shell Shell; UK, current from late 1940s, with the follow-on line **Keep Going Well – Keep Going Shell**. Both were featured in early TV commercials, most notably with Bing Crosby singing the jingle in 1962 and Sammy Davis junior in 1964.

Grace . . . Space . . . Pace Jaguar; UK, current 1960s.

I Can Be Very Friendly Sun Oil; US, from 1973. Jane Maas records: 'The chairman and founder of Wells, Rich, Greene, Mary Lawrence, is responsible for the line "I Can Be Very Friendly". During the gasoline crisis, when everyone (customers and dealers) were grouchy about no supplies and long waiting lines, this campaign showed the Sun Oil dealers declaring their intent to win customers over with extra care, concern and good will. It was summed up in the slogan which not only changed the image of Sun Oil in customers' eyes, but also motivated the Sun Dealers to be, indeed, very friendly.'

I Told 'Em, Oldham Oldham car batteries; UK, current late 1950s. Created by Joan Bakewell.

King Of The Road Lucas cycle lamps and batteries; UK, current 1920.

Look At All Three! Chrysler Plymouth; US, from 1932. J.V. Tarleton, of J. Stirling Getchell Inc., recalled: 'The one big fact that gave rise to the whole "Look at all three" idea was that Henry Ford, whose plants had been out of production for almost a year while he tooled up production of the new V-8, was planning to introduce this radically new model in the very same week when Mr Chrysler was planning to announce his new Plymouth . . . Getchell and a writer proceeded to bat their brains out for a day or two looking for a unique and different way of announcing a new car – a way that would take advantage of the suspenseful situation created by Mr Ford and get Plymouth through the swinging door on his push . . . One of their advertisements showed a large picture of Mr Chrysler in a very informal pose with his foot on the bumper of a new Plymouth. The headline on this ad had originally read "Look at all three low priced cars before you buy." In the process of making the layout, the writer had boiled this down to four big words, "Look At All

Three" . . . The day when [it] was published in newspapers all over the country, the reaction was unmistakable. Chrysler Corporation dealers reported that their doors started swinging early in the morning and didn't stop until late at night. Plymouth, over night, had become a real contender in the low priced field.'

Put A Tiger In Your Tank Esso; US, from 1964. This was a slogan that really took off and gave rise to endless jokes and cartoons. I can remember taking part in a revue sketch about Noah's Ark at Oxford in 1965, the sole purpose of which seemed to be to lead up to the punch line, 'Put A Tiger In Your Tank'. The Esso Tiger had been around in the US and UK a long time before this, however. He first appeared on a poster for Esso Extra in the UK in 1952, realistic, fierce and far from friendly. In 1959 he reappeared in more human form in the US. The line 'Put A Tiger In Your Tank' was thrown away. In 1964, the cartoon tiger was launched in the US, a year later in the UK, and it became a national craze, with countless tiger tails adorning the petrol caps of the nation's cars. Subsequently, he went abroad: 'Mettez un tigre dans votre moteur' appeared in France; in Germany, 'Pack den Tiger in den tank'. In the US, particularly, he gave rise to numerous tiger derivatives. A sample: 'If You Feel Like A Tiger Is In Your Throat Reach For Guardets Lozenges . . .'. A hamburger stand advertised: 'Put A Tiger In Your Tummy.' Tiger Beer in the Japanese *Times* slogromed: 'Put A Tiger In Your Tankard.' Standard Rochester Beer countered: 'Put A Tankard In Your Tiger.'

There may be a connection with a song (by W. Dixon) which Muddy Waters had been singing by 1960: 'I Want to Put A Tiger in Your Tank'. This gave double meanings to a number of motoring phrases.

The UK campaign ran for two years before it flagged, hence:

Save The Esso Tiger Esso; UK, from 1967. Dennis Page recalls how he was hired to revive the tiger. He told *Campaign* (7 November 1980): 'I had the ad manager on television advertising the end of the Esso tiger and the tiger saying he was not going to go. Far from saving the tiger, it actually hastened his demise [in 1968].'

PUT A TIGER IN YOUR TANK

NEW POWER-FORMULA ESSO EXTRA BOOSTS POWER THREE WAYS...

1. QUICK STARTING. New Esso Extra gives quick starting, in summer and winter, and *smooth controlled power* with that extra acceleration when you need it.
2. SMOOTH FIRING. Esso Extra's new Power formula improves ignition, helps your engine to fire smoothly and efficiently.

3. HIGH QUALITY. New Esso Extra has the high quality that modern cars need for peak performance. *So call at the Esso sign and fill up with new Esso Extra –and feel the difference.* PUT A TIGER IN YOUR TANK.

Safety Fast MG Motors; UK, current before the Second World War.

Standard Of The World Cadillac; US, current 1912. Created by MacManus, John & Adams (Detroit), the copy ran: 'You know it to be true — you know that the Cadillac is a criterion wherever motor cars are discussed . . . all the Cadillac arguments we could advance in a score of announcements would not be one-hundredth part as impressive as the positive knowledge you hold in your mind at this moment. You know that the Cadillac is *in very fact* the standard of the world. What more is there to be said?'

That's Shell — That Was! Shell; UK, current from early 1930s. A one-headed man with the slogan 'That's Shell — That Is', current in 1929, was developed into a two-headed man with the more widely known slogan. A possibly apocryphal story is that the two-headed man was devised by a member of the public called Horsfield, who received £100 for his trouble.

Think Small Volkswagen; US, from c1959. Created at Doyle, Dane, Bernbach, this slogan led to the connection between DDB and the Democratic Party. It is said that John F. Kennedy had enjoyed the 'Think Small' campaign — it appealed to his sense of humour — and he suggested the link-up.

Time To Re-Tire Fisk Rubber Co. tyres; US, from 1907. Burr Griffin did the original sketch for the long-running pun of an ad which showed a yawning child with candle, night-shirt, and tyre. The original slogan was **When It's Time To Re-Tire, Buy A Fisk**.

Watch The Fords Go By Ford Motor Co.; US, from 1908. Started off as a baseball cry in support of the team at the company's Highland Park factory. Applied to ads upon the introduction of the Model T.

When Better Automobiles Are Built . . . Buick Will Build Them Buick; US, current 1923.

When You're Only No. 2, You Try Harder. Or Else Avis Rent-A-Car; US, from 1963. Avis had been in the red for

We try harder.

fifteen years when, in 1962, Doyle, Dane, Bernbach were hired to do its advertising. A $3 million loss in 1962 became a $3 million profit in 1963, despite warnings that admitting you were not No. 1 was 'un-American' and would merely provide Hertz with a free advertisement.

Where The Rubber Meets The Road Firestone tyres; US, quoted 1976.

You Can Be Sure Of Shell Shell; UK, from c1931.

You Can Trust Your Car To The Man Who Wears The Star Texaco; US, current 1961.

TEETH 'N' SMILES

Cleaning your teeth is not all that a toothpaste does for you. Name the brands supported by the following lines. The answers are overleaf.

1 For People Who Can't Brush Their Teeth After Every Meal

2 You'll Wonder Where The Yellow Went

3 Did You ********** Your Teeth Today?

4 Cleans Your Breath While It Cleans Your Teeth

5 The Toothpaste For Thinking People

6 Gets Rid Of Film On Teeth

7 It's Tingling Fresh

8 Looks Like Fun, Cleans Like Crazy

ANSWERS

1 Gleem; US, quoted 1957. Research showed that many people felt guilty about not brushing their teeth after every meal. So a slogan was coined which gave these people the perfect excuse not to do so.

2 **When You Brush Your Teeth With Pepsodent**; US, current 1950s. An appeal to vanity rather than health.

3 **Did You Maclean Your Teeth Today?**; US, current 1934.

4 Colgate Dental Cream; US, current 1946. Every toothpaste can do it but no one had made it a claim before. Also **The Colgate Ring Of Confidence**.

5 Pebeco; US, current 1931.

6 Pepsodent; US, current early twentieth century. Another of Claude C. Hopkins's great coups — to claim something that every toothpaste could claim and get away with it. He said: 'People do not want to read of penalties. They want to be told of rewards . . . People want to be told the ways to happiness and cheer . . . I resolved to advertise this toothpaste as a creator of beauty.'

7   Gibbs S.R. toothpaste; UK, current 1955. 'It's fresh
    as ice, it's Gibbs S.R. toothpaste, the tingling fresh
    toothpaste that does your gums good, too. The
    tingle you get when you brush with S.R. is much
    more than a nice taste. It's a tingle of health. It tells
    you something very important. That you're doing
    your gums good and toughening them to resist
    infection. . . .' – accompanied by the visual of a
    tube embedded in a block of ice, this was the first
    commercial ever shown on British TV, in 1955.

8   Stripe toothpaste; US, quoted 1958. A man who had
    invented a tube nozzle which coloured the sides of
    the emerging ribbon of toothpaste was discovered
    by J. Walter Thompson in New York. Copywriters
    picked the name 'Stripe' and coined the slogan, then
    took the package to Lever Brothers, who found
    themselves with a ready-made product – a com-
    plete reversal of the usual process. (Mayer)

I'M BACKING BRITAIN

However you phrase them — **Made In England, British Made** or **Buy British** — appeals to patriotism in advertising have had a rough ride and a limited response. Swan Vesta matches were using the slogan **Support Home Industries** as long ago as 1905. There was a campaign dedicated to the idea of buying British goods in preference to others in the wake of the First World War — part of an effort to revive British trade. But, as a commentator wrote in 1925: 'The slogan has never from its birth rung like true metal. There is nothing satisfying about it. It savours of a cry of distress — an S.O.S. — and does not begin to represent the spirit of a commerce that is reconstructing itself and paying its debts simultaneously.'

Somehow, patriotism (which can be appealed to legitimately in time of war) does not mix with commerce. Besides, there is a suspicion of boycott about such phrases. There is also the obstacle of identification — how does the consumer *know* what is British and what is not? How can he make the choice when he does not know what component parts are used in making a product?

All this has not prevented such slogans reappearing whenever things have looked bleak for the economy. **British Is Best** has been used at regular chauvinistic intervals. The most curious revival of the 'Buy British' theme was in January 1968 when, in the wake of the Labour Government's decision to devalue the pound sterling, all kinds of peculiar reactions filled the air. Valerie, Brenda, Joan, Carol and Christine — typists at the Colt Heating and Ventilation offices at Surbiton — responded to a Christmas message from their boss to make some special work-effort. From 1 January they declared they would work half an hour extra each day for no extra pay. Was this spontaneous, or were they pushed? Whatever the case, the media leapt in. The slogan **I'm Backing Britain** appeared from somewhere and Prime Minister

Harold Wilson said, 'What we want is "Back Britain" not back-biting.' The Industrial Society launched an official campaign on 24 January. Bruce Forsyth recorded a song 'I'm Backing Britain'. Two million badges and stickers were manufactured. A press ad listed 'three things retired folk could do' to help the economy or 'seven things a manufacturer could do'. People actually started sending money to the Chancellor of the Exchequer. It was as barmy as that. Then things turned sour. 'Back Britain' T-shirts were found to have been made in Portugal. Trade unions objected to the idea of anyone working extra hours for no more pay. A rival 'Help Britain' group led by Robert Maxwell MP conflicted with the Industrial Society's effort. The whole thing had fizzled out by August.

IN THIS STYLE 10/6

The price-ticket on the Mad Hatter's hat in the Tenniel illustration for Lewis Carroll's *Alice's Adventures In Wonderland* (ten shillings and sixpence being the equivalent of 52½p in post-1971 British currency) introduces a selection of fictional slogans – or perhaps one should say 'slogans in fiction', because some of them are quite convincing . . .

It's A Far, Far Butter Thing . . . A suggested slogan for margarine from *Murder Must Advertise* by Dorothy L. Sayers. The whole of this novel (1933) is set in Pym's, an advertising agency modelled on the firm of S.H. Benson, where Sayers worked in the 1920s and 30s. The book positively teems with suggested and mostly rejected advertising lines – some devised by Lord Peter Wimsey himself, disguised as Death Bredon, a trainee copywriter:

Bigger And Butter Value For Money
You'd Be Ready To Bet It Was Butter
If You Kept A Cow In The Kitchen You Could Get No Better Bread-Spread Than G. P. Margarine
Don't Say Soap, Say Sopo!
Makes Monday, Fun-Day

Are You A Whiffler? If Not, Why Not?
It Isn't Dear, It's Darling
Everyone Everywhere Always Agrees
On The Flavour And Value Of Twentyman's Teas

'P.P.' What About You? In *Keep The Aspidistra Flying* (1936), George Orwell describes an advertising campaign by the Queen of Sheba Toilet Requisites Co. for the deodorant, 'April Dew'. The firm was after a phrase like 'Night Starvation' that would 'rankle in the public consciousness like a poisoned arrow'. The idea of smelly feet becomes 'Pedic Perspiration' or 'P.P.'

If You Can't Sleep At Night, It Isn't The Coffee — It's The Bunk Dick Powell's winning coffee jingle in the film *Christmas in July* (1940).

All Animals Are Equal, But Some Animals Are More Equal Than Others
Napoleon Is Always Right
Vote For Snowball And The Three Day Week
Vote For Napoleon And The Full Manger
                    from *Animal Farm* (1945) by George Orwell

If You Ain't Eatin' Wham
You Ain't Eatin' Ham
In the film *Mr Blandings Builds His Dream House* (1948), Cary Grant portrays an advertising man in search of a slogan which eludes him until his black cook utters these immortal words.

Big Brother Is Watching You
Freedom Is Slavery
Ignorance Is Strength
War Is Peace
                    from *Nineteen Eighty-Four* (1949) by George Orwell

Bowen's Beer Makes You Drunk In the Kingsley Amis novel *I Like It Here* (1958) Garnet Bowen suggests that this is the only type of beer slogan that will really appeal.

McKay: The Better Way

Robert Redford won on this slogan in the film *The Candidate* (1972). It caught only too well the uninspired quality of most modern political slogans.

KIKES, KOONS, AND KATHOLICS

Popular protest — for and against — kikes (Jews), black people, and other vocal minorities and causes in the UK and the US:

When Adam Delved And Eve Span, Who Was Then A Gentleman? A rhyme from the Peasants' Revolt, 1381. Taken as the text for a sermon preached by John Ball to Wat Tyler's men at Blackheath.

No Popery, No Tyranny, No Wooden Shoes Defoe said that there were a hundred thousand fellows in his time ready to fight to the death against popery, without knowing whether popery was a man or a horse. After the initial impact of the Restoration had worn off, this was the cry that came to be heard. The wife of Charles II, Catherine of Braganza, was a Roman Catholic and so was his brother (later James II). They were surrounded by priests and the Fire of London (1666) was put down to papist action and foreign interference. Hence, the anti-Roman Catholicism of the slogan coupled with general English distrust of foreigners (wooden shoes=French *sabots*). The variation **No Jews — No Wooden Shoes** (obvious rhyming slang) occurred in 1753 when an anti-Jewish Bill was before Parliament.

The cry 'No Popery' is chiefly associated, however, with the Gordon Riots of 1780, when Lord George Gordon fomented a violent protest against legislation which had lightened penalties on Roman Catholics. The riots in London were put down by George III's troops (and form the background to Charles Dickens's novel *Barnaby Rudge*). The slogan was again used by supporters of the Duke of Portland's government opposed to Catholic Emancipation, in 1807.

Wilkes And Liberty Cry of the London mob, 1764, in support of John Wilkes (1727-97), the radical politician, who was repeatedly elected to Parliament despite ministerial attempts to exclude him because of his scurrilous attacks on the government. He was a popular champion of parliamentary reform and of the cause of the colonies in the War of American Independence.

One Man, One Vote A phrase first coined in the nineteenth century for a campaign led by Major John Cartwright (1740-1824), a radical MP ('The Father of Reform'), in the fight against plural voting. It was possible in those days for a man to cast two votes, one on the basis of residence and the other by virtue of business or university qualifications. This right was not abolished until 1948. The phrase arose again during the period of the illegal Unilateral Declaration of Independence in Rhodesia (1965-80) to indicate a basic condition required by the British government before the breakaway could be legitimized. The phrase has also been used in the US, in civil rights contexts.

Home Rule (For Ever) First used about 1860 in its usual sense of home rule for Ireland, then under British rule. The Home Rule Movement led by Sinn Fein ultimately led to the founding of the Irish Free State — with Northern Ireland remaining part of the UK.

Ulster Will Fight, And Ulster Will Be Right In an open letter to a Liberal-Unionist in May 1886, Lord Randolph Churchill wrote: 'Ulster will not be a consenting party; Ulster at the proper moment will resort to a supreme arbitrament of force; Ulster will fight and Ulster will be right.' Taken up by Ulster Volunteers, loyal to the British Crown, and opposing Irish Home Rule, 1913-14.

The Saloon Must Go Anti-Saloon League, founded in 1893. When saloons were a proliferating, noisy, smelly nuisance, the League used political pressure to bring the temperance movement to a successful climax in Prohibition.

Kill The Kikes, Koons, And Katholics Ku Klux Klan, from the late nineteenth century.

Bring Back The Cat The cat-o'-nine-tails was the nine-thong whip once used to enforce discipline in the Royal Navy. This phrase has long been the cry of corporal punishment enthusiasts demanding its return. Usually associated with right-wing 'hangers and floggers' within the Conservative Party.

Not A Penny Off The Pay, Not A Minute On The Day (and variants)   Coined by A.J. Cook, Secretary of the Union of Mineworkers, and used in the run-up to the miners' strike of 1926 (which led to the General Strike). (Compare:

> In his chamber, weak and dying
> While the Norman Baron lay,
> Loud, without, his men were crying
> 'Shorter hours and better pay.'
>
> Anon.)

You Gave Us Beer, Now Give Us Water   Dustbowl farmers' plea (US), 1933. The year of the great drought, which destroyed crops and created dust-storms was, ironically, when Prohibition ended.

A Vote For Hogg Is A Vote For Hitler   A famous by-election took place at Oxford in the month after the Munich agreement in 1938. Quintin Hogg (later Lord Hailsham) stood as the champion of Munich and the Prime Minister, Neville Chamberlain; A.D. Lindsay, Master of Balliol and a member of the Labour Party, stood as a representative of the anti-fascist Popular Front. Hogg won.

Ban The Bomb   One of the simplest and best-known alliterative slogans, current in the US from 1953 and marginally later in the UK. The Campaign for Nuclear Disarmament was not publicly launched until February 1958. (Richard Crossman refers to 'Scrap the Bomb' in a 1957 press article.)

Better Red Than Dead   A slogan of the British nuclear disarmament movement. Bertrand Russell wrote in 1958: 'If no alternative remains except communist domination or the extinction of the human race, the former alternative is the lesser of two evils' — hence the slogan. The counter-cry **Better Dead Than Red** became almost equally well established.

Marples Must Go   Ernest Marples (1907-78) was the hyperactive Conservative Minister of Transport (1959-64). This slogan first arose in October 1962 (and was quoted as such in a *Daily Herald* headline) after he had intervened in the build-up to the publication of the Beeching Report, which recommended sweeping cuts in rail services. 'Trades union leaders

and Labour MPs have started a Marples Must Go campaign,'
the *Herald* reported, 'convinced that Marples must be sacked
to save a head-on clash between railway unions and government.' When the report was finally published in March 1963,
Marples was judged to have given a poor defence of it in the
House of Commons.

However, it was because of motoring matters that the
slogan was taken up at a more popular level. Marples had
already introduced Britain to parking zones, car tests, and
panda crossings. He could claim that London's traffic was
moving 37½ per cent faster as a result of his draconian
measures. But many saw them as an infringement of individual liberty. In May 1963, Marples introduced 'totting up'
for motoring convictions and, shortly afterwards, a 50 m.p.h.
speed limit at peak summer weekends in an effort to reduce
the number of road accidents. It was this last measure that
produced a rash of car stickers bearing this cry. It appeared
daubed on a bridge over the M1 motorway in August.

When Barbara Castle became Labour Transport Minister
in 1965 and introduced breath-tests to combat drunken driving, car stickers appeared saying 'Marples Come Back, All Is
Forgiven.

The 'Must Go' formula can be traced back in politics
through **Eden Must Go** (during Suez) to **Balfour Must Go**
(c1905).

If You Want A Nigger For A Neighbour – **Vote Labour**   appeared in one constituency – Smethwick – during the 1964
UK general election. The seat was won from Labour by Peter
Griffiths, later described by the incoming Prime Minister,
Harold Wilson, as 'a member who, until another election
returns him to oblivion, will serve his time here as a parliamentary leper'.

Hearts And Minds   The Vietnam War (c1959-73) produced
almost no patriotic American slogans – reflecting the mixed
support for an unpopular and ultimately unsuccessful operation. 'Hearts And Minds', meaning what had to be won, was
a slogan of sorts for the US government. Its origins go back to
Theodore Roosevelt's day when Douglas MacArthur, as a
young aide, asked him in 1909 to what he attributed his
popularity. The President replied: 'To put into words what is

in their hearts and minds but not in their mouths.' (Safire) Before that, the phrase is biblical in origin.

A ribald Green Beret use of the phrase could be observed during the war above the bar in the den of Charles W. Colson (later indicted over the Watergate cover-up): **If You Got 'Em By The Balls, Their Hearts And Minds Will Follow**.

Abolish The Draft and **Hell, No, We Won't Go**   US anti-draft slogans, 1960s.

America, Love It Or Leave It   The most memorable of the few patriotic slogans, current from 1969.

Make Love, Not War   A 'peacenik' and 'flower power' sentiment expressed from the mid-1960s, not just applied to Vietnam. It was written up in English at the University of Nanterre during the French student revolution of May 1968.

Turn On, Tune In, Drop Out   Hippie slogan and LSD motto associated with Dr Timothy Leary, from c1967.

Peace Now   On poster, quoted 1968 − echoing the 'now' theme also used in civil rights slogans.

Build Not Burn   Students For A Democratic Society, late 1960s.

Flower Power   Hippie slogan, 1960s, inspired no doubt by 'Black Power'. Flowers were used as a love symbol.

Shoot To Live   The Weathermen (militant revolutionary group), c1969.

Support Your Local Police, Keep Them Independent Police bumper sticker, 1969. The film *Support Your Local Sheriff* had appeared in 1968, but the idea of supporting or consulting your local or neighbourhood whatever was already well established.

Out Of The Closets And Into The Streets   Gay Liberation Front, c1969.

Say It Loud, We're Gay And We're Proud   Gay Liberation Front.

2-4-6-8,
Gay Is Just As Good As Straight
3-5-7-9
Lesbians Are Mighty Fine   Gay Liberation Front, 1970s.

Register Communists Not Guns   John Birch Society, 1970.

Guns Don't Kill People, People Kill People   National Rifle Association, current 1981.

YOUR OWN, YOUR VERY OWN

A phrase describing the nature of their act was a distinctive feature of billing for music-hall and variety artists in the UK and vaudeville performers in the US. At times, such 'bill matter' was used as more than a tag. As an up-and-coming comedian, Tommy Trinder bought space on hoardings all over London to proclaim:

It It's Laughter You're After, Trinder's The Name.

The World's Greatest Entertainer	Al Jolson
The Man With The Golden Trumpet	Eddie Calvert
Creating An Impression	Peter Cavanagh
The One And Only	Phyllis Dixey
A Song, A Smile, And A Piano	Norman Long
The Human Hairpin	Carlton
The Wigan Nightingale	George Formby senior
Fiddling And Fooling	Ted Ray
The Essence of Eccentricity	Nellie Wallace
America's Beloved Baritone	John Charles Thomas
The Velvet Fog	Mel Tormé
The Singer With The Smile In His Voice	Jack Smith
Almost A Gentleman	Billy Bennett
The Casual Comedian	Geep Martin (*whose hands shook so much you could hear his script rattling at the microphone*)
The Cheeky Chappie	Max Miller
The Chocolate Coloured Coon	G.H. Elliott

The Last Of The Red Hot Mamas	Sophie Tucker (*from the title of a song by Jack Yellen, introduced by her in 1928*)
The Prime Minister Of Mirth	George Robey
She's No Lady!	George Lacy (*female impersonator*)
The Long And The Short Of It	Ethel Revnel and Gracie West
The Man With The Orchid-Lined Voice	Enrico Caruso (*coined by his publicist, Edward L. Bernays*)
Two Ton Tessie	Tessie O'Shea
The Girl Who Made Vaudeville Famous	Eva Tanguay
Radio's Bouncing Czech	Egon Regon
A Concert-in-a Act	Peter and Mary Honri
Fills the Stage With Flags	Kardomah
The Clown Prince Of Wales	Wyn Calvin
Oh No, There Isn't!	The Two Pirates
Britain's Favourite American Performers/America's Favourite British Performers	Kimberly & Page (*in UK and US*)
Too Mean To Tell You What They Do	The Three Aberdonians

LET'S MAKE AMERICA
GREAT AGAIN

American presidential elections have given rise to some of the quirkiest political slogans and, increasingly of late, to some of the dullest. 'Let's Make America Great Again', for example, has been used more than once and could apply to any candidate, Democratic or Republican, incumbent or challenger. Here, taken from some of the past campaigns, are the more pointed rallying cries, both official and unofficial:

1828 **Bargain And Corruption** No one candidate in the previous election had received a majority of the electoral vote although Andrew Jackson was in the lead. When the election came to be decided by the House of Representatives, John Quincy Adams struck a deal with fellow candidate Henry Clay (Speaker of the House) by which Adams won and Clay became

Secretary of State. In 1828, using the slogan 'Bargain And Corruption', Jackson unseated President Adams.

1840 **Tippecanoe And Tyler Too** 'Tippecanoe' refers to General William Henry Harrison, the Whig candidate, who had defeated Indians at Tippecanoe Creek in 1811. John Tyler stood as Vice-President. The Democrats renominated President Van Buren and characterized Harrison as the 'Log Cabin And Hard Cider' candidate — a challenge the Whigs turned to their advantage by forming log cabin clubs and serving hard cider at rallies. Van Buren, in turn, was characterized as an effete New Yorker drinking wine from 'coolers of silver', and acquired the nickname 'Old Kinderhook' from the name of his birthplace in New York State. **O.K.** became a slogan in the 1840 campaign, too, adding to the colourful etymology of that phrase. It was not O.K. for Van Buren, however — he was unseated.

1844 **Who's Polk?** James K. Polk, the first 'dark horse' candidate, took the Democratic nomination from ex-President Van Buren. As a compromise candidate he was little known (just as more than a century later Jimmy Carter initially gave rise to the cry 'Jimmy Who?'). He campaigned with the expansionist slogan **54-40 Or Fight**, seeking to reoccupy the territory of Oregon, then jointly held by Britain and the US, up to a northern boundary with Canada at 54° 40'. The Democrats won the election but President Polk negotiated a compromise settlement at the 49th Parallel. Coinage of the phrase is credited to Samuel Medary, an editor from Ohio, though William Allen, a Democratic Senator from that state, used it in a speech before the US Senate.

1852 **We Polked You in 1844, We Shall Pierce You In 1852** The next 'dark horse' was Franklin Pierce, who was not considered as the Democrats' candidate until the 35th ballot at the party convention. When he was selected on the 49th, the slogan was inevitable. He won the election, too.

1856 **Free Soil, Free Men, Free Speech, Frémont** The new Republican Party's first candidate was John C. Frémont, a soldier and explorer. When formed two years before, the party had absorbed abolitionists including the Free Soil Party (which was dedicated to free land for settlers as well as to the abolition of slavery) who used the slogan **Free Soil, Free Speech, Free Labour, And Free Men**, which the Republicans adapted. Meanwhile, the American (Know Nothing) Party which supported ex-President Fillmore in the race used the slogan **Peace At Any Price** to mean that they were willing to accept slavery for blacks in order to avoid a civil war. This phrase had been coined in 1848 by the French foreign affairs minister, Alphonse de Lamartine. Neither Frémont nor Fillmore won. James Buchanan did.

1872 **Anything To Beat Grant** After only one term it was apparent that President Grant, though a war hero, was unsuited to the presidency. The Liberal Republican Party emerged to unseat him with Horace Greeley as candidate — but failed to do so.

1876 **Hayes, Hard Money And Hard Times** A Democratic challenge to the Republican candidate Rutherford B. Hayes, who won after a disputed election

1884 **Rum, Romanism, Rebellion** Samuel Dickinson Burchard, speaking on behalf of clergymen who supported the Republican candidate, James G. Blaine, said: 'We are Republicans, and don't propose to leave our party and identify ourselves with the party whose antecedents have been Rum, Romanism, and Rebellion.' His Irish-Catholic audience in New York took none too kindly to this. Blaine lost the state's vote, and the presidency, to Grover Cleveland.

1900 **Full Dinner Pail** A Republican phrase which helped secure the re-election of President McKinley. Prosperity of this type was plainly more appealing to the average voter than William Jennings Bryan's call for 'Immediate Freedom For The Philippines'. A remark made by McKinley supporter Senator Mark Hanna, 'We Will Stand Pat', gave rise to the idea that 'Stand Pat With McKinley' was used as a slogan in this election but this appears to be a fallacy.

1904 You Can't Beat Somebody With Nobody And President Theodore Roosevelt was re-elected over the Democratic challenger Alton B. Parker.

1916 He Kept Us Out Of War and **Wilson's Wisdom Wins Without War** Woodrow Wilson's slogans for re-election were true at the time (although he had nothing to do with them) but he took the US into the First World War the following year.

1920 Back To Normalcy and **Return To Normalcy With Harding** were used effectively in the Republican campaign which took Warren G. Harding to the White House. Both were based on his remark of that year: 'America's present need is not heroics but healing, not nostrums but normalcy.'

1924 Keep Cool With Coolidge and **Coolidge Or Chaos** Calvin C. Coolidge had assumed the presidency in 1923 on the death of Harding. He won this election by a wide margin.

1928 Hoover And Happiness, Or Smith And Soup Houses Herbert Hoover easily defeated the Democrat Alfred E. Smith in the prosperous calm before the economic storm. 'Two Chickens For Every Pot' is said, erroneously, to have been used by Hoover in the campaign. The suggestion appears to have arisen because Smith mocked a Republican flysheet headed 'A Chicken in Every Pot' — using the phrase coined by King Henry IV of France (1553-1610) when he said: 'I wish that there would not be a peasant so poor in all my realm who would not have a chicken in his pot every Sunday.'

1932 In Hoover We Trusted, Now We Are Busted After the stock-market and financial crash, Hoover was roundly defeated by the Democratic challenger Franklin D. Roosevelt.

1936 Land Landon With A Landslide and **Land a Job With Landon** Roosevelt's New Deal policies were challenged by the Republican Governor, Alfred M. Landon. Telephone operators at the switchboard of the *Chicago Tribune* answered calls with 'Only X more days to **Save The American Way Of Life**.' Democrats encouraged the incumbent to **Carry On, Roosevelt**. He did.

1940 **We Want Wilkie** At the Republican convention, the balconies were packed with supporters of Wendell Wilkie. They helped sway the nomination in his direction. 'Win With Wilkie' did not help unseat FDR. The President had his own slogan for crowd repetition: **Martin, Barton And Fish**. Seeking to blame Republicans for US military unpreparedness, he cited three Congressmen — Joseph Martin, Bruce Barton (later of the advertising firm, Batten, Barton, Durstine & Osborn), and Hamilton Fish. The speech in which the phrase arose was written by Judge Samuel I. Rosenman and Robert E. Sherwood, the dramatist. Crowds loved to join in the rhythmic line echoing 'Wynken, Blynken and Nod'.

1944 **Time For A Change** Twelve years of FDR led to his Republican challenger, Thomas E. Dewey, saying: 'That's why it's time for a change.' But the call was ignored, as it was when he repeated it four years later. It was finally effective for the Republicans in 1952.

1948 **Don't Let Them Take It Away** Fears that a Republican president might re-enter the White House after sixteen years of Democratic rule gave rise to this unofficial slogan. It worked this time for Harry S. Truman's election but not when the slogan was revived in 1952. At the beginning of the 1948 campaign Truman told Alben Barkley, his running mate, 'I'm going to fight hard. I'm going to give them hell.' So **Give 'Em Hell, Harry** became a battle-cry.

1952 **I Like Ike** This slogan began appearing on buttons in 1947 as the Second World War general, Dwight David Eisenhower, began to be spoken of as a possible presidential nominee (initially as a Democrat). By 1950 Irving Berlin was including one of his least notable songs, 'They Like Ike', in *Call Me Madam* and 15,000 people at a rally in Madison Square Gardens were urging Eisenhower to return from his military sojourn in Paris and run as a Republican in 1952, with the chant 'We Like Ike'. It worked. The three sharp monosyllables and the effectiveness of the repeated 'i' sound in 'I Like Ike' made it an enduring slogan throughout the fifties. A sign observed during the 1960 campaign said 'We Like Ike But We Back Jack.' **K_1C_2** or **Korea, Communism And Corruption** was the hard-hitting slogan of the 1952 campaign, representing the three charges against the incumbent Democrats — that they were unable to end the war, were soft on communism, and had created a mess in Washington. **I Shall Go To Korea** was an Eisenhower promise made in a campaign speech. **Had Enough?** pointed up the Republicans' long absence from power. **You Never Had It So Good** was a Democratic slogan which failed to deliver for Adlai Stevenson.

1960 **Let's Get America Moving Again** (John F. Kennedy) and **Keep The Peace Without Surrender** (Richard M. Nixon) were interchangeable slogans from the election that JFK won.

1964 **All The Way With LBJ** and **USA For LBJ** were employed by Lyndon B. Johnson in the election that gave him a landslide victory over the Republican, Barry M. Goldwater, in the year following the Kennedy assassination. 'All The Way With LBJ' had first been used when Johnson was seeking the presidential nomination which eventually went to Kennedy in 1960. 'All through the fall and winter of 1959 and 1960,' wrote Theodore White, 'the noisemakers of the Johnson campaign . . . chanted "All The Way With LBJ" across the South and Far West, instantly identifiable by their Texan garb, their ten-gallon hats (and, said their enemies, the cowflap on their boots).' **In Your Heart You Know I'm/He's Right** was the much-parodied Goldwater slogan — 'In Your Gut You Know He's Nuts'; 'You Know In Your Heart He's Right — Far Right.' **$AuH_2O = 1964$** gave rise to the riposte '$AuH_2O = H_2S$' and 'Goldwater in '64, Hot Water in '65, Bread and Water in '66'.

1968 **Nixon's The One** So, indeed, he was, if his official slogan can be said to have any meaning at all. Later in the campaign there appeared **This Time Vote Like Your Whole Life Depended On It**. Democratic opponent Hubert H. Humphrey countered in vain with **The Politics Of Joy**, and third-party candidate George C. Wallace sniped at the big boys with the charge that there was **Not A Dime's Worth Of Difference**. Nixon won.

1972 **Send Them A Message**   George C. Wallace's plea, by which he sought to attract votes away from Nixon and the Democrat George McGovern by pointing up the gulf between the little people in the electorate and the aloof politicians in power, failed to stop Nixon winning again.

1976 **He's Making Us Proud Again**   Gerald R. Ford needed to, having assumed the presidency in the wake of Watergate. He was rejected in favour of the Democrat who used the catchphrase/slogan **My Name Is Jimmy Carter And I'm Running For President** as well as the loftier cry, **Why Not The Best?**

1980 **The Time Is Now**   Another incontestable statement that helped bring Ronald Reagan to power. His long-time supporters continued to use **Win This One For The Gipper** — a reference to Reagan's earlier existence as a film actor. In *Knute Rockne* he played a football star, George Gipp, who died young. The team's coach sent his team-mates out on to the field with this exhortation. Jimmy Carter's detractors within and without his own party came up with **A.B.C.** — **Anyone But Carter**.

MAKE BRITAIN GREAT AGAIN

No general election is complete without slogans. Here are some of the more intriguing ones from British Conservative and Labour campaigns:

1923 **Yesterday The Trenches, Today The Unemployed** was used in the aftermath of the First World War and prior to the first Labour election victory, under Ramsay MacDonald.

1929 **Safety First** was a Tory slogan under which Stanley Baldwin fought for re-election. Posters showed the 'wise and honest' face of the Prime Minister, who, inevitably, was smoking a pipe, and the further words: 'Stanley Baldwin, The Man You Can Trust.' He was even shown as a sea-captain, wearing a sou-wester, accompanied by the slogan **Trust Baldwin, He Will Steer You To Safety**. Conservative Central Office had thought that the General Strike of not so long before (1926) called for this reassuring approach but, with growing unemployment and the depression on the way, the slogan proved a loser. The party chairman, J.C.C. Davidson, who had accepted the idea from Benson's agency, took the blame for the Tories' defeat at the hands of Ramsay MacDonald and the Labour Party. The phrase came into use in the 1890s when railway companies maintained that 'the Safety of the Passenger is our first Concern'. In 1916, the London General Bus Company formed a London Safety First Council. The 1922 general election saw the phrase in use as a political slogan for the Conservatives. In 1934 the National Safety First Association was formed, concerned with road and industrial safety.

1945   Send Him Back To Finish The Job   Used by Winston
Churchill seeking to return as Conservative Prime Minister
after his leadership of an all-party War Cabinet. The slogan
backfired when it was seen to be supported by those who
had tried to keep Churchill out of power in 1940. A Labour
victory brought in Clement Attlee as Prime Minister.

**1950   Your Future Is In Your Hands/A Vote For The Liberals
Is A Vote Wasted/Make Britain Great Again**   led to defeat
by a yet smaller margin. The Tories were returned under
Churchill the following year.

**1959   Life's Better With The Conservatives – Don't Let
Labour Ruin It**   A Tory slogan which helped bring them a
further period of office after an election in which many
broadcasting and advertising techniques were applied to
UK politics for the first time. There was much to justify the
claim: material conditions had improved for most people;
the balance of payments surplus, gold and dollar reserves
were at a high level; wages were up; and taxation had gone
down. The slogan emerged from consultations between
Central Office and the Colman, Prentis & Varley agency. In
his book *Influencing Voters*, Richard Rose says he knew of
four people who claimed to have originated the slogan.
Ronald Simms was the PR chief at Central Office from 1957 to
1967. He is said to have come up with 'Life Is Good With The
Conservatives, Don't Let The Socialists Spoil It'. Lord Hailsham wanted 'better' instead of 'good' and CPV changed
'spoil' to 'ruin'. On the other hand, Maurice Smelt writes:
'The slogan was so successful that many people have claimed
it (that always happens): but it was just a perfectly routine
thing I did one afternoon in 1959, as the copywriter on the
Conservative account at CPV. The brief from Oliver Poole
was to say something like "You've Never Had It So Good"'
but with less cynicism and more bite. The first five words
were the paraphrase: and the whole ten told what I still think
was a truth for its time. It's the slogan I am proudest of.'

As is shown elsewhere, the phrase 'You Never Had It So
Good' was used by the Democrats in the 1952 US presidential
election. Given the way Harold Macmillan's 'You've Never
Had It So Good' came to dog him, it would be surprising if it
had been used in any official campaign. The phrase was

rejected by the Conservatives' publicity group, partly because it 'violated a basic advertising axiom that statements should be positive, not negative', but it hovered about unofficially, and there was an official poster which came very close with **You're Having It Good, Have It Better**.

1964 **Let's Go With Labour, And We'll Get Things Done** At this election, the Labour Party overcame its earlier inhibitions about bringing in help from the advertising world, as the Conservatives had done for many years. As early as January 1963, Labour's advertising group agreed to use a thumb's-up sign derived from Norman Vaughan, compère of the ITV show *Sunday Night at the London Palladium*. (They shrank, however, from incorporating his catchphrases 'swinging' and 'dodgy' in the slogan 'Tories Dodgy — Labour Swinging' for fear that not all the electorate would know what they were on about.) Anthony Howard and Richard West say in *The Making of the Prime Minister* that 'everybody agreed that the word "Go" was necessary to the slogan. It implied dynamism and action; it was short and pithy.' Suggestions included 'Labour's Got Go', 'Labour Goes Ahead', 'All Systems Go', 'Labour For Go', and 'Labour's On The Go'. Of this last one, Harold Wilson said that it sounded like 'Labour On The Po' and Percy Clark from Labour Party HQ said that it might sound as if the party had diarrhoea. The group finally hit on its successful slogan and 'Let's Go With Labour' was used for the eighteen months prior to the election. David Kingsley, one of the advertising people involved, says the phrase was coined by Ros Allen, Labour won by a narrow margin.

1966　**You Know Labour Government Works**　After almost four years in power, the Labour Government went to the country in an effort to increase its majority and used a slogan intended to reflect its credibility (it had previously been out of power for thirteen years). David Kingsley says that the slogan was 'largely my own creation but it grew out of team-work with Dennis Lyons and Peter Lovell-Davis'. A version of its creation is that Lovell-Davis suggested 'Labour Government Works' and Kingsley added the 'You Know'.

1970　**Yesterday's Men**　David Kingsley says that this phrase 'came from the three of us in the team and we never could untangle precisely who created it' — perhaps as well, as it had to be dropped for reasons of taste during the campaign. A colour poster showing crudely coloured models of Conservative politicians (Edward Heath, Iain Macleod, Lord Hailsham and others) and the additional line 'They failed before' was felt to 'degrade' politics. Labour lost the election to 'Yesterday's Men' but the phrase continued to cause trouble. In 1971 it was used as the title of a BBC TV programme about the defeated Labour leaders and how they were faring in Opposition. This soured relations between the BBC and the Labour Party for a long time afterwards.

1974　**Britain Will *Win* With Labour**　Used from August onwards in the second election of that year, which secured

Labour's majority for a further four and a half years.

1979 **Labour Is The Answer** Labour lost to the Conservatives under Margaret Thatcher. (A graffito added: 'If Labour is the answer, it's a bloody silly question'.) The Conservative slogan – **Labour Isn't Working** – **Britain's Better Off With The Conservatives** – first appeared in 1978 on posters showing a long queue outside an employment office. Created by Saatchi & Saatchi, it was later widely used in the campaign that took Margaret Thatcher to Downing Street. When unemployment continued to rise under the Conservatives the poster was recalled with irony. ('Put A Woman On Top For A Change' was a semi-official slogan, coined by Young Conservatives in 1976.)

LIKE MOTHER USED
TO MAKE

Drinka Pinta Milka Day   UK, from 1958. The target was to get everyone drinking one pint of milk a day and the slogan was a piece of 'bath-tub inspiration' that came from the client, namely Bertrand Whitehead, Executive Officer of the National Milk Publicity Council of England and Wales. Francis Ogilvy, Chairman of Mather & Crowther, apparently insisted on it being used over the protests of the creative department, which wanted it strangled at birth. It was the sort of coinage to drive teachers and pedants to apoplexy, but the 'pinta' achieved its own entry in *Chambers Twentieth Century Dictionary*.

Drink More Milk   UK, quoted 1928. A later campaign from the Milk Marketing Board drew a response from the British Medical Association in January 1938 — an ad headed 'Is *All* Milk Safe To Drink?' (suggesting that milk should be tested for tuberculosis). The BMA had to modify this 'knocking copy' to 'Drink Safe Milk'.

Full Of Natural Goodness   UK, current 1980.

If It's Borden's, It's *Got* To Be Good   US, current 1940s. Used on dairy products from the Borden company and featuring 'Elsie the Cow'.

Milk From Contented Cows   US, from 1906. Elbridge A. Stuart was the man who gave rise to Carnation evaporated milk in 1899. Seven years later he went to Chicago to lay on an advertising campaign with the Mahin agency. John Lee Mahin and Stuart, having decided on the main lines of the campaign, called in a new young copywriter called Helen Mar.

'Mr Stuart gave me a description of the conditions under which Carnation was produced,' she recalled many years later. 'In his own sincere and quiet way he spoke of the ever-verdant pastures of Washington and Oregon, where grazed the carefully kept Holstein herds that supplied the raw milk. He described in a manner worthy of Burton Holmes the picturesque background of these pastures from which danced and dashed the pure, sparkling waters to quench the thirst of the herds and render more tender the juicy grasses they fed on. He spoke of the shade of luxuriant trees under which the herds might rest. Remembering my lectures in medical college and recalling that milk produced in mental and physical ease is more readily digested − I involuntarily exclaimed: "Ah! The milk of contented cows!" Mr Mahin's pencil tapped on the table top and he and Mr Stuart spoke almost together: "That's our slogan."'

And so it has remained − or almost. The words on the can have usually read:'*From* Contented Cows'.

Watch Out There's A Humphrey About   UK, current 1974. The Humphreys were a mythical race supposed to steal milk when nobody was looking. They were not seen (in TV ads) − only the red-striped straws through which they sipped.

GOLDEN MOTTOES IN IN THE MOUTH*

If a slogan promotes a cause, then mottoes and war-cries can on occasion fulfil the same purpose. The word slogan or 'slug-horn' derives from the Gaelic *sluagh-ghairm*, meaning 'host-cry' or 'army-shout'. The Scottish Home family's famous cry **A Home, A Home, A Home!** not only identified them but spurred the soldiers on to action, despite the legend that on hearing it at the Battle of Flodden Field in 1513 they turned tail and headed for home.

As for the Medicis in Florence, taking their cue from the family arms, their supporters would cry: **Palle, Palle** (which translated means 'Balls, Balls!').

Most mottoes are less aggressive than slogans. Sometimes they are indistinguishable — as with the motto of the Nation Life Assurance company which collapsed in 1974: **Safe And Sure**. From the large number available, here is a small sample of mottoes which have the force of slogans or which just go to show how difficult it is to categorize phrases of this type:

All For One, And One For All ('Tous pour un, un pour tous')   The motto of the fictional Three Musketeers in the novel by Alexandre Dumas.

Be Prepared   The motto of the Boy Scout movement, based on the initials of its founder Sir Robert Baden-Powell. (Also used as an advertising slogan by Pears' Soap.)

Courtesy And Care   The Automobile Association (UK). Devised by Viscount Brentford, chairman, 1910-22. Included in its armorial bearings.

*Herman Melville

The Difficult We Do Immediately, The Impossible Takes A Little Longer *Bartlett's Familiar Quotations* attributes this motto, now widespread, to the US Army Service Forces and traces it back to Charles Alexandre De Calonne (1734-1802): 'Madame, si c'est possible, c'est fait; impossible? cela se fera.'

Every Day And In Every Way I Am Getting Better And Better (though sometimes found as **Every Day In Every Way . . .** or **Day By Day In Every Way** The French psychologist Émile Coué was the originator of a system of 'Self-Mastery Through Conscious Auto-suggestion' which had a brief vogue in the 1920s. His patients had to repeat this phrase over and over and it became a popular catchphrase of the time, though physical improvement did not noticeably follow. Couéism died with its inventor in 1926. (It gave rise to this joke: a woman became pregnant and went to Coué to ask how she could ensure that her child grew up with good manners. She was told to say many times every day: 'My Child Will Be Polite And Good-Mannered', or words to that effect. Nine months passed and no child was born. Years went by and still no child appeared. Eventually, the lady, now quite old, died and a post-mortem was held. As the body was opened, there stood two tiny old men with long white hair and beards, saying to each other: 'Après vous, m'sieur'; 'Non, non, après vous.')

Fidelity, Bravery, Integrity The US Federal Bureau of Investigation, based on its initials FBI.

How To Win Friends And Influence People More than the title of a book. Dale Carnegie's courses incorporating the principle had been aimed at business people for a quarter of a century when, in 1936, an ad campaign launched Carnegie's book on self-improvement. As a result, a million copies were sold between December 1936 and November 1939.

The Mounties Always Get Their Man Unofficial motto of the Royal Canadian Mounted Police. John J. Healy, editor of the Fort Benton Montana, *Record*, wrote on 13 April 1877 that the Mounties: 'Fetch their man every time.' The official motto since 1873 has been **Maintain The Right/Maintiens Le Droit**.

My Word Is My Bond Bargains are made 'on the nod' at the London Stock Exchange, with no written pledges given or documents exchanged. Hence the motto.

Nation Shall Speak Peace Unto Nation The British Broadcasting Corporation's motto was suggested by Dr Montague Rendall, one of the first five governors, when the coat of arms was chosen in 1927. It echoes a passage in Micah 4:3 'Nation shall not lift up a sword against nation'. In 1932, however, it was decided that the BBC's mission was not to broadcast to other nations but to provide a service for home consumption — and for the Empire. **Quaecunque** ('whatsoever') was introduced as an alternative reflecting the Latin inscription, also composed by Dr Rendall, in the entrance hall of Broadcasting House, London, and based on Philippians 4:8: 'Whatsoever things are beautiful and honest and of good report'. In 1948 'Nation Shall Speak Peace Unto Nation' came back into use as the Corporation's main motto — appropriately, after the BBC's notable role promoting international understanding during the Second World War.

No Destitute Child Ever Refused Admission Dr Barnardo's Homes; UK, from c1872. When a child died after being turned away for lack of room, this motto was inscribed over the door of one of these homes for deprived children. Later came **The Ever-Open Door**.

Peace Is Our Profession US Strategic Air Command.

Small Is Beautiful Professor E.J. Schumacher's prescription for economics on a human scale (used as the title of his 1973 book) does not promote a product or a cause within a specific organisation or framework. Therefore it is a maxim or guiding principle, although one could imagine it being used as a motto or slogan.

We Never Sleep Pinkerton's national detective agency which opened its first office in Chicago, 1850.

Who Dares, Wins   UK Special Air Service regiment (SAS).
(After they had shot their way into the Iranian Embassy in
London in May 1980 and ended the siege there, wags sug-
gested that the motto should be: 'Who dares use it, wins.')

MONEY, MONEY, MONEY

Access Takes The Waiting Out Of Wanting Access credit card; UK, c1973. Withdrawn after protests about the ethics of the pitch and replaced by **Makes Sensible Buying Simple**. More recently: **Access − Your Flexible Friend** (UK, current 1981).

At The Sign Of The Black Horse Lloyd's Bank; UK, current 1980. This slogan capitalized upon the bank's black horse symbol, which dates back to 1666.

Before You Invest − Investigate The National Better Business Bureau Inc.; US, current 1941. Suggested by S.P. Halle, President of Halle Brothers, while a member of the Cleveland Better Business Bureau. Designed to warn prospective investors.

Come And Talk To The Listening Bank Midland Bank; UK, from 1980. A slogan that turned sour when a twenty-year-old student was *arrested* when she went to see her manager about her overdraft.

Don't Leave Home Without It American Express credit card; US, current 1981. In the UK in the late 1970s. **That'll Do Nicely, Sir!**, a fawning line from an Amex TV ad which became a catchphrase.

For God's Sake Care, Give Us A Pound Created by the KMP Partnership in 1968 for the Salvation Army. David Kingsley says: 'This was a product of a team led by myself. The truth is, I put up "For God's Sake, Give Us A Pound" to the then General of the Salvation Army and he and I revised it to "For God's Sake Care . . ." for obvious reasons.'

Get The Abbey Habit Abbey National Building Society; UK, current late 1970s.

His Hands Are Insured For Thousands, But He Suffers From Athlete's Foot/He's A Big Shot In Steel, But He's A Dental Cripple All The Same insurance company (name unknown); US, current c1934.

The Man From The Pru Prudential Assurance Co. Ltd; UK, current from late 1940s. The firm was founded in 1848 and the phrase evolved from what people called the person who collected their life-insurance premiums. It had become a music-hall joke by the end of the century but there was no serious use of it as a slogan by the company until after the Second World War, when it appeared in ads as **Ask The Man From The Pru**.

Merrill Lynch Is Bullish On America Merrill Lynch bank; US, current 1972. Also **A Breed Apart** (current 1980) — though not quite as apart as all that: the phrase has also been used by Triumph motorcycles in the UK.

The Prudential Has The Strength Of Gibraltar Prudential Insurance Co. of America; US, from 1896. Mortimer Remington of JWT was commuting to work in New York when, crossing the New Jersey meadows, he passed Snake Rock. This made him think of Gibraltar in answer to the Prudential President's demand for some 'symbol of lasting, enduring strength'.

We're With The Woolwich Woolwich Equitable Building Society; UK, current late 1970s. In response to the question 'Are You With The Woolwich?' in TV ads. From the accompanying jingle came the phrase 'The Safe Place, With The Nice Face', and the nice face had a peculiarly ingratiating way of saying 'Good Morning'.

PARDON MY BOAST

The danger in all sloganeering is that people will remember your slogan but not the cause or product that it promotes. Nowhere is this danger greater than in the field of 'corporate apologias' — institutional advertising where, as Daniel Boorstin says in *The Image*, we are made to think of the Du Pont Corporation not as 'Merchants of Death' but as providing **Better Things For Better Living, Through Chemistry**.

In 1955, Ronald Reagan became host of the popular programme *General Electric Theater*. Each edition ended with his intoning the line: **At General Electric Progress Is Our Most Important Product**. At least, that corporate tag was closely linked to the name of the company.

Here are twenty more phrases to be matched to twenty companies. They seem, for the most part, interchangeable. Link them up and compare your answers with the correct ones. (In Britain, corporate goo is less prevalent, so only the first five slogans may be known to most readers.)

---

1 **Simply Years Ahead**

2 **The Pathfinders**

3 **Yours Faithfully**

4 **Home Of Good Health**

5 **Getting Bigger By Being Better**

6 **Today Something We Do Will Touch Your Life**

7 **A Powerful Part Of Your Life**

---

8   Getting People Together

9   We Make Things That Bring People Closer

10   Computers Help People Help People

11   Ideas To Build On

12   Making Machines Do More, So Men Can Do More

13   We're Working To Keep Your Trust

14   A Concern For The Future

15   Think What We Can Do For You

16   We Build Your Kind Of Truck

17   We Guarantee Tomorrow Today

18   Always The Leader

19   Take Stock In America

20   A Household Name, At Work

a	Union Carbide	k	Scott Paper
b	Boeing	l	Wander Foods
c	Texaco	m	Westinghouse
d	Johns-Manville	n	IBM
e	PPG Industries	o	Philips
f	International Harvester	p	New York Life
g	Mack Trucks	q	Amoco
h	Trust Houses Forte	r	Bank of America
i	Western Electric	s	Sperry Rand
j	US Savings Bonds	t	ICI

ANSWERS

1:o	5:q	9:i	13:c	17:p
2:t	6:a	10:n	14:e	18:g
3:h	7:m	11:d	15:r	19:j
4:l	8:b	12:s	16:f	20:k

NOW IS THE TIME FOR ALL GOOD MEN . . .

Just in case there is anybody under the impression that **Now Is The Time For All Good Men To Come To The Aid Of The Party** has anything to do with communism, let it be said that it is as much a slogan as **The Quick Brown Fox Jumps Over The Lazy Dog**. They are both typewriter exercises. Charles E. Weller, a court reporter, originated 'Now Is The . . .' in Milwaukee in 1867 to test the efficiency of the first practical typewriter, which his friend Christopher L. Scholes had made. Unfortunately, he did not do a very good job because the phrase only contains eighteen letters of the alphabet, whereas 'The Quick Brown Fox . . .' has all twenty-six. The latter was once thought to be the shortest sentence in English containing all the letters of the alphabet but it was superseded by 'Pack My Box With Five Dozen Liquor Jugs' (which has three fewer letters overall).

Workers Of The World, Unite!   The current slogan of Industrial Workers of the World is taken from the *Communist Manifesto* (1848) of Marx and Engels: 'Let the ruling classes tremble at a communist revolution. The proletarians have nothing to lose but their chains. They have a world to win. Working men of all lands, unite!'

All Power To The Soviets   Petrograd workers, November 1917.

Toilers in Agriculture! Strengthen The Fodder Basis Of Animal Husbandry! Raise The Production And Sale To The State Of Meat, Milk, Eggs, Wool And Other Products!   One of seventy-five May Day slogans prepared by the Soviet Communist Party's Central Committee in 1980.

PEACE FOR OUR TIME

In the run-up to the Second World War, the hollowest slogan of all was Neville Chamberlain's phrase **Peace For Our Time**. On 30 September 1938 he returned from signing the Munich agreement with Hitler. He hoped that his concessions (including the virtual dismemberment of Czechoslovakia) would pave the way for peace. If Hitler honoured the agreement, well and good. If he did not, then at least the world would be able to see that he was clearly guilty. And, to be fair to Chamberlain, such was the desire for peace in Europe that, whatever personal misgivings he may have had (and there is evidence that he experienced great discomfort at the role he had to play), he was swept along with the tide. That night he spoke from a window at 10 Downing Street, 'not of design but for the purpose of dispersing the huge multitude below' (according to his biographer, Keith Feiling). He said: 'My good friends. This is the second time in our history that there has come back from Germany to Downing Street peace with honour. I believe it is peace for our time. Go home and get a nice quiet sleep.'

Two days before, however, when someone had suggested the Disraeli phrase **Peace With Honour**, Chamberlain had impatiently rejected it, as Feiling records. A week later, Chamberlain was asking the House of Commons not to read too much into words 'used in a moment of some emotion, after a long and exhausting day, after I had driven through miles of excited, enthusiastic, cheering people'.

Disraeli had been talking about the Berlin Treaty of 1878 which forced the Russians to make a number of concessions but created rather more problems than it solved. In an impromptu speech from the steps of his railway carriage at Dover on 16 July, he said: 'Gentlemen, we bring you peace; and I think I may say, peace with honour.' Later that day in London he repeated the claim: 'Lord Salisbury and myself have brought you back peace — but a peace, I hope, with honour, which may satisfy our sovereign and tend to the welfare of the country.'

Chamberlain's phrase is often misquoted as 'Peace *in* our time', as by Noel Coward in the title of a play set at the time of the Munich agreement. Perhaps he, and others, were influenced by the phrase from the *Book of Common Prayer:* 'Give Peace in our time, O Lord.'

THE PURSUIT OF HAPPINESS

Taking their cue from the title of a 1962 Peanuts book by Charles M. Schulz, *Happiness is a Warm Puppy*, sloganeers went nuts on the 'Happiness is . . .' theme from the mid-1960s onwards, gradually watering down the original:

Happiness Is Egg-Shaped   (UK, selling eggs)

Happiness Is A Quick-Starting Car   (US, Esso)

Happiness Is A Cigar Called Hamlet   (UK)

Happiness Is Being Elected Team Captain – And Getting A Bulova Watch   (US)

Happiness Is A $49 Table   (US, Brancusi Furniture)

Happiness Is Giving Dad A Terry Shave Coat For Christmas   (US, Cone Sporterry)

Happiness Is The Sands   (US, Las Vegas hotel)

Happiness Is A Bathroom By Marion Wieder   (US, decorator)

Happiness Can Be The Color Of Her Hair   (US, Miss Clairol)

Happiness Is Being Single   (bumper sticker, seen in NYC, 1981)

Happiness Is Slough In My Rear-View Mirror   (car sticker, seen in London, 1981)

No wonder Lennon & McCartney wrote a song called 'Happiness is a Warm Gun'.

READ ALL ABOUT IT

When newspapers and magazines come to promote themselves we are generally not impressed. Even the brightest
and sanest publications can be made to sound smug and
off-putting. There is something about the ethos of newspapers and magazines which is incompatible with their
attempts at sloganeering. How can they appear to be sensible
and reasonable organs when they have to pitch for custom
like soap powders?

All Human Life Is There *News of the World*; UK, from
c1958-9. The only reference to this phrase in the *Oxford
Dictionary of Quotations* appears under Henry James. Even if
we had never read his 'Madonna of the Future' (1879) – and
we had not – we were told that it contained the line: 'Cats
and monkeys, monkeys and cats – all human life is there.'
What was the connection, if any, with the steamy British
Sunday newspaper?

   Maurice Smelt takes up the story: '"All Human Life Is
There" was my idea, but I don't, of course, pretend that they
were my words. I simply lifted them from the *Oxford Dictionary of Quotations*. I didn't bother to tell the client that they
were from Henry James, suspecting that, after the
Henry–James–Who–He? stage, he would come up with
tiresome arguments about being too high-hat for his read-
ership. I did check whether we were clear on copyright,
which we were by a year or two. The agency I was then
working for was Colman, Prentis & Varley. I do recall its use
as baseline in a tiny little campaign trailing a series that
earned the *News of the World* a much-publicized but tooth-
less rebuke from the Press Council. The headline of that
campaign was: '"I've Been A Naughty Girl" Says Diana
Dors". The meiosis worked, as the *News of the World* knew it
would. They ran an extra million copies of the first issue of
the series.'

All The News That's Fit To Print   *New York Times*; US, from 1896. This slogan was devised by Adolph S. Ochs when he bought the *New York Times* and it has been published in every edition since — at first on the editorial page, on 25 October 1896, and from the following February on the front page. It became the paper's war-cry in the 1890s battle against formidable competition from the *World, Herald,* and *Journal.* It has been parodied by Howard Dietz as 'All The News That Fits We Print' and at worst sounds like a slogan for the suppression of news. However, no paper prints everything.

Forward With The People   *Daily Mirror*; UK, from c1935 until 1959. This slogan appeared on the paper's mast-head, though some who thought the paper had a way of anticipating the inevitable said the slogan ought to have been 'Sideways With The People'.

Never Underestimate The Power Of A Woman   *Ladies' Home Journal*; US, from c1941. Gordon Page of N.W. Ayer recalled: 'It came off the back burner of a creative range where ideas simmer while the front burners are preoccupied with meeting closing dates . . . it was just a more direct way of stating the case for the leading woman's magazine of the day. But always believing that you can do things with a twinkle that you can't do with a straight face, it was trotted to Leo Lionni . . . it's largely *his* fault that you can't say "never underestimate the power of *anything*," today, without echoing the line.' (Watkins). Even in 1981, the following ad was appearing in the *New York Times:* 'Ladies' Home Journalism — Never Underestimate Its Power'.

Sunday Isn't Sunday Without The Sunday Times   *Sunday Times*; UK, from 1968. Peter Phillips recalls: 'In 1968 I asked the whole creative department at Thomson Group Marketing to come up with a slogan for the *Sunday Times* and the person who presented me with this deathless slogan was Frank Page, later motoring correspondent of *The Observer*. I was not aware that the *Empire News* had already used it (as **Sunday Isn't Sunday Without The Empire News**) — nor were the countless people who have claimed authorship since then.' (*Campaign*, 17 April 1981)

Top People...

take THE TIMES

Top People Take The Times   *The Times*; UK, from 1957. In
the mid-1950s, the London *Times* was shedding circulation,
the end of post-war newsprint rationing was in sight, and an
era of renewed competition in Fleet Street was about to
begin. In 1954, the paper's agency, the London Press Exchange, commissioned a survey to discover people's atti-
tudes towards 'The Thunderer'. They chiefly found it dull,

but the management of *The Times* was not going to change anything, least of all allow contributors to be identified by name. *The Times* would have to be promoted for what it was. A pilot campaign in provincial newspapers included one ad showing a top hat and a pair of gloves with the slogan **Men Who Make Opinion Read The Times**.

It was not the London Press Exchange but an outsider who finally encapsulated that idea in a more memorable slogan. G.H. Saxon Mills was one of the old school of advertising copywriters and had been copy director at Crawford's. But he was out of a job when he bumped into Stanley Morison of *The Times*. As a favour, Mills was asked to produce a brochure for visitors to the newspaper. When finished, it contained a series of pictures of the sort of people who were supposed to read the paper – a barrister, a trade-union official, and so on. Each was supported by the phrase: 'Top People Take The Times'.

This idea was adopted for the more public promotional campaign and first appeared in poster form during 1957, running into immediate criticism for its snobbery. But sales went up and, however toe-curling it may have been, the slogan got the paper noticed and ran on into the early 1960s.

REMEMBER, REMEMBER . . .

Remember **********! has been a common theme of slogans, particularly enabling wars to begin or continue by keeping alive a cause of anger:

Remember The River Raisin! A war-cry of Kentucky soldiers dating from the War of 1812. In the Raisin River massacre, 700 Kentuckians, badly wounded trying to capture Detroit, were scalped and butchered by Indians who were allies of the British.

Remember The Alamo! The Alamo Mission in San Antonio, Texas, was used as a fort during the rebellion against Mexican rule in 1836. On 6 March, five days after Texas declared her independence, President Antonio López de Santa Anna with more than 3,000 men attacked the Alamo. In it were a hundred or so Texans, including Davy Crockett. After a thirteen-day siege, every Texan had been killed or wounded, and even the wounded were put to death. López was defeated and captured at the Battle of San Jacinto, 21 April 1836, by a Texan army under Commander-in-Chief Sam Houston. Sidney Sherman, a colonel in this army, is credited with devising the battle-cry. **Remember Goliad!** from the same conflict refers to Santa Anna's shooting of 330 Texans who had retreated from Goliad.

Remember The Maine! The US battleship *Maine* exploded and sank in Havana harbour on 15 February 1898, taking 258 American lives with it. The vessel had been sent to protect US residents and their property during the Cuban revolution. The cause of the explosion was never established, but the Spanish-American War started ten weeks later. (Graffito reported shortly after: 'Remember the Maine, To hell with Spain, Don't forget to pull the chain'.)

Remember The Lusitania!   The *Lusitania* was a British liner carrying many American passengers which was sunk off the Irish coast on 7 May 1915 by a German submarine. The sinking helped bring the US into the First World War.

Remember Belgium!   Originally a recruiting slogan referring to the invasion of Belgium by the Germans at the start of the First World War. It eventually emerged with ironic emphasis amid the mud of Ypres, encouraging the rejoinder: 'As if I'm ever likely to forget the bloody place!' (Partridge)

Remember Pearl Harbor! The initial war-slogan and battle-cry of the US after the bombing of Pearl Harbor by the Japanese in December 1941.

Remember The Pueblo!   A bumper sticker with one of the rare battle-cries of the Vietnam War. Coined by Young Americans For Freedom following the capture of the USS *Pueblo* by North Korea in 1968.

THE SHOUT HEARD
ROUND THE WORLD

Coca-Cola bids fair to be the most widely advertised product in the world. It would be hard to find a country unfamiliar with the logo and the simple injunction (in whatever language) to **Drink Coca-Cola**. Dr John Pemberton invented the drink in 1886. By 1890 the company was spending $11,000 a year on advertising. The drink was first sold outside the US in 1899. Coca-Cola today spends $184 million world-wide on advertising.

Much of the emphasis has been on driving away competitors. Among them: Caro-Cola, Fig Cola, Candy Cola, Cold Cola, CayOla, Koca-Nola, Coca, Cola, Coca-Kola, Kora-Nola, Kola Nola, KoKola, Co Kola, Coke Ola, Kos Kola, Toca-Cola, Soda Cola. Hence the continuing necessity to maintain that 'Coke' is 'the real thing'. This idea appeared in 1942 as **The Only Thing Like Coca-Cola Is Coca-Cola Itself. It's The Real Thing** followed in 1970. Pepsi Cola is the only major rival.

Do you remember these other slogans out of the scores that have been used?

Coke Adds Life (from 1976)

Have A Coke And A Smile (current 1980)

I'd Like To Buy The World A Coke (from 1971) The jingle became a hit in its own right when retitled 'I'd Like to Teach the World to Sing'.

It's The Refreshing Thing To Do (current 1937)

The Pause That Refreshes (from 1929)

Things Go Better With Coke (from 1963)

Thirst Knows No Season (from 1922)

Pepsi Cola is now consumed in as many countries as Coca-Cola and has achieved this in a shorter time and, for many

Makes a light lunch refreshing

Your favorite soda fountain, your favorite sandwich, and America's favorite refreshment ... ice-cold Coca-Cola. Quick-as-a-wink you're refreshed and on your way. That's why you hear so many busy people at lunch saying: "and a Coca-Cola." Try it yourself.

Drink

Coca-Cola

Delicious and Refreshing

5¢

THE PAUSE THAT REFRESHES

years, with considerably less expenditure on advertising. Value for money was always aimed at in the product itself:

Come Alive — You're In The Pepsi Generation US, from 1964. This slogan presented certain problems in translation. In German it came out as 'Come alive out of the grave', and in Chinese 'Pepsi brings your ancestors back from the dead'.

Lipsmackin thirst quenchin (ace tastin motivatin good buzzin cool talkin high walkin fast livin ever givin cool fizzin) Pepsi UK, from 1974. From a jingle written by John Webster at Boase Massimi Pollitt.

Twice As Much For A Nickel, Too US, current 1930s. Walter Mack is credited with writing this 'first advertising jingle in history' (it was sung to the tune of 'John Peel'), much used on American radio in the 1930s — indeed, an estimated six million times. After the Second World War, the value-for-money principle went out of the window and the price of Pepsi had to be raised to six and then seven cents. Consequently, the jingle had to be revised to **Twice As Much And Better, Too**. (Louis)

You've Got A Lot To Live, Pepsi's Got A Lot To Give US, current 1960s. James B. Somerall, Pepsi's President at the time of the Vietnam War, claimed that this slogan drew attention to America's 'new national pastime — living, and making every second count.'

Best By Taste Test Royal Crown Cola; US, current 1944.

Drink Tizer, The Appetizer Tizer; UK, current from 1920s.

Freshen-Up With 7-Up 7-Up; US, current 1962. Alternatively, **Bring On The *Real* Thirst-Quencher!** and **The Un-Cola**.

It's In The Public Eye Squirt; US, quoted 1958. Well, it would be, from a product called Squirt.

One Crazy Calorie Tab; US, quoted 1980.

LEGAL, DECENT, HONEST, TRUTHFUL

That 'All advertisments should be legal, decent, honest and truthful' is one of the essences of good advertising, according to the British Code of Advertising Practice. However, if you are feeling a mite punch-drunk from the assertiveness of the slogans in this book, it may come as some balm to be told of ones that backfired because they failed to achieve their end — and left egg all over the face of those who coined them.

America Cannot Stand Pat In the 1960 presidential election, John F. Kennedy quoted **Stand Pat With McKinley** as an example of Republican reaction. So Richard Nixon countered with 'America Cannot Stand Pat' — until it was politely pointed out that he was married to a woman with that name. **America Cannot Stand Still** was rapidly substituted.

Flat Out On Ethyl Well, you see, there was this brand of petrol in the 1920s derived from tetraethyl lead. It is no longer available.

Grieve For Lincoln A Conservative candidate's slogan. He lost.

Once You've Driven One, You're Unlikely To Drive Another Say that again? Mercedes-Benz ad, quoted 1980.

Sounds Better Than it Looks Perhaps it is as well that we do not know the name of the TV set which is advertised all over India thus.

Vote For Any Candidate, But If You Want Well-Being And Hygiene, Vote For Pulvapies The town of Picoaza in Ecuador was treated to this slogan during a local campaign for mayor in 1967. Pulvapies was not the name of a candidate but of a locally produced foot-powder. And, when it came to the ballot, 'vote for Pulvapies' was exactly what the Picoazans did.

You're Never Alone With A Strand   The slogan of a, by now, classic British ad which caught the public imagination and yet failed to achieve its purpose — selling cigarettes. Devised in 1960 by John May of S.H. Benson for the W.H. & H.O. Wills tobacco company, the campaign was to launch a new, cheap filter cigarette called Strand. Wills had rejected the first plan put to them and so, at rather short notice, John May thought up a new concept. This amounted to appealing to the youth market by associating the cigarettes not with sex or social ease but with 'the loneliness and rejection of youth'. 'The young Sinatra was the prototype of the man I had in mind,' says May. 'Loneliness had made him a millionaire. I didn't see why it shouldn't sell us some cigarettes.'

And so a Sinatra-clone was found in the shape of a 28-year-

old actor called Terence Brook, who was also said to bear a resemblance to James Dean. He was shown mooching about lonely locations in raincoat and hat. In no time at all he had his own fan-club. Music from the TV ad, 'The Lonely Man Theme', became a hit in its own right.

But the ads did not work. Viewers revised the slogan in their own minds to mean: 'If you buy Strand, then you'll be alone.' However much the young may have identified with the figure in the ad they did not want to buy him or his aura. Or perhaps it was just not a very good cigarette. Either way, it has not been forgotten.

SOFT SOAP

Body Odour (or **B.O.**)   Lifebuoy soap; US, current from 1933. A notable phrase given to the language by advertising. On US radio in the 1930s they used to sing the jingle:

> Singing in the bathtub, singing for joy,
> Living a life of Lifebuoy —
> Can't help singing, 'cos I know
> That Lifebuoy really stops B.O.

The initials 'B.O.' were sung *basso profundo*, emphasizing the horror of the offence. In the UK, TV ads showed pairs of male or female friends out on a spree, intending to attract partners. When one of the pair was seen to have a problem the other whispered helpfully, 'B.O.'

Good Morning! Have You Used Pears' Soap?   UK, current 1888 (still in use 1928). Thomas J. Barratt (1842-1914) has been dubbed, with good reason, the 'father of modern advertising', in the UK at least. With remorseless energy and unflagging invention he flooded the country with ads for Pears' soap from 1875 onwards. 'Any fool can make soap,' he said. 'It takes a clever man to sell it.' Some of his work also appeared in the US. Early on, Barratt 'decided he must have a catchphrase which would make the whole country say "Pears' Soap". His staff were invited to nominate the commonest phrase in daily use. Inevitably, somebody suggested "Good morning". The result was the notorious "Good Morning! Have You Used Pears' Soap?" which scourged two continents. There were many who never forgave Thomas Barratt for debasing this traditional, friendly greeting. The sensitive shrank from saying "Good morning", knowing that it would only spark off the exasperating counter-phrase in the mind of the person addressed.' (Turner)

Mrs. LANGTRY says—
Since using PEARS' SOAP for the hands and complexion I have discarded all others.

How Do You Spell Soap? Why P-E-A-R-S, Of Course UK, current 1880s, can hardly have been a less trying catchphrase.

Cleanliness Is Next To Godliness Although this phrase appears in one of John Wesley's sermons, it is within quotation marks and without attribution. Thomas J. Barratt could hardly be expected to leave it alone. On a visit to the US in the 1880s, he sought a testimonial from a man of distinction. Shrinking from an approach to President Grant, he ensnared the eminent divine, Henry Ward Beecher. Beecher happily complied with Barratt's request and wrote a short text beginning: 'If cleanliness is next to Godliness . . .' and received no more for his pains than Barratt's 'hearty thanks'.

He Won't Be Happy Till He Gets It   UK, current 1880s (US, current 1888). Coupled with the picture of a baby stretching out of his bath to pick up a cake of Pears' soap. 'Cartoonists freely adapted this poster, converting the baby into the Czar or the Kaiser, and the cake of soap into the disputed territory of the day.' (Turner). There was also a companion picture with the slogan **He's Got It And He's Happy Now**. In early editions of *Scouting for Boys*, Robert Baden-Powell used the original slogan (with acknowledgement to Pears) to refer to the achievement of the scouts' first-class badge.

Lillie Langtry, the noted actress of the period, came near to coining the phrase **Since When I Have Used No Other** when she wrote in a testimonial: 'Since using Pears' Soap I have discarded all others.' The precise wording came from a cartoon parody drawn by Harry Furniss which appeared in *Punch*, 26 April 1884. This showed a grubby tramp penning his own testimonial with the words: 'Two years ago I used your soap since when I have used no other.' Not missing a trick, Pears, with permission from *Punch*, added the firm's name to the cartoon and issued it as one of thousands of handbills distributed in the 1880s and 1890s.

Preparing To Be A Beautiful Lady   UK, from 1932 – when young girls, some with their mothers, were featured using Pears' soap. In 1981, an announcement for the 'Miss Pears Contest' was still employing the phrase: 'We're looking for a radiant little girl who is preparing to be a beautiful lady by using pure transparent Pears' Soap every day.'

Keep That Schoolgirl Complexion   Palmolive soap; US, from 1917. Coined by Charles S. Pearce, a Palmolive executive. Beverley Nichols wrote in *The Star-Spangled Manner* (1928) that in his 'riotous youth' he was comforted through 'numberless orgies' only by the conviction that if he used a certain soap he would retain his schoolboy complexion:
   'It did not matter how much I drank or smoked, how many nameless and exquisite sins I enjoyed – they would all be washed out in the morning by that magic soap . . . I bought it

merely because years ago a bright young American sat down in an office on the other side of the Atlantic and thought of a slogan to sell soap. And he certainly sold it.'

During the Second World War, Palmolive was still plugging the old line in the UK: 'Driving through blitzes won't spoil that schoolgirl complexion'.

99 44/100 Per Cent Pure Ivory Soap; US, from c1882. One of the clumsiest but most enduring slogans of all. Nobody remembers who first coined this bizarre line but it has stuck, along with the claim that **It Floats**. A story has it that the floating character of the soap was not recognised until a dealer asked for another case of 'that soap that floats'. (In 1974, a gangster film with Richard Harris was entitled *99 And 44/100 Per Cent Dead*. For the benefit of non-Americans who would not understand the allusion, the film was tardily retitled *Call Harry Crown*. *Variety* opined crisply that it was 'As clumsy as its title'.)

Nine Out Of Ten Screen Stars Use Lux Toilet Soap For Their Priceless Smooth Skins Lux Toilet Soap; US, from 1927. The campaign ran for twenty years and among the stars who were listed as Lux users were Fay Wray, Mary Astor, Louise Brooks, Myrna Loy, Bebe Daniels, Clara Bow and Joan Crawford.

Pearline Keeps White Things White And Bright Women Bright Pearline soap; US, current 1896.

People Who Like People Like Dial Dial soap; US, quoted 1965. Also **Aren't You Glad *You* Used Dial: Don't You Wish *Everybody* Did?** quoted 1969.

The Skin You Love To Touch Woodbury's Facial Soap; US, from 1910. The records of the Andrew Jergens Company show that 'The Skin You Love To Touch' was originally the title of a booklet about the skin and how to care for it. The *Ladies' Home Journal* for May 1911 carried it first. Carl Naether commented in *Advertising To Women* (1928): 'It is a lure to make women believe that, by using the soap in question, she will be able to cultivate a skin sufficiently beautiful to constitute an infallible safeguard against the waning of male affection. In other words, the promise was that the soap would do more for her than just cleanse her skin.'

Why Does A Woman Look Old Sooner Than A Man? Sunlight soap; UK, from c1890. William Hesketh Lever (the first Lord Leverhulme) recorded in a diary of his tour studying American publicity methods (1888) that he bought this slogan from a Philadelphia soapmaker, Frank Siddal.

You'll Look A Little Lovelier Each Day/With Fabulous Pink Camay Camay soap; UK, current c1960. One of the catchiest phrases from the early days of British commercial TV. The soap boasted **Perfume Worth 9 Guineas An Ounce** and led to a parody about a Labour politician on the BBC TV *That Was The Week That Was* show:

> You'll look a little lovelier each day
> With fabulous Douglas Jay.

You Should See Me On Sunday Knight's Family Health Soap; UK, quoted 1941.

THE EFFECT IS
SHATTERING

Born 1820 − Still Going Strong Johnnie Walker whisky; UK, from 1910. There *was* a John Walker but he was not born in 1820 − that was the year he set up a grocery, wine and spirit business in Kilmarnock. In 1908, Sir Alexander Walker decided to incorporate a portrait of his grandfather in the firm's advertising. Tom Browne, a commercial artist, was commissioned to draw the founder as he might have appeared in 1820. Lord Stevenson, a colleague of Sir Alexander's, scribbled the phrase 'Johnnie Walker, Born 1820 − Still Going Strong' alongside the artist's sketch of a striding, cheerful Regency figure. It has been in use ever since.

The Brandy Of Napoleon Courvoisier brandy; UK, from 1909. Napoleon really did drink it. When the former French Emperor gave himself up to the British in 1815 and was sent into exile on St Helena, a supply of the best cognac from Jarnac, selected by Emmanuel Courvoisier, travelled with him. Originally it had been intended to accompany him on a projected escape to the United States. British officers who escorted Napoleon to St Helena had many opportunities to taste the exile's cognac. In this way, Courvoisier came to be known, in English, as 'The Brandy Of Napoleon'.

Don't Be Vague − Ask For Haig Haig whisky; UK, since c1936. The origin of this slogan is to some extent shrouded in a Scotch mist because many of the John Haig & Co. archives were destroyed during the Second World War. However, the agency thought to be responsible was C.J. Lytle Ltd. An ad survives from 1933 with the wording 'Don't Be Vague, Order Haig', another from 1935 with 'Why Be Vague? Ask for Haig', and it seems that the enduring form arose in about 1936. (In

The Perfect Round—

DON'T BE VAGUE
ORDER

JOHN HAIG & Co LTD
HAIG
GOLD LABEL
LIQUEUR SCOTCH WHISKY

Haig

NO FINER WHISKY GOES INTO ANY BOTTLE

1981, a graffito in a Belfast Protestant slum declared: 'Don't Be Vague — Starve A Taig' — 'taig' being slang for a Catholic.) It has been jocularly suggested that Haig's premium brand, Dimple, which is sold as Pinch in North America, should be promoted with the slogan 'Don't Be Simple, Ask For Dimple'.

Emigrate To Canada Dry (For The Sake Of Your Scotch) Canada Dry tonics and mixers; UK, current 1980. An earlier version of the slogan was used in his act by the American comedian Pat Henning: 'He was a drinkin' man, my fadder. One day he's standin' onna banks of the river, wonderin' what the hell folks can do with all that water, when suddenly he sees a great sign on the other side — DRINK CANADA DRY. [Pause] So he went up there.'

For Men Of Distinction Lord Calvert custom-blended whiskey; US, current 1945. 'For years', the copy ran, 'the most expensive whiskey blended in America, Lord Calvert is intended especially for those who can afford the finest.' Marshall McLuhan wrote in *The Mechanical Bride* (1951): 'Snob appeal might seem to be the most obvious feature of this type of ad, with its submerged syllogism that since all sorts of eminent men drink this whiskey they are eminent because they drink it. Or only this kind of whiskey is suited to the palate of distinguished men, therefore a taste for it confers, or at least displays an affinity for, distinction in those who have not yet achieved greatness.'

It Never Varies Dewar scotch whisky; UK, from 1922.

J & B Rare Can Be Found J & B Rare Whisky; UK, current 1980. Accompanying pictures of J & B bottles secreted in mazes, tulip fields, etc.

I Thought St Tropez Was A Spanish Monk Until I Discovered Smirnoff Smirnoff vodka; UK, from c1973. The common advertising technique of the 'before' and 'after' type was given memorable form in the series of Smirnoff slogans accompanying escapist visuals from 1970 to 1975. The variations included:

It Was The 8.29 Every Morning . . .
Accountancy Was My Life . . .
I Never Saw Further Than The Boy Next Door . . .
I Was The Mainstay Of The Public Library . . .
I'd Set My Sights On A Day Trip To Calais . . .
I Thought The Kama Sutra Was An Indian Restaurant . . .
Until I Discovered Smirnoff.

The original copywriter at Young & Rubicam was John Bacon and the art director David Tree. Tree recalled how the pair of them struggled for weeks to get the right idea. One day, after a fruitless session, he was leaving for lunch when he happened to glance at a magazine pin-up adorning the wall of the office he shared with Bacon. 'If we really get stuck,' he said, 'we can always say, "I was a boring housewife in Southgate until . . ."' (Southgate was where he was living at the time.) (Kleinman)

There were objections to the 'leg-opener', inhibition-banishing promise implicit in all this. In 1975 the Advertising Standards Authority tightened up its rules on alcohol ads, laying down that 'advertisments should neither claim nor suggest that any drink can contribute towards sexual success' and that they 'should not contain any encouragement . . . to over-indulgence'. This last requirement ruled out the tag-line **The Effect Is Shattering** because it might be taken as an inducement to 'get smashed'.

The Right One Martini; UK, from 1970. In a conscious attempt to switch Martini from being a 'woman's drink' to a 'his and hers' drink, McCann-Erickson created a romantic, high-life world full of young, beautiful people engaged in skiing, speedboating, even ballooning. Not the least ingredient was the song composed by Chris Gunning:

> Try a taste of Martini
> The most beautiful drink in the world,
> It's the bright one, the right one.
> There's much more to the world than you guess,
> And you taste it the day you say yes
> To the bright taste, the right taste
> Of Martini . . .

Barry Day 'admits responsibility' for the phrase 'The Right One'. When it comes to **Any Time, Any Place, Anywhere**, Day agrees that there is more than a hint of Bogart in the line: 'As a Bogart fan of some standing, with my union dues all paid up, I think I would have known if I had lifted it from one of his utterances, but I honestly can't place it.' Also, **Martini is . . .**

Vladivar From Warrington. The Greatest Wodka In The

'It was the 8.29 every morning until I discovered Smirnoff.'

The effect is shattering

SMIRNOFF VODKA

Vorld Vladivar vodka; UK, from 1972. The unlikely positioning of Greenall-Whitley's distillery in Warrington, far from Russia or Poland, gave rise to a distinctive and enjoyable series of campaigns. The original usage was coined by Len Weinreich at the Kirkwood Company.

What Is The Secret Of Schhh? Schweppes tonic waters and mixers; UK, from c1963. A phrase which caught on in a really big way. It was thought up, jointly, by Royston Taylor, copywriter, and Frank Devlin, art director, at Mather & Crowther. Taylor recalls: 'Schweppes had largely been handling their own advertising, featuring Benny Hill on TV and Stephen Potter's whimsical copy in the press. The problem was, "What can we say instead of **Schweppervescence Lasts The Whole Drink Through**"? Our idea grew very much out of the spy fever that was raging at the time. The James Bond films were just beginning, *Danger Man* was on TV (indeed, we wanted Patrick Magoohan to appear in our ads, at one stage). I came up with the idea of **Tonic Water By You-Know-Who . . .** — the sort of thing you might say confidentially out of the side of your mouth in a bar. Frank Devlin suggested "The Secret of Schhh . . ." which accorded with the old copywriter's dream of not showing or even naming the product if it could possibly be avoided. We compromised, just using the first three letters of the brand name and half a bottle. The comedians soon picked it up. It "made" William Franklyn, who used to appear in various comic spy situations. I suppose you could say it took Schweppes advertising out of *Punch*-style whimsy and into another area of popular whimsy — substituting one form of obscurity for another!'

You Can Take A White Horse Anywhere White Horse whisky; UK, from 1969. The campaign which featured a white horse (but which failed to communicate any product benefit to the consumer) was masterminded in its original form by Len Heath at the KMP partnership.

STICKER SNICKER

Mid-way between the official slogan and the unofficial graffito, there is the ever-growing craze for promotional phrases emblazoned on T-shirts, lapel badges, bumper stickers and hand-drawn placards. Whereas graffiti are anonymous, this form of sloganeering suggests a measure of identification with the cause by the wearer or bearer. 'I am what I wear,' he says. He is not afraid to be counted. The slogan may not be his own work — indeed, a lapel button has probably been commercially produced — but it has a jokey, amateurish, instant appeal, which may not be true of official slogans. From the many, just a handful of the ones which do not seek to provoke a smile alone but also promote a point of view:

Lousy But Loyal London East End slogan at George V's Jubilee, 1935.

Eleanor Start Packing, The Wilkies Are Coming US, 1940.

Madly For Adlai Stevenson button, US, 1952.

We Don't Like Anyone Very Much Placard during 1964 US election.

Hitler Is Alive — In The White House button, US, 1968

The Family That Prays Together Stays Together poster/bumper sticker; US, from 1947.

My God Is Not Dead . . . Sorry 'Bout Yours Bumper sticker, US, current 1969.

Don't Blame Me, I'm From Massachussetts Comment on snarled peace negotiations with Hanoi, December 1972. The state had voted for George McGovern in the November election. He had promised immediate peace.

Betty Ford's Husband For President Best-selling button of the 1976 campaign, US.

Peanut Butter Is Love — Spread Some Around Today   Placard at 1976 Democratic Convention, US.

Chile Out   Wall slogan, London, c1978. (Out of what? one might ask.) Neatly mocked by another on a Martello tower near Dublin which said 'Napoleon Out'.

A Reactor Is A Safer Place Than Ted Kennedy's Car   Window sticker, US, 1979.

More Lives Were Lost At Chappaquiddick Than At Harrisburg   Ditto.

A Blonde In Every Pond
Reagan For President, Kennedy For Chauffeur
Re-Elect Carter, Free Joan Kennedy
Nobody For President   Buttons, US, 1980.

There Is Nothing Worth Dying For   Anti-draft registration placard, US, 1980.

Piss On Disco   T-shirt, UK, 1980.

If You Can Read This — Thank A Teacher   Bumper sticker, US, 1981

Mrs Thatcher Helps Small Businesses (Get Smaller All The Time)   Window-sticker, UK, 1981.

The Sun Never Sets On The British Empire Because God Doesn't Trust The Brits In The Dark   Irish Republican placard during New York visit of Prince Charles, June 1981.

Don't Do It, Di!   Feminist badge prior to royal wedding, UK, 1981.

STOP ME AND
BUY ONE

Sweets, candies, cookies or ice cream . . . whatever it takes to bridge that gap:

And All Because The Lady Loves Milk Tray   Cadbury's Milk Tray chocolates; UK, from 1968. The pay-off line to action ads showing feats of daring of a James Bond kind and leading up to the presentation of a box of the chocolates to a suitably alluring female.

Are You A Cadbury's Fruit And Nut Case? (or 'Everyone's A . . .')   Cadbury's Fruit and Nut chocolate; UK, current 1964.

Award Yourself The CDM   Cadbury's Dairy Milk chocolate; UK, from 1967-77. Devised by Dennis Auton at Young & Rubicam, this campaign invited the public, through TV, posters and press ads, to nominate worthy recipients of an award. These people then had their citations published in a style parodying the royal honours lists. Recipients included 'Miss S. Pollak, Eton Villas, London NW3, "for walking in her mini-skirt within whistling distance of the building site" (nominated by Mr T. Taylor)' and Arkle, the Grand National Steeplechase winner.

Bridge That Gap With Cadbury's Snack   Cadbury's Snack; UK, current 1967.

Chocolates With The Less Fattening Centres   Maltesers; UK, current 1965.

Desperation, Pacification, Expectation, Acclamation, Realization   Fry's chocolate; UK, current after the First World War. Ads featured the faces of the famous 'five boys' anticipating a bite.

POLO

Oh!

POLO

The Mint with the Hole

Made by Rowntrees

WAFER BISCUITS 1

STOP ME
AND
BUY ONE

20 T. WALL & SONS LTD
THE FRIARY ACTON.

WALL'S ICE CREAM

PURE DAIRY PRODUCTS
FRESH FRUIT JUICES
SOUND FOOD VALUE

LARGE BRICKS 1/6
SMALL BRICKS 9D
TUBS 4D
CHOC BARS 3D
BRICKETTES 2D
SNOFRUTES 1D

Have a break... have a Kit Kat

Don't Forget The Fruit Gums, Mum Rowntree's Fruit Gums; UK, from 1958 to 1961. Coined by copywriter Roger Musgrave at S.T. Garland Advertising Services. Market research showed that most fruit gums were bought by women but eaten by children. One Friday evening, Kenneth Gill, who was in charge of the campaign, gave Musgrave this information. Over the following weekend Musgrave conceived these words as part of a jingle which was used, word for word, as written. Later on, the phrase fell foul of advertising watchdogs, who were keen to save parents from nagging. So 'mum' was amended to 'chum'.

Double Your Pleasure, Double Your Fun Wrigley's Doublemint chewing gum; US, from 1959.

Full Of Eastern Promise Fry's Turkish Delight; UK, current late 1950s. One of the longest-running British TV ads, appealing to escapist fantasies. One of the first showed a male slave unrolling a carpet containing a woman captive before an eastern potentate. The phrase was still in use on wrappers in 1981.

Have A Break, Have A Kit-Kat Rowntree's Kit-Kat; UK, from c1955.

Jungle Fresh Golden Wonder salted peanuts; UK, current late 1970s.

A Mars A Day Helps You Work, Rest And Play Mars bar; UK, from 1960. Also **Mars Are Marvellous**.

Melts In Your Mouth, Not In Your Hand Treets; UK, quoted 1980. Also adopted for Minstrels, current 1982.

The Mint With The Hole Life-Savers; US, current 1920. The full phrase is: **The Candy Mint With The Hole**. Also used for Rowntree's Polo mints; UK, from 1947.

Roses Grow On You Cadbury's Roses chocolates; UK, current mid-1960s. Norman Vaughan, who presented the TV ads, recalls: 'This was shouted at me wherever I went from about 1965. The campaign only ran for two years but on personal appearances even now (1979) people still ask me, "Where are your roses?"' Maurice Drake, who was with Young & Rubicam at the time, adds: 'This was a famous line that originally went into the waste-paper basket, but was rescued a couple of hours later, just before the cleaners came in.'

Sharp's The Word For Toffee Sharp's toffee; UK, from 1927. Sir Edward Sharp first manufactured toffee in 1880. The old firm became Trebor Sharps Ltd during the 1960s. (Trebor is 'Robert' backwards.)

Stop Me And Buy One Wall's ice cream; UK, from 1923. The phrase is believed to have been invented by Lionel and Charles Rodd, who were on the board of T. Wall & Sons. 8,500 salesmen with the slogan on their tricycles pedalled round Britain out of a national network of 136 depots. One salesman whose brakes failed as he descended a very steep hill introduced a slight variation as he hurtled to destruction: 'If you can stop me, you can have the lot.'

Flavour Of The Month   A generic phrase aimed at persuading people to try new varieties of ice cream and not just stick to their customary choice (principally in the US). Latterly it has become an idiom for any quickly discarded fad, craze or personal relationship.

The Sweet You Can Eat Between Meals (Without Ruining Your Appetite)   Milky Way; UK, from 1960.

Too-Good-To-Hurry-Mints   Murraymints; UK, from late 1950s. Howard 'Boogie' Barnes wrote the lyric for one of the

most catchy early British TV jingles. A typical situation was an army parade ground (in cartoon):

Sergeant: Hey, that man there!
Soldier (rifle leaning against the wall): Sorry, you'll just have to wait — I'm finishing my Murraymint, the too-good-to-hurry-mint.
Chorus of soldiers: Murraymints, Murraymints,
Too-good-to-hurry-mints.
Why make haste
When you can taste
The hint of mint
In Murraymints.

A Woman Never Forgets The Man Who Remembers Whitman's Sampler chocolates and confections; US, current 1954. Also **Give Whitman's Chocolates — It's The Thoughtful Thing To Do**, coined in 1933 to remind people that 'social graces had not been lost in the slump'. (Lambert)

Wot A Lot I Got Smarties; UK, from c1958 to 1964. Anthony Pugh of J. Walter Thompson recalled in 1965:

'For a long time we did dotty advertising which said that everybody likes Smarties. This was palpably untrue, because only kids did . . . What we discovered was that children like collecting lots of little things — so we thought of the phrase "What a lot". Then I taped my own children playing with lots of Smarties, and they said "WOTALOTIGOT" and "WOTALOTUGOT" . . . Then I thought, why don't we show the people who are supposed to be eating them, let's just get ordinary kids, not television children. The sales soared.' (Pearson)

At the end of the TV ads came the tag **Buy Some For Lulu**.

A TASTE OF HOME

Ahh Bisto!   Bisto gravy browning; UK, from 1919. The name of the product is a hidden slogan, too. When the Cerebos company first put it on the market in 1910, the product did not have a name. According to legend, the initial letters of the proposed slogan 'Browns, Seasons, Thickens In One' were rearranged to give the brand name. The Bisto Kids, drawn by Will Owen, first appeared in 1919, sniffing a wisp of gravy aroma and murmuring, 'Ahh Bisto!' This is a phrase which has endured ever since and has been parodied in numerous cartoons over the years, providing almost a pocket history of the century – 'Ah! Ribso'; 'I Smell Bristowe!'; 'Ah, Blitzo!'; 'Ah, Bizerta!'; 'Ah, Crippso!'; 'Ah! Winston!'; 'Ah! Coupon free!'; and 'Arrgh!'

Alas! My Poor Brother   Bovril meat extract; UK, current 1896. Bovril came on to the market in Britain when bold, modern advertising techniques were being applied for the first time. John Lawson Johnston, a Scot who emigrated to Canada, developed a way of blending meat extract with other raw materials. The product was first sold as Johnston's Fluid Beef in 1874. In London, S.H. Benson, a Johnston employee, set up his own business as an 'advertiser's agent' with Bovril as his first client. By the end of the century he had made Bovril a household name – and launched an advertising business that kept the Bovril account until the agency folded in 1969. 'Alas! My Poor Brother' is the most famous of the early Bovril captions, appearing with W.H. Caffyn's poster of a tearful bull eyeing a jar.

The Glory Of A Man Is His Strength   dates from this time, too. Coupled with the picture of a youth in a leopard-skin wrestling with a lion, it endured on the Bovril label for more than fifty years.

The Two Infallible Powers. The Pope And Bovril is advertising chutzpah of the first order. It appeared in the late 1890s.

I Hear They Want More, spoken by one nervous bull to another in 1903, again pointed up the somewhat uncomfortable fact of where the product originated.

It *Must* Be Bovril stemmed from an endorsement by Sir Ernest Shackleton, the explorer, in 1909. 'The question of the concentrated beef supply (on expeditions) is most important — it must be Bovril.' The phrase was still in use as late as 1936.

Give Him/Her/Them Bovril appeared in the last campaign before the outbreak of the First World War. The Bovril airship bearing 'Give Him Bovril' on one side and 'Give Her Bovril' on the other made numerous flights over London at heights of between 100 and 1,000 feet and engaged in mock battles with a biplane, anticipating the more realistic encounters to come.

Bovril Prevents That Sinking Feeling, on H.H. Harris's cheery poster of a pyjama-clad man astride a jar at sea, ushered in the post-war years in 1920, although the slogan was born in a golfing booklet issued by Bovril in 1890 which included the commendation: 'Unquestionably Bovril . . . supplies . . . the nourishment which is so much needed by all players at the critical intermediate hour between breakfast and luncheon, when the *sinking feeling* engendered by an empty stomach is so distressing, and so fruitful of deteriorated play.' It is said that Bovril had intended to use this slogan earlier but withheld it because of the *Titanic* disaster. With updated illustrations the slogan endured until 1958.

Aunt Bovril Sandwiches Grandma? One of numerous awful puns perpetrated in Bovril advertising, especially on the railways, in the 1920s and 1930s. Others included **Bovril 2.40fy You; Scotch Express Great Faith In Bovril; If You've Mr Train Don't Miss Bovril; Noel Feelings To Bovril; Isn't The Milkmaid Attractive With Bovril? To All In Tents Bovril Is As Good As A Blanket.**

America's Most Famous Dessert Jell-O; US, current 1900.

Babies Are Our Business Gerber Products; US, current 1954.

Beanz Meanz Heinz Heinz baked beans; UK, current 1967. The kind of phrase that drives teachers into a frenzy because of its apparent encouragement of poor spelling. Johnny Johnson wrote the music for the jingle which went:

> A million housewives every day
> Pick up a tin of beans and say
> Beanz meanz Heinz.

'I created the line at Young & Rubicam,' says Maurice Drake. 'It was in fact written — although after much thinking — over two pints of bitter in the Victoria pub in Mornington Crescent.'

Bet You Can't Eat Just One Lay's potato chips; US, quoted 1981.

Can *You* Tell Stork From Butter? Stork margarine; UK, from c1956. One of the earliest slogans on British commercial

TV — endlessly referred to at the popular level. Housewives in TV ads from the Lintas agency were asked to take part in comparative tests between pieces of bread spread with real butter and Stork.

C'mon Colman's Light My Fire Colman's mustard; UK, current 1979. A clear echo of the Jim Morrison song 'Com' on baby, light my fire' to accompany the picture of a voluptuous woman on a tiger rug who is clearly in no need of any such encouragement. Or perhaps she is the little bit on the side.

Come Home To Birds Eye Country Birds Eye frozen vegetables, etc.; UK, current early 1960s.

Don't Say Brown — Say Hovis Hovis bread; UK, current from mid-1930s. Originally called Smith's Patent Germ Bread and created by Richard Smith in the 1880s, Hovis takes its name from the Latin 'hominis vis' (strength of man). In the 1930s one of the firm's paper bags showed a radio announcer saying: 'Here's a rather important announcement . . . I should have said Hovis and not just "brown".' The slogan occurred in its final form from 1956 to 1964. It still reverberates: in May 1981, when a British golfer, Ken Brown, was deserted by his caddie during a Martini championship, a *Sunday Mirror* headline was: 'Don't Say Brown, Say Novice'.

Do You Know Uneeda Biscuit? Uneeda soda crackers; US, from 1898.

Eat More Fruit British Fruit Trades Federation; UK, from 1923. The Federation launched a well mounted broadside 'stressing the enjoyment and good health to be derived from eating fruit. Fortuitously, an influenza epidemic broke out, enabling the promoters to point out how fruit fortified the human frame against illness.' (Turner). The campaign was a great success and paved the way for rival 'Eat More' and 'Drink More' campaigns.

The reverse form of this kind of approach was contained in the First World War slogan **Eat Less Bread**. A poster of about 1917 explained: 'The sinking of foodships by German submarines and the partial failure of the World's wheat crop have brought about a scarcity of wheat and flour which makes it imperative that every household should at once reduce its consumption of BREAD. The Food Controller asks that the weekly consumption of Bread throughout the Country should be reduced by an average of 4 lbs. per head.'

Eventually — Why Not Now?   Gold Medal Flour; US, from c1907. The story has it that when Benjamin S. Bull, advertising manager of the Washburn Crosby company, requested members of his department to suggest catchphrases to be used in support of Gold Medal Flour, nobody came up with anything worthwhile. Mr Bull demanded: 'When are you going to give me a decent slogan?' His underlings staved him off by saying, 'Eventually.' 'Eventually!' thundered Mr Bull, 'Why not now?'

Fresh To The Last Slice   Sunblest bread; UK, current early 1960s. Compare the famous Maxwell House slogan.

Glaxo Builds Bonny Babies   Glaxo (dried, skimmed milk); UK, from 1913. The slogan 'swept the country', prompting the music-hall quip about the young husband who asked: 'Who takes it — me or the wife?'

Go To Work On An Egg   British Egg Marketing Board; UK, from 1957. Fay Weldon, now known as a novelist and TV playwright, was a copywriter on the 'egg' account at Mather & Crowther. She has taken the trouble to put the record straight over her involvement in creating one of the more memorable British slogans:

'I was certainly in charge of copy at the time "Go To Work On An Egg" was first used as a slogan as the main theme for an advertising campaign. The phrase itself had been in existence for some time and hung about in the middle of paragraphs and was sometimes promoted to base lines. Who invented it, it would be hard to say. It is perfectly possible, indeed probable, that I put those particular six words together in that particular order but I would not swear to it. Mary Gowing, a very creative and talented advertising copywriter, was in charge of the account before I took over. She died, suddenly, when I was working under her and I, as the phrase goes, stepped over the cook; that is, I took over because there was nobody else to do it. If she wrote "Go To Work On An Egg" I don't want to claim it, but I can't be sure. I certainly devised, along with the art director, Ruth Gill,

Happiness Is Egg Shaped and **You Can Rely On The Lion** but I think **There Is A Lion On My Egg** was Mary Gowing's' (The lion device was stamped on eggs as a kind of hallmark, but after all this effort, campaigns on behalf of eggs went out of favour.)

Graded Grains Make Finer Flour   Homepride flour; UK, current 1969. The tag-line of a series of popular TV ads featuring the Homepride flour graders, a likeable race of bowler-hatted men.

The Ham What Am   Armour & Co. meat products; US, current 1917. Accompanied by the logo of a negro chef — suggested by a lithographer. Latterly used as a trademark for all the company's meat products, not just the ham.

Heinz 57 Varieties   Heinz canned foods; US, from 1896. In that year Henry Heinz was travelling through New York City on the overhead railway. He saw a streetcar window advertising 21 styles of shoe, the idea appealed to him and, although he could list about 58 or 59 Heinz products, he settled on 57 because it sounded right. Heinz commented later: 'I myself did not realise how successful a slogan it was going to be.' In fact, it is now as much a brand name as a slogan. (In housey-housey or bingo, 'all the beans' is now the cry for '57'.)

It's Fingerlickn' Good   Kentucky Fried Chicken; US, current 1973. Also **Real Goodness From Kentucky Fried Chicken** and **Corn And Cluck For A Buck.**

It's Not Fancy, But It's Good   Horn & Hardart (restaurants using vending machines); US, current 1966.

It Takes A Tough Man To Make A Tender Chicken   Perdue Farms chicken; US, current 1976. The ads featured Mr Perdue himself.

It Takes Two Hands To Hold A Whopper   Whopper (hamburger); US, quoted 1981.

The Kind Mother Used To Make   New England Mincemeat; US, current 1900. One of numerous advertising lines playing on assumptions about the goodness of home produce and the good old days (reminding one of the small ad said to have made the pitch: 'Buckwheat cakes like mother used to make $1.25. Like mother thought she made $2.25.') (The title of this section also plays upon the same theme. It was devised by Barry Day as an all-purpose food slogan — but has not, to my knowledge, actually been used.)

Makes You Feel Like A Queen   Summer County margarine; UK, current 1960s.

Mr Kipling Does Make Exceedingly Good Cakes   Mr Kipling Cakes; UK, current from early 1970s.

Nobody Does It Like McDonald's Can   McDonald's hamburger restaurants; US, current 1970s.

The Only 'Sauce' I Dare Give Father   Burma sauce; UK, current in the early twentieth century.

Out Of The Strong Came Forth Sweetness   Lyle's Golden Syrup; UK, current 1930s onwards. A quotation from the Book of Judges 14:14: 'Out of the eater came forth meat, and out of the strong came forth sweetness' − Samson's riddle. More recently the Tate & Lyle company has completely reversed the phrase by saying **Out Of Sweetness Came Forth Strength** as part of its occasionally necessary campaigns featuring 'Mr Cube' to ward off nationalisation of the British sugar industry.

Oxo Gives A Meal Man-Appeal   Oxo beef extract, for cooking and drinks; UK, from 1958. The Oxo cube first appeared in 1910 and has been supported by numerous slogans over the years. In the late 1950s, the Oxo company wanted TV to 'take it off the streets and put it in the home'. Copywriter Joan Drummond was told to come up with a husband-and-wife domestic situation which would dramatize the youthful image J. Walter Thompson wished to project. 'We want the idea that the chap is after the girl for her sexiness as well as her good cooking,' she was told, 'and we need a slogan to keep us on that line.' 'Oxo Gives A Meal Man-Appeal' was what she came up with. (Pearson)

See How It Runs   Cerebos salt; UK, from 1919. Cerebos salt was invented in 1894 by George Weddell, who discovered that his compound flowed much better than ordinary table salt. This property was emphasized when in 1906 the Cerebos company bought up a rival, Birdcatcher salt, whose trademark was a little boy pouring salt on a chicken's tail. He first appeared on the Cerebos packs after the First World War.

Spreads Straight From The Fridge   Blue Band margarine; UK, current late 1960s.

Sweet As The Moment When The Pod Went 'Pop'   Birds Eye peas; UK, from c1956. Written by Len Heath at the Lintas agency.

Try Our Rivals, Too   Van Camp's pork and beans; US, current in the late nineteenth century. Claude C. Hopkins said: 'I urged people to buy the brands suggested and compare them with Van Camp's . . . if we were certain enough of our advantage to invite such comparisons, people were certain enough to buy.' (He had found that the executives of the company could not tell their own product and its competitors apart.)

When It Rains, It Pours   Morton salt; US, from 1911. This phrase could apply to other products, but with the logo of a girl in the rain, sheltering the salt under her umbrella, it capitalized on the fact that the Morton grade ran freely from salt cellars even when the atmosphere was damp. In a small booklet describing the product a copywriter used the phrase as a paragraph heading and the slogan developed from there.

Where's George? – He's Gone To Lyonch   Lyons Corner Houses; UK, current 1936. W. Buchanan-Taylor, advertising chief at Lyons, recalled: 'I resorted to the unforgivable and invented "Lyonch" as a descriptive of lunch at Lyons . . . then I heard a story within the office of how a man on the advertising staff of *The Times* called one day a little later than was his wont to pick up his pal, George Warner, the head of my studio. He was so much later than usual that when he looked into the room and asked "Where's George?" the artist replied, without looking up from his work, "Gone to Lyonch, you fool." I made a note on my desk pad . . . and I sent one of the staff to Somerset House to tot up the number of registered Georges in the country.' When the count had reached more than a million, the slogan was adopted. It had to be carefully obliterated during the funeral of King George V in 1936.

Where's The Beef?   Wendy International hamburger chain; US, from 1984. In a TV commercial, three elderly women are eyeing a small hamburger on a huge bun — a Wendy competitor's product. 'It certainly is a big bun,' asserts one. 'It's a very big fluffy bun,' the second agrees. But the third asks, 'Where's the beef?' The line caught on hugely. Walter Mondale, running for the Democratic presidential nomination, used it to question the substance of his rival Gary Hart's policies.

With A Name Like Smuckers It Has To Be Good Smucker's preserves; US, from c1960. Lois Wyse of Wyse Advertising, New York, recalls: 'Slogans come and go but "With A Name Like . . ." has become a part of the language. I wrote it for a company with an unusual name in answer to a challenge from Marc Wyse who said that he didn't feel our Smucker advertising differed from the competition. The real job, however, was not thinking up the slogan but selling it to Paul Smucker. The then sales manager said: "If you run that line, Paul, we'll be out of business in six months"! But it's still in use after twenty years.'

You Don't Have To Be Jewish To Love Levy's Real Jewish Rye Levy's rye bread; US, current 1967. The point of this slogan was reinforced memorably by its being positioned under pictures of very obviously un-Jewish people — Indians, Chinese, or whoever. Nobody had heard of the brand until Doyle, Dane, Bernbach got to work on it. There had been a show of Jewish humour with the title *You Don't Have To Be Jewish* running on Broadway in 1965. (Graffiti additions have been plentiful. They include: '. . . to be offended by this ad'/'. . . to be called one'/'. . . to go to Columbia University, but it helps'/'. . . to wear levis'/'. . . to be circumcised'.)

GOOD TO THE
LAST DROP

Chock Full O'Nuts Is That Heavenly Coffee Chock Full O'Nuts coffee; US, current 1950s. Included in a jingle by Shirley Polykoff.

Good To The Last Drop Maxwell House coffee; US, from 1907. President Theodore Roosevelt was visiting Joel Cheek, perfector of the Maxwell House blend. After the President had had a cup, he said of it that it was 'Good . . . to the last drop'. It has been used as a slogan ever since, despite the various smart-alecs who have inquired 'What's wrong with the last drop then?' Professors of English have been called in to consider the problem and have ruled that 'to' can be inclusive and not just mean 'up to but not including'.

Grateful And Comforting Like Epps's Cocoa Epps's cocoa; UK, from c1900. In Noel Coward's play *Peace In Our Time* (1947), one character says: 'One quick brandy, like Epps's Cocoa, would be both grateful and comforting.' When asked 'Who is Epps?' he replies: 'Epps's Cocoa — it's an advertisement I remember when I was a little boy.' Also, **The Food For Strong and Weak**.

Horlicks Guards Against Night Starvation Horlicks milk drink; UK, from 1930. J. Walter Thompson evolved the concept of 'night starvation' (to add to the worries of the twentieth century — nobody had been aware of it before): 'Right through the night you've been burning up reserves of energy without food to replace it. Breathing alone takes twenty thousand muscular efforts every night.' Eric Partridge records that the phrase became a popular term for sexual deprivation. Before this, there had been the memorable picture ad of a man turning out his suitcase with the phrase **I Know I Packed It**. During the 1950s, JWT ran comic-strip sagas of the refreshing qualities of Horlicks for tired housewives, run-down executives, etc., which customarily ended with the slogan: **Thinks . . . Thanks To Horlicks.**

Hot Chocolate, Drinking Chocolate – The Late, Late Drink Cadbury's Drinking Chocolate; UK, current 1960s.

Join The Tea-Set Typhoo tea; UK, current 1970s.

Ready, Aye, Ready Camp coffee; UK, from c1883. This is almost a slogan in the old sense of a war-cry. It was used as such by several Scots clans, including the Johnstons, Stewarts, Napiers and Scotts. Various institutions used it as a motto, too – Merchiston Castle School, Edinburgh, is one. But it has travelled farthest on the distinctive label for Camp coffee, manufactured by R. Paterson & Sons of Glasgow. The label was virtually unchanged for nearly a hundred years. Today the basic elements still remain: a Scots officer being served coffee by a turbanned attendant with the slogan up a flagpole. Additional phrases have adjured: **Drink Camp – It's The Best!** and **Don't Be Misled!!!**

Salada Is Delicious Tea Salada tea; US, from c1890.

Sleep Sweeter, Bournvita Bournvita night drink, UK, current 1960s. Featured memorably in a TV commercial which simply consisted of a smiling mug and the slogan followed by a yawn and 'Goodnight'.

Spend Wisely – Save Wisely Brooke Bond Dividend tea; UK, current 1930s.

The Tea You Can Really Taste Brooke Bond P.G. Tips; UK, current 1960s. Also **Tea You Can Taste To The Last Delicious Drop.**

Tetley Make Tea-bags Make Tea Tetley's tea; UK, current 1970s.

Typhoo Puts The 'T' In Britain Typhoo tea; UK, current 1970s.

We Are The Ovaltineys/Happy Girls And Boys   Ovaltine milk drink; UK, from 1935. From one of the most evocative jingles of all. The Ovaltiney Club was launched over Radio Luxembourg. Children were given badges, rule books, secret codes and comics, and by 1939 there were five million active members. In 1946 the show was revived to run for several more years.

UP IN SMOKE

Ah, Woodbine – A *Great* Little Cigarette   Woodbine cigarettes; UK, current 1957 – using Norman Hackforth's voice-over.

. . . Anyhow Have A Winfield   Winfield cigarettes; Australia, current 1975. From long-running TV campaigns featuring Paul Hogan came the distinctive pronunciation of 'anyhow' as 'ennyeeiaouww . .!'

...anyhow* have a Winfield

The Best Tobacco Money Can Buy   Rothman's cigarettes; UK, current 1981. With equal modesty: **The Greatest Name In Cigarettes** and **The World's Most Popular King Size Filter Cigarette**.

Blow Some My Way   Chesterfield cigarettes; US, from 1926. Used – some said suggestively – when a woman made her first appearance in US cigarette advertising. **I'll Tell The World – They Satisfy** was current the same year.

Call For Philip Morris   Philip Morris cigarettes; US, current 1941. The jingle went: 'You get all the flavour and you get it mild/When you call for Philip Morris cigarettes.'

Come To Where The Flavor Is. Come To Marlboro Country   Marlboro cigarettes; US, current from mid-1950s. Originally devised by the Leo Burnett agency in Chicago as a means of shifting the appeal of Marlboro from women to men by showing it in use by rugged cowboy types. Hence **Man-Sized Flavour** but, hedging the bet, **A Man's Cigarette That Women Like Too**.

Cool As A Mountain Stream   Consulate cigarettes; UK, current early 1960s. Also **Menthol-Fresh, Cool, Clean, Consulate** (changed following the 1963 cancer scare to: **Cool, Fresh, Consulate**).

For Your Throat's Sake, Smoke Craven "A" – They Never Vary   Craven "A" cigarettes; UK, current 1920s and 1930s. A quite unbelievable line nowadays, but at the time there were others, too: **Smoke Craven "A" – Will Not Affect Your Throat** and **Craven "A" – It's Kind To Your Throat**.

Have A Capstan   Capstan Cigarettes; UK, current 1930s.

I'd Walk A Mile For A Camel   Camel cigarettes; US, current early twentieth century. One day a sign-painter was painting a billboard – according to the story – when a man came up and asked him if he had a cigarette. The painter gave him a Camel. The stranger thanked him and uttered the immortal words: 'I'd walk a mile for a camel.' The painter passed the line on and from this incident came one of the best ever cigarette slogans. It was dropped in 1944.

Internationally Acknowledged To Be The Finest Cigarette In The World   Dunhill cigarettes; UK, quoted 1981.

The International Passport To Smoking Pleasure   Peter Stuyvesant cigarettes; UK, current from 1960s. Do you remember the line from the cinema ads: 'In City After City, Country After Country, More And More People Are Turning To . . .'? Also **So Much More To Enjoy**

It's That Condor Moment   Condor pipe tobacco; UK, current 1970s.

It's Toasted   Lucky Strike cigarettes; US, current from late 1920s. Sometimes **They're Toasted** – as indeed are all cigarettes, but Lucky Strike seized the pitch. From the same period comes the line **Reach For A Lucky Instead Of A Sweet**. George Washington Hill of the American Tobacco

Company was driving through New York City one day when he grabbed his colleague Vincent Riggio and cried, 'I've got it!' He had noticed a stout woman waiting to cross the street, eating a big piece of candy. Alongside, a taxi pulled up in which a 'nice-looking' woman was smoking a cigarette. The contrast precipitated this slogan. Understandably, the confectionery industry was not very pleased but it is said that this campaign created more women smokers than any other promotion. Also **No Throat Irritation — No Cough**; the 1940s radio catchphrase **LS/MFT** (Lucky Strike Means Finer Tobacco); and **So Round, So Firm, So Fully Packed** (quoted 1958).

Not A Cough In A Carload   Old Gold cigarettes; US, current 1928.

People Are Changing To Guards   Guards cigarettes; UK, current 1960s.

Player's Please   John Player & Sons cigarettes; UK, from 1927. Three years earlier this enduring slogan appeared in the form 'Player's Will Please You'. By 1925 this had become 'They're Player's And They Please'. George Green, the firm's advertising manager entered a tobacconist's shop and overheard a customer asking for 'Player's, please'. He went back to his office, wrote the phrase out in his own immaculate hand (the one used in the ads) and the slogan took on its final form. **It's The Tobacco That Counts** was current in 1927, too. **People Love Player's** — 'a classic campaign revealing the romantic promise implicit in a puff of smoke' — was launched in 1960.

Pure Gold   Benson & Hedges cigarettes; UK, current 1964. Originally this campaign used the phrase (to reflect the gold packs) with lines like 'What's too precious to leave lying round?' Later the brand took to providing visual images that would inevitably recall the slogan, without actually using it.

Senior Service Satisfy   Senior Service cigarettes; UK, current 1981. Before 1950, there was the bizarre line **A Product Of The Mastermind**.

Winston Tastes Good Like A Cigarette Should   Winston cigarettes; US, current 1965. The slogan dealt a blow to standard usage ('as a cigarette should . . .').

You've Come A Long Way Baby (To Get Where You Got To Today) Virginia Slims cigarettes; US, from 1968. A slogan that reflected the feminist mood of the time — indeed, the phrase has been used on Women's Lib posters.

And something to light up with:

Flick Your Bic Bic lighters; US, from 1975. Coined by Charlie Moss, the original usage occurred in an ad that showed how smart, sophisticated people did not use lighters — they simply 'flicked their Bics'. The line became a household word in the US and was picked up by many comedians.

During the energy crisis, Bob Hope said: 'Things are getting so bad that the Statue of Liberty doesn't light up any more. She just stands there and flicks her Bic.'

Smokers Are Requested To Use Swan Vestas matches; UK, current 1920s and 1930s. The captions on the matchboxes themselves have changed to reflect current conditions: **The Smoker's Match** (1905); **Use Matches Sparingly** (1941).

Not forgetting, in the UK from 1971, on all cigarette advertising and packs:
DANGER; H.M. GOVERNMENT HEALTH DEPARTMENT'S WARNING: CIGARETTES CAN SERIOUSLY DAMAGE YOUR HEALTH. The 'seriously' was added in 1977, the 'Danger' in 1980. David Simpson, Director of ASH (Action on Smoking and Health), comments:

'There is no law that the words should be on the packs but it is one provision of the "voluntary" agreement which the tobacco industry has entered into with the Department of Health as a preference to the possibility of legislation. For a product which will kill one in four of those who smoke twenty a day all their lives, the warnings are hopelessly inadequate.'

And in the USA: packs started carrying the message **CAUTION: CIGARETTE SMOKING MAY BE HAZARDOUS TO YOUR HEALTH** in 1965. Five years later, this was strengthened to read: **WARNING; THE SURGEON-GENERAL HAS DETERMINED THAT CIGARETTE SMOKING IS DANGEROUS TO YOUR HEALTH**.

Also, just in case that failed to scare you:

Kiss A Non-Smoker . . . Enjoy The Difference!
Your Money *And* Your Life!
You Can't Scrub Your Lungs Clean
Cancer Cures Smoking
all current in the UK in 1981.

THE WAR TO
END WARS

'I launched the phrase **The War To End Wars** and that was not the least of my crimes,' confessed H.G. Wells long after the First World War was over. (*The War That Will End War* was the title of a book he had written in 1914.)

Most of the slogans that came out of the war, however, are related to recruitment:

'Arf A Mo, Kaiser!   became a catchphrase after a recruiting poster had shown a British 'Tommy' lighting a pipe prior to going into action. (The phrase even surfaced again in the Second World War as "Arf A Mo, Hitler!')

Berlin By Christmas   Initially, it was thought that the war would not last very long. (In 1939, the phrase 'All Over By Christmas' was used by some optimists as it had been in several previous wars — none of which was over by Christmas.)

Business As Usual   H.E. Morgan (later Sir Herbert Morgan) was an advertising man working for W.H. Smith & Sons, who promoted this slogan which had quite a vogue until it was proved to be manifestly untrue and hopelessly inappropriate. Morgan was an advertising consultant to H. Gordon Selfridge, who consequently also became associated with the slogan. On 26 August 1914, Selfridge said: '"Business As Usual" must be the order of the day.' In a Guildhall speech on 9 November, Winston Churchill said: 'The maxim of the British people is "Business as usual".'

Daddy, What Did *You* Do In The Great War? (accompanied by the picture of an understandably appalled family man puzzling over what to reply to the daughter on his

Daddy, what did __YOU__ do in the Great War?

knee)   This recruiting slogan became a catchphrase in the form 'What did you do in the Great War, Daddy?' and gave rise to such responses as 'Shut up, you little bastard. Get the Bluebell and go and clean my medals.' (Partridge)

England Expects That Every Man Will Do His Duty And Join The Army Today   An obvious extension of Lord Nelson's message to the British fleet before the Battle of Trafalgar in 1805. The original form of *that* slogan was 'Nelson Confides That Every Man Will Do His Duty' but it was suggested to him that it would be better to substitute 'England' for 'Nelson'. The signals officer, one Lieutenant Pasco, also pointed out that if 'expects' was substituted for 'confides' he need only run up one flag instead of seven (as 'expects' was a common enough word to be represented by one flag in the signals book).

Enlist Today (or rather **To-Day** as it was usually put)   A key phrase in almost all recruitment copy from this war.

Hang the Kaiser   Pressure was strong for retribution at the 1918 General Election (fuelled by the newspapers). The Treaty of Versailles (1919) committed the Allies to trying the Kaiser but the Government of the Netherlands refused to hand him over. He lived until 1941.

A Land Fit For Heroes (sometimes **A Country Fit For Heroes**) When the war was over, Lloyd George gave rise to this slogan in a speech at Wolverhampton on 24 November 1918, the exact words of which are: 'What is our task? To make Britain a fit country for heroes to live in.'

Who's Absent? Is It You? (plus a picture of John Bull)

Women Of Britain Say — 'GO!'

Your Country Needs You   The most famous recruiting slogan of all. It was used to accompany a picture of Field-Marshal Lord Kitchener, with staring eyes and pointing finger. Kitchener was appointed Secretary of State for War on 6 August 1914, two days after the outbreak. He set to work immediately, intent on raising the 'New Armies' required to supplement the small standing army of the day, which he rightly saw would be inadequate for a major conflict.

In fact, work on advertising for recruits had started the

year before, with some success. Then, towards the end of July 1914, Eric Field of the tiny Caxton Advertising Agency (owned by Sir Hedley Le Bas) received a call from a Colonel Strachey, who 'swore me to secrecy, told me that war was imminent and that the moment it broke out we should have to start advertising at once'. That night, Field wrote an advertisement headed **Your King And Country Need You** with the royal coat of arms as the only illustration. The day after war was declared, 5 August, this appeared prominently in the *Daily Mail* and other papers.

The appeal appeared in various forms but Kitchener preferred this first slogan and insisted on finishing every advertisement with 'God Save The King'. The drawing was by the humorous artist Alfred Leete and it was taken up the same month by the Parliamentary Recruiting Committee for poster use. The original is in the Imperial War Museum. (Margot Asquith commented: 'If Kitchener was not a great man, he was, at least, a great poster.')

The idea was widely imitated abroad. In the US, James Montgomery Flagg's poster of a pointing Uncle Sam bore the legend **I Want *You* For The US Army**. (There was also a version by Howard Chandler Christy featuring a woman with a mildly come-hither look saying, **I Want You For The Navy**.)

TODAY PEORIA, TOMORROW THE WORLD

Slogans help keep the wheels of democracy turning, not only in presidential election years. Here are political cries from all over the political spectrum during two centuries and more of American history:

No Taxation Without Representation was current in the years before the War of Independence, or in the form **Taxation Without Representation Is Tyranny**, attributed to the lawyer and statesman James Otis in 1763. He opposed British taxation on the grounds that the colonies were not represented in the House of Commons. (Echoed many years later by Arnold Toynbee: 'No annihilation without representation.')

Liberty And Property, And No Stamps The motto of various American newspapers following the Stamp Act of 1765, which was the first direct tax levied upon the American colonies by the British Parliament.

United We Stand, Divided We Fall Jonathan Dickinson wrote 'The Patriot's Appeal' in 1768:

> Then join hand in hand, brave Americans all!
> By uniting we stand, by dividing we fall.

The State of Kentucky gave it the precise form in its 1792 motto. The idea can, however, be traced back to 550 BC and Aesop's Fable of the Four Oxen and the Lion.

Vote As You Shot Used by veterans' groups for many years after the Civil War.

Speak Softly And Carry A Big Stick Speaking at the Minnesota State Fair in September 1901, President Theodore Roosevelt gave strength to the idea of backing negotiations with threats of military force when he said: 'There is a homely adage which runs, "Speak softly and carry a big stick; you will go far." If the American nation will speak softly and yet build and keep at a pitch of the highest training a thoroughly efficient navy, the Monroe Doctrine will go far.' The homely adage is said to have started life as a West African proverb.

Share The Wealth and **Everyman A King (But No Man Wears A Crown)** Slogans of Louisiana Governor Huey P. Long from 1928 to his assassination in 1935. The thrust of his campaign was that 10 per cent of the people owned 70 per cent of the wealth and that this should be shared. The second of the slogans is a quotation from William Jennings Bryan's 'Cross of Gold Speech' to the 1896 Democratic Convention

The Buck Stops Here President Truman had a sign on his desk bearing these words, indicating that the Oval Office was where the passing of the buck had to cease. The phrase seems to be of his own making. When President Nixon published his memoirs, people opposed to its sale went around with buttons saying: 'The book stops here.'

Had Enough? A Republican slogan aimed at President Truman during the 1946 mid-term elections when things were going badly for him.

Over The Hump With Humphrey A sign on Hubert Humphrey's campaign bus when he sought the Democratic nomination, in vain, in 1960.

More With Gore Gore Vidal's slogan during his unsuccessful campaign as Democratic candidate for Congress in a New York district. (Unhappily, 'Vidal So Soon' appears to have been considered and rejected.)

You'll Be Safe In The Park/Every Night After Dark/With Lefkowitz, Gilhooley And Fino A dotty local election ditty from New York in 1961. There was even a version in Spanish for the Puerto Ricans (who otherwise appeared unrepresented on this cosmopolitan ticket).

Your Home Is Your Castle – Protect It A 'code-word' slogan, designed to appeal to white voters concerned that property values would decline if blacks moved in. Used by various candidates in mayoralty and state elections. Lester Maddox won a narrow victory in the contest for the 1966 Georgia governorship with it.

Gordon Liddy Doesn't Bail Them Out, He Puts Them In Lawyer G. Gordon Liddy (later the mastermind behind Watergate) contested a Republican congressional nomination in 1968 with this slogan and lost narrowly.

He Is Fresh When Everyone Is Tired A John Lindsay campaign slogan from his years as Mayor of New York, giving rise to the graffiti emendation: 'He is fresh when everyone is polite.'

Would You Buy A Used Car From this Man? A devastating slur which has attached itself permanently to the personality of Richard M. Nixon. It was recalled in poster form during the 1968 election, though it began to circulate as a joke as early as 1952. Compare the phrase applied to Governor George Romney: 'Would you buy a *new* car from this man?'

Give The Presidency Back To The People Eugene McCarthy's cry, seeking the Democratic nomination in 1968 — without success.

Winning In Politics Isn't Everything, It's The Only Thing Slogan of the Committee to Re-Elect The President in 1972. Look where it got them.

Impeach Nixon Common cry in 1974.

Nobody Drowned At Watergate In the early days of Watergate Nixon supporters made this pointed reference to the stonewalling by Senator Edward Kennedy after the Chappaquiddick incident.

Dog Litter — An Issue You Can't Sidestep Corny, but a candidate for local office in Washington won with it.

WE EXCHANGED MANY FRANK WORDS IN OUR RESPECTIVE LANGUAGES

A foreign language slogan occasionally impinges upon English speech. One which I believe to be of Nazi origin is still with us and, as a construction capable of innumerable variations, has passed into the language: **Today ************, **Tomorrow the world!** The idea lies behind the slogan for the National Socialist Press: 'Heute Presse der Nationalsozialitsen, Morgen Presse der Nation' ('Today the press of the Nazis, tomorrow the press of the nation'.) Dating from the early 30s, this reaches its final form in: 'Heute gehort uns Deutschland — morgen die ganze Welt' ('Today Germany belongs to us — tomorrow the whole world'.) By the outbreak of the Second World War, as John Osborne recalled, an English school magazine was declaring: 'Now soon it will be our turn to take a hand in the destinies of Empire. Today, scholars; tomorrow, the Empire.'

So common is the construction now that a New York graffito (reported in 1974) stated: 'Today Hollywood, tomorrow the world', and one from El Salvador (March 1982) ran: 'Ayer Nicaragua, hoy El Salvador, manana Guatemala!' ('Yesterday Nicaragua, today El Salvador, tomorrow Guatemala!').The *Guardian* (6 July 1982) carried an advertisement with the unwieldy headline: 'Self-Managing Socialism: Today, France — Tomorrow, the World?'

What causes did the following foreign phrases promote? What do they mean?

1   Enosis

2   Ils Ne Passeront Pas

3   Cymru Am Byth

4   Vive Le Québec Libre

5   Blut Und Eisen

6   On Les Aura

7   Ein Reich, Ein Volk, Ein Führer

8   Liberté, Égalité, Fraternité

9   E Pluribus Unum

10   Sinn Fein

11   Algérie Française

12   Mussolini A Sempre Ragione

13   Travail, Famille, Patrie

14   Yanqui Go Home

ANSWERS

1 ('One') Modern Greek slogan referring to the proposed union of Cyprus with mainland Greece, from about 1952.

2 ('They Shall Not Pass') First said to have been uttered by Marshal Pétain at Verdun, 26 February 1916. The official record appears in General Nivelle's Order of the Day (23 June 1916) as: 'Vous ne les laisserez pas passer!' The inscription on the Verdun medal is 'On ne passe pas'. Subsequently, as 'No pasarán', the phrase was used at the end of a radio speech by Dolores Ibarruri (La Pasionara), 18 July 1936, calling on the women of Spain to help defend the Republic. It became a Republican watchword in the Spanish Civil War. (Bartlett)

3 ('Wales For Ever') The motto of the Welsh Guards (and everybody else in the principality).

4 ('Long Live Free Quebec!') 'Extempore remarks' made by French President Charles de Gaulle during a visit to Montreal, 25 July 1967, led to his rapid departure for home, having incurred the displeasure of the Federal Government for interfering in Canada's internal affairs.

5 ('Blood And Iron') 'It is desirable and it is necessary that the conditions of affairs in Germany and of her constitutional relations should be improved; but this cannot be accomplished by speeches and resolutions of a majority, but only by iron and blood' (i.e. 'Eisen und Blut' in the original) – Bismarck, in a speech to the Budget Commission of the Prussian House of Delegates, 30 September 1862. (The Roman orator Quintilian first used the phrase 'sanguinem et ferrum' ('blood and iron') in the first century AD.)

6 ('Let 'Em Have It') From a French poster of the First World War seeking war loans (revived in the Second World War).

7 ('One Realm, One People, One Leader') Nazi slogan, first used at the Nuremberg Rally, September 1934.

8 ('Liberty, Equality, Fraternity') Of earlier origin than the French Revolution, it was adopted by the revolutionary Club des Cordeliers as its official motto on 30 June 1793. At first, the words 'Ou la mort' ('or death') were added but were dropped from 1795.

9 ('One out of many') A line from Virgil's *Moretum* was chosen by Benjamin Franklin, Thomas Jefferson and John Adams as the US motto in 1776. It appears on the Great Seal of the United States and on all coins and banknotes, although 'In God We Trust' was formally adopted by Congress as the country's motto in 1956.

10 ('Ourselves Alone' or 'We Alone') The motto of the Irish Nationalist Movement, Sinn Fein, since about 1907. (Also adopted by Breton separatists.)

11 ('Algeria is French') Slogan of right-wing opponents of President de Gaulle, from May 1958. The rhythm of the slogan was tooted on car horns and the actual phrase often delivered as part of the longer chant, 'Vive l'Algérie Française, Vive la République, Vive la France!'

12 ('Mussolini Is Always Right') Italian fascist slogan, 1936.

13 ('Work, Family, Fatherland') Slogan of Vichy France, 1940-4.

14 Mexican version of 'Yankee Go Home', widely used throughout Latin America from 1950 on, protesting against US military and business presence.

A DIAMOND IS
FOREVER

It is odd, at first glance, that diamonds should need advertising. Are they not their own best advertisement? But in 1939 the South Africa-based De Beers Consolidated Mines launched a campaign to promote further the diamond engagement ring tradition. It was devised by the N.W. Ayer agency of Chicago and the original copy was written by B.J. Kidd. The idea was not new. Anita Loos in her novel *Gentlemen Prefer Blondes* (1925) enshrined it in: 'Kissing your hand may make you feel very, very good but a diamond and safire bracelet lasts for ever.' Ian Fleming gave a variation of the phrase as the title of his 1956 James Bond novel *Diamonds Are Forever*. Technically speaking, however, diamonds are not forever. It takes a high temperature, but, being of pure carbon, they will burn.

YOU KNOW IT
MAKES SENSE

The voice of officialdom in the UK as reflected in cajoling slogans:

Clunk Click *Every* Trip   The sound of a car door closing and seat-belt being fastened, used in road safety ads featuring Jimmy Savile from 1971.

Don't Ask A Man To Drink And Drive   First used 1964.

Dull It Isn't   Metropolitan Police, 1972. The day after the brief TV and poster campaign using this slogan started, it was apparent that the phrase was catching on. A young policeman went to break up a fight at White Hart Lane football ground. Having seized a young hooligan, the constable emerged, dishevelled but triumphant, from the mêlée. A voice from the crowd cried out: 'Dull it effing isn't' eh?'

It's A Man's Life   Army recruitment, quoted 1963.

Join The Army And See The World   Current 1920s and 1930s. (Eric Partridge gives the response 'Join the Army and see the world — the next one!' as c1948.) (Compare: 'I joined the Navy to see the world. And what did I see? I saw the sea' — the song by Irving Berlin.)

Join The Professionals   Regular army recruitment campaign, current 1968. The phrase emerged from extensive research which showed that it 'encapsulated all that young men who were in the target range most admired'.

Keep Britain Tidy   The simplest of messages and one of the most enduring. Promoted through the Central Office of Information (as were most of these slogans), it first appears in their records as a sticker produced for the Ministry of Housing and Local Government in 1952. However, it was probably coined around 1949. Two years before *that*, the word 'litterbug' was coined for use by the New York City Department of Sanitation.

Keep Death Off The Road (Carelessness Kills) Nobody knows who created this message — the best known of any used in government-sponsored advertising campaigns through the COI. It was used in the memorable poster by W. Little, featuring the so-called 'Black Widow', in 1946.

Save It Energy conservation campaigns from April 1975 to May 1979 used this phrase – on behalf of the government's Department of Energy. Specifically, during the long, dry summer of 1976, it was applied to conservation of water supplies. (Variations have included **Turn If Off** and the informal **Save Water – Bath With A Friend**.)

Watch Out, There's A Thief About Home Office crime prevention campaigns run by the COI first used this slogan c1966.

Would You Be More Careful If It Was You Who Got Pregnant? Quoted 1978. Headline of a Health Education Council poster showing a pregnant male.

You Know It Makes Sense The pay-off line to all road safety campaigns from 1968 to 1970; not so much a slogan as a summing-up of all the different road safety campaigns. However, the phrase was used with emphasis on the BBC TV programme *That Was The Week That Was* in 1963 which suggests that it was current before this.

YOU, TOO, CAN
HAVE A BODY

Taking care of yourself — inside and out:

Acts Twice As Fast As Aspirin   Bufferin; US, current 1951.

All Over The World Good Mornings Begin With Gillette
Gillette razor blades; UK, current c1952.

Avoid Five O'Clock Shadow   Gem razors and blades; US,
current 1945.

Be Careful How You Use It   Hai Karate deodorant; US,
quoted 1979.

Because You Are The Very Air He Breathes   Veto deodorant; US, quoted 1958. Norman B. Norman of the Norman,
Craig, Kummel agency asks: 'Why advertise what everybody expects? Of course it should stop perspiration, people
expect that. We gave them a slogan with empathy, that gets at
the very heart of the matter.'

Dr Williams' Pink Pills For Pale People   UK, current 1900.
'The artful alliteration . . . may have done much to build up
the £1,111,000 fortune which George Taylor Fulford acquired
from this property.' (Turner)

Every Picture Tells A Story   Sloan's Backache and Kidney
Pills; UK, current 1907. The picture showed a person bent
over with pain.

**First Thing Every Morning Renew Your Health With
ENO's**   Eno's fruit salts laxative; UK, current 1927.

Helps The Plain, Improves The Fair   Pomeroy Face Cream;
UK, quoted 1925.

Bufferin

TRADE-MARK

Acts twice as fast as aspirin!

Helps You Break The Laxative Habit
Carter's Little Liver Pills; US, quoted
1958.

**I Can't Believe I Ate The Whole
Thing**   Alka-Seltzer; US, from 1972.
Howie Cohen and Bob Pasqualine of
Wells, Rich, Greene created two
extraordinary lines on the 'morning
after' theme for Alka-Seltzer. 'I Can't
Believe . . .' featured in a memorable
TV ad delineating the agonies of
over-indulgence, as did **Try It, You'll
Like It**. Both these phrases entered the
language, especially the latter, which
was used by every comic, every mother,
and certainly every waiter in the US for
the entire year of the campaign (1971).

Inner Cleanliness   Andrews Liver Salts
(laxative); UK, current from 1950s. 'To
complete your inner cleanliness,
Andrews cleans the bowels. It sweeps
away troublemaking poisons, relieves
constipation, and purifies the blood . . .'

BE PREPARED!

AVOID 5 O'CLOCK SHADOW WITH

GEM
RAZORS and BLADES

GEM

KEEP YOUR EYE ON THE INFANTRY—
The Doughboys are on the job!

An earlier generation of Andrews ads featured a man searching through his suitcase and saying **I Must Have Left It Behind**.

Keep 'Regular' With Ex-Lax   Ex-Lax chocolate laxative; US, current 1934. Also **When Nature Forgets — Remember Ex-Lax**

Life. Be In It   Health campaign; Australia, from 1975. The Department of Youth, Sport and Recreation in the State of Victoria initiated a campaign to get people off their backsides and join in sports. Amid debate as to its worth, the slogan was taken up nationally and the Federal Government declared 2 December as 'Life. Be In It' day. Rejoinders include 'Life. Be Out Of It' and (from Barry Humphries) 'Life. Be Up It'.

Make Your Armpit Your Charm Pit Stopette spray deodorant; US, current early 1950s.

Mennen For Men The Mennen Company's talcum powder; US, current 1941. Obvious play on words designed to overcome male resistance to using the product.

Nothing Acts Faster Than Anadin Anadin analgesic tablets; UK, current from 1960s. (It inspired the graffiti retort: 'Then why not use Nothing?') From earlier TV ads: 'Headache? Tense, nervous headache? Take Anadin.'

Often A Bridesmaid, But Never A Bride Listerine mouthwash; US, from c1923. One of the best known lines in advertising, written by Milton Feasley of Lambert & Feasley, though there is an echo of the British music-hall song 'Why am I always a bridesmaid?', made famous by Lily Morris. Also **Her Honeymoon — And It Should Have Been Mine!/ Even Your Best Friends Won't Tell You/The Taste You Love To Hate (Twice A Day)**.

Phyllosan Fortifies The Over-Forties Phyllosan tonic; UK, current late 1940s. (We can hear an echo in the BBC saying: 'Radio 4 over-fortifies the over-forties.')

One Degree Under Aspro headache pills; UK, current 1960s.

The Priceless Ingredient Of Every Product Is The Honor And Integrity Of Its Maker Squibb drug products; US, from 1921. Before that year, 'Squibb had never advertised to the public . . . the problem given to Raymond Rubicam, then a writer at N.W. Ayer & Son, was to produce a series of advertisements which would sell Squibb to the public and not offend the publicity sensitive medical profession . . . One night at two in the morning he seemed as far away from the solution as ever. Wearily gathering up his yellow sheets before going to bed, he took one more look through the mass of headlines he had written. "Suddenly," he writes, "two separate word combinations popped out at me from two different headlines. One was 'The Priceless Ingredient' and the other 'Honor and Integrity'. Instantly, the two came together in my mind . . ." The phrase became a permanent part of Squibb advertising.' (Watkins). 'Raymond Rubicam's famous slogan . . . reminds me of my father's advice: when a company boasts about its integrity, or a woman about her virtue, avoid the former and cultivate the latter.' (Ogilvy). A later slogan was: **For Years We've Been Making Our Products As If Lives Depend On Them**.

Someone Isn't Using Amplex Amplex (breath purifier); UK, current 1957.

That Kruschen Feeling Kruschen salts; UK, current 1920s and 1930s. The ads featured an athletic man who attributed all his powers to Kruschen salts.

Things Happen After A Badedas Bath Badedas bath additive; UK, from 1966. Helicopters land on your lawn, dashing men lurk beneath your window. But it is an old fantasy: two hundred years ago a bath additive claimed to be: 'Admirable for those who have been almost worn out by women and wine . . . it will render their intercourse prolific.'

Stops Halitosis! Listerine mouthwash; US, from 1921. At first, Listerine was promoted as a 'safe antiseptic' with countless hygienic uses. Then in 1921 the Lambert Company decided to use a clinical term for the ordinary unpleasantness known as 'bad breath' — halitosis. An anxiety was not only stimulated, it was labelled. Listerine sales climbed from 115,000 a year in 1921 to 4 million a year in 1927. (Atwan). 'Who can steal "Stops Halitosis" from Listerine? Dozens of other mouthwashes stop halitosis. Many tried to move in on this great classic Unique Selling Proposition, until it became almost a source of embarrassment to them, seeking ways to phrase their imitation, so that they did not advertise the leader. This U.S.P., in the public's mind, belongs to Listerine.' (Reeves). Also **For Halitosis, Use Listerine**.

Within The Curve Of A Woman's Arm Odorono toilet water; US, from 1919. James Young of J. Walter Thompson wrote the original. Two hundred *Ladies Home Journal* subscribers cancelled their subscriptions when the ad tackled 'a frank discussion of a subject too often avoided', but the deodorant's sales increased by 112 per cent in that year.

Worth A Guinea A Box Beecham's pills; UK, from 1859. This slogan appeared in the first advertisement Thomas

Beecham ever placed in a newspaper, the *St Helens Intelligencer*, on 6 August 1859. Family tradition had it that the saying was inspired by a woman in St Helens market who approached Thomas and asked for another box, saying: 'They're worth a guinea to me, lad.' But in 1897 Thomas stated categorically that he had struck out from the metal anvil 'that spark of wit which has made the pills a household word in every quarter of the globe'. A probably apocryphal story has it that an ad was inserted in a church hymnal which led a congregation one day to chorus:

> Hark, the Herald Angels sing
> Beecham's Pills are just the thing.
> For easing pain and mothers mild,
> Two for adults, one for a child.

You Too Can Have A Body Like Mine   Charles Atlas bodybuilding courses; US, current from 1930. 'Charles Atlas' was born Angelo Siciliano in Italy in 1894. In his youth he actually was 'a skinny, timid weakling of only seven stone', as the later ads said. 'I didn't know what real health and strength

were. I was afraid to fight — ashamed to
be seen in a bathing costume.' After
watching a lion rippling its muscles
at the zoo he developed a method of
pitting one muscle against another
which he later called **Dynamic
Tension**. In 1922 he won the title
of **The World's Most Perfectly
Developed Man** in a contest
sponsored by Bernarr Macfadden
and his *Physical Culture*
magazine. He started giving
mail-order lessons:
'Hey! Quit kicking that
sand in our faces!' He died
in 1972.

*Charles
Atlas*

—actual photo of the
man who holds the
title. "The World's
Most Perfectly
Developed Man."

YOURS TO ENJOY
IN THE PRIVACY OF
YOUR OWN HOME

It takes a dirty mind to know one. But sex sells — or at least that is the conventional wisdom. No amount of protest from the women's movement can prevent some leggy model being stuck on the front of a combine harvester to advertise her charms, if not those of the product. Verbally, too, sex is thrown in to nudge you along — sometimes with quite shameless audacity:

Howard Makes Clothes For Men Who Make Babies

Make-Up To Make Love In
Mary Quant

Are You Getting It Every Day?
Sun newspaper

Give Him A Right Good Hemeling Tonight
Wouldn't You Rather Be Hemeling?
Hemeling beer

That Gleam Is Back In George's Eye Again
Serta Perfect Sleeper mattress

After The Pill: Posturpedic
Sealy mattress

When Should A Blonde Give In?
Clairol

You Know What Comes Between Me And My Calvins? Nothing!
Brooke Shields in Calvin Klein jeans ad, 1980

My Men Wear English Leather Or They Wear Nothing At All

Get Into Fellas
Fellas men's underwear (New Zealand)

A Buck Well Spent On A Spring-Maid Sheet

Is Your Man Getting Enough?
Milk Marketing Board (UK)

Is Your Wife Cold?
National Oil Fuel Institute (US)

Kayser Is Marvelous In Bed

What Makes A Shy Girl Get Intimate?

When A Chic Woman Undresses, What Do You See?

Perhaps We Could, Paul. If . . . You Owned A Chrysler

What's The Difference Between A Male Policeman And A Female Policeman? Six Inches
Police recruiting, UK

The First Time Is Never The Best
Campari, US

ACKNOWLEDGEMENTS
CATCHPHRASES

As I mentioned earlier, show business history remains largely unwritten — except in the form of often haphazardly-compiled memoirs, sometimes little better than fan-fodder — so this makes any attempt at compiling a reference work doubly difficult. However, I am grateful to a large number of people who have helped me with my inquiries, including: Edwin Apps and Pauline Devaney; Arthur Askey; George Bartram; Jan Bastiaenssens; Bernard Bresslaw; Max Bygraves; Edward Carey; Judy Carne; James Casey; Charlie Chester; Gerry Collins; Mat Coward; Colin Crompton; Barry Cryer; Paul Daniels; Ken Dodd; Barry Day; Arthur English; Alan Freeman; Ken Goodwin; Terry Hall; Patrick Iredale; Grant Lockhart; Cliff Michelmore; Bob Monkhouse; Nat Mills; Frank Muir; Janice Nicholls; Vernon Noble; Matthew Norgate; Jon Pertwee; Sandy Powell; Beryl Reid; Jenny Searle; Marion Somerville; Ed Stewart; Edward Taylor; Barry Took; Alfonso Torrents dels Prats; Norman Vaughan; L. Vilhjalmsson; Margaret Walsh; E. H. Loxley.

A number of sources, some of which I have quoted, were useful memory-joggers. To the authors and publishers of the following books my thanks are due:

Askey, Arthur, *Before Your Very Eyes* (Woburn Press, 1975).
Barker, Eric, *Steady Barker* (Secker & Warburg, 1956).
Black, Peter, *The Biggest Aspidistra in the World* (BBC, 1972).
Bridgmont, Leslie, *Leslie Bridgmont Presents* (Falcon Press, 1949).
Brooks, Tim and March, Earle, *The Complete Directory to Prime Time Network TV Shows 1946 — Present* (Ballantine Books, 1981).
Brough, Peter, *Educating Archie* (Stanley Paul, 1955).
Bygraves, Max, *I Wanna Tell You A Story* (W.H. Allen, 1976).
Campbell, Commander, *When I was in Patagonia* (Christopher Johnson, 1953).
Chester, Charlie, *The World is Full of Charlies* (New English Library, 1974).
Clark, Kenneth, *The Other Half* (John Murray, 1977).
Edwards, Jimmy, *Take it from Me* (Werner Laurie, 1953).
Fisher, John, *No Way to be a Hero* (Muller, 1973).

Fletcher, Cyril, *Nice One, Cyril* (Barrie & Jenkins, 1978).

Flexner, Stuart Berg, *Listening to America* (Simon & Schuster, 1982).

Hall, Henry, *Here's to the Next Time* (Odhams, 1956).

Halliwell, Leslie, *Halliwell's Television Companion* (Granada, 1982).

Howerd, Frankie, *On the Way I Lost it* (W.H. Allen, 1976).

Kavanagh, Ted, *The ITMA Years* (Woburn Press, 1974).

Kavanagh, Ted, *Tommy Handley* (Hodder & Stoughton, 1949).

Maxwell, John, *The Greatest Billy Cotton Band Show* (Jupiter, 1976).

Midwinter, Eric, *Make 'Em Laugh* (George Allen & Unwin, 1979).

Milligan, Spike, *More Goon Show Scripts* (Woburn Press, 1973).

Parker, Derek, *Radio: The Great Years* (David & Charles, 1977).

Partridge, Eric, *A Dictionary of Catch Phrases* (Routledge & Kegan Paul, 1977).

Pickles, Wilfred, *Wilfred Pickles Invites You to have Another Go* (David & Charles, 1978).

Randall, Alan and Seaton, Ray, *George Formby* (W.H. Allen, 1974).

Ray, Ted, *Raising the Laughs* (Werner Laurie, 1952).

Silver, Stuart and Haiblum, Isidore, *Faster than a Speeding Bullet* (Playboy Paperbacks, 1980).

Took, Barry, *Laughter in the Air* (Robson/BBC, 1976).

Took, Barry and Feldman, Marty, *Round the Horne* (Woburn Press, 1974).

Took, Barry and Feldman, Marty, *The Bona Book of Julian and Sandy* (Robson, 1976).

Train, Jack, *Up and Down the Line* (Odhams, 1956).

Warner, Jack, *Jack of all Trades* (W.H. Allen, 1975).

Wentworth, Harold and Flexner, Stuart Berg, *Dictionary of American Slang* (Thomas Y. Crowell, 1960).

Worsley, Francis, *ITMA 1939-1948* (Vox Mundi, 1948).

ACKNOWLEDGEMENTS
SLOGANS

Many people have helped me with my inquiries, on both sides of the Atlantic, and I am much indebted to them. My wife, Sue Bates, helped compile the original list of slogans. Helpful suggestions came from Ron and Pat Lehrman, Keith and Avril Ravenscroft, and especially Barry Day, President of McCann & Company. Among the other individuals from advertising agencies and elsewhere who provided information were:

Don Arlett; Paul Beale; John Bessant (Central Office of Information); Paul Best; Tony Brignull; Jill Craigie; Julian Bradley (New Scotland Yard); Maurice Drake; Alan Evans (Birds Eye Wall's Ltd); David Hall (Arthur Guinness Son & Co. (Park Royal) Ltd); Dany Khosrovani; David Kingsley; David Lamb (Rowntree Mackintosh Ltd); Terry Lovelock; Jane Maas; Charles Moss; Chris Munds; David McLaren; E.N. Monahan (Shell UK Oil); Roger Musgrave; John Paine; Valerie Simmonds; David Simpson (Action on Smoking and Health); Maurice Smelt; Edward Taylor; Royston Taylor; Peter Thomson (Advertising Standards Authority); Len Weinreich; Fay Weldon; David White (Start-Rite Shoes Ltd); Lois Wyse.

I am also most grateful to many companies and organisations for providing me with research facilities. Among them:

Austin Reed Ltd; Bass Ltd; Bovril Ltd; British Rail; Carnation Foods Company Ltd; Design & Art Directors Association of London; Hoover Historical Center; John Haig & Co. Ltd; John Lewis Partnership Ltd; John Player & Sons Ltd; Leo Burnett USA; Hovis Ltd; Institute of Practitioners in Advertising; Kentucky Fried Chicken (Great Britain) Ltd; Mars Ltd; R. Paterson & Sons Ltd; A. & F. Pears Ltd; Prudential Assurance Company Ltd; RHM Foods Ltd; Jos. Schlitz Brewing Company; The J.M. Smucker Company; Tate & Lyle Ltd; Texaco Ltd; Wm Whiteley Ltd; F.W. Woolworth & Company Ltd.

To the authors and publishers of the following books (from some of which I have quoted or reproduced illustrations) my thanks are due:

Atwan/McQuade/Wright, *Edsels, Luckies & Frigidaires* (Dell, 1979).
Baglee, Christopher, and Morley, Andrew, *Street Jewellery: A History of Enamel Advertising Signs* (New Cavendish Books, 1978).
Baker, Samm Sinclair, *The Permissible Lie* (Peter Owen, 1969).
Boorstin, Daniel, *The Image* (Weidenfeld & Nicolson, 1960).
Calder, Angus, *The People's War* (Cape, 1969).
Day, Barry (ed.), *100 Great Advertisements* (Times Newspapers, Mirror Group Newspapers, Campaign, 1978).
Feiling, Keith, *The Life of Neville Chamberlain* (Macmillan, 1946).
Flexner, Stuart Berg, *I Hear America Talking* (Simon & Schuster, 1979).
Gable, Jo, *The Tuppenny Punch and Judy Show* (Michael Joseph, 1980).
Hadley, Peter (compiler), *The History of Bovril Advertising* (Bovril, 1970).

Howard, Anthony, and West, Richard, *The Making of the Prime Minister* (Jonathan Cape, 1965).

Jones, Edgar R., *Those Were the Good Old Days* (Simon & Schuster, 1979).

Kleinman, Philip, *Advertising Inside Out* (W.H. Allen, 1977).

Lambert, I.E., *The Public Accepts* (University of New Mexico Press, 1941).

Longmate, Norman, *How We Lived Then* (Arrow, 1973).

Louis, J.C., and Yazijian, Harvey, *The Cola Wars* (Everest House, 1980).

McLaine, Ian, *Ministry of Morale* (George Allen & Unwin, 1979).

Mayer, Martin, *Madison Avenue, USA* (Weidenfeld & Nicolson, 1971).

Nicholl, David Shelley, *Advertising: its Purpose, Principles and Practice* (Macdonald & Evans, 1978).

Ogilvy, David, *Confessions of an Advertising Man* (Atheneum, 1980).

Partridge, Eric, *Dictionary of Slang and Unconventional English* (Routledge & Kegan Paul, 1970).

Partridge, Eric, *Dictionary of Catch Phrases* (Routledge & Kegan Paul, 1977).

Polykoff, Shirley, *Does She . . . Or Doesn't She?* (Doubleday, 1975).

Pearson, John, and Turner, Graham, *The Persuasion Industry* (Eyre & Spottiswoode, 1965).

Safire, William, *Safire's Political Dictionary* (Ballantine, 1980).

Sayers, Dorothy L., *Murder Must Advertise* (Gollancz, 1933).

Stiling, Marjorie, *Famous Brand Names, Emblems and Trade Marks* (David & Charles, 1980).

Turner, E.S., *The Shocking History of Advertising* (Michael Joseph, 1952).

Watkins, Julian Lewis, *The 100 Greatest Advertisements* (Dover, 1959).

White, Theodore H., *The Making of the President 1961/1964/1968/ 1972* (Jonathan Cape, 1962, 1965, 1969, 1973).

Yanker, Gary, *Prop Art* (Darrien House, 1972/Studio Vista, 1972).

INDEX

INDEX